KU-308-818

The Cousins

THE COUSINS

The friendship, opinions and activities of
Wilfrid Scawen Blunt and George Wyndham

Max Egremont

STIRLING
DISTRICT
LIBRARY

COLLINS
St James's Place, London
1977

William Collins Sons & Co Ltd
London · Glasgow · Sydney · Auckland
Toronto · Johannesburg

821·8
EGR

First published 1977
© Max Egremont 1977
ISBN 0 00 216134 6
Set in Linotype Pilgrim
Made and Printed in Great Britain by
William Collins Sons & Co Ltd Glasgow

To my parents, and Carlyn and Harry

Contents

Illustrations

Acknowledgements

Many people have helped me with this book. I should particularly like to thank the Duke of Westminster for permission to use the papers of George Wyndham and Wyndham's wife Sibell Grosvenor that are in the Grosvenor Estate office in Davies Street; the Earl of Lytton, Lady Anne Lytton and Lady Winifrid Tryon for the use of papers of Wilfrid Scawen Blunt and the first Earl of Lytton that are in their possession; the Syndics of the Fitzwilliam Museum, Cambridge, for allowing me to consult the original manuscripts of the Blunt diaries and to quote from Blunt's writings and correspondence; the Governors of Dunford House for permission to quote from the Cobden papers in the West Sussex County Record Office; Francis Wyndham for the use of papers in his possession; Ian Anstruther for the use of the papers of Lady Currie; and the Taoiseach for permission to quote from a letter in the Irish State Paper Office at Dublin Castle.

At the Fitzwilliam Museum the director, Professor Michael Jaffé, the librarian, Mr Paul Woudhuysem, and Mrs Robertson have been unfailingly kind and helpful. At every stage the Earl of Lytton, Wilfrid Scawen Blunt's grandson and his biographer, has supplied encouragement and advice, and shown exceptional patience in the face of endless questioning. Guy Acloque at the Grosvenor Estate office went out of his way to make my researches there easy and comfortable. Blunt's official biographer, the Countess of Longford, not only showed immense tolerance of my trespassing on her terrain but urged

ACKNOWLEDGEMENTS

me on at every opportunity. Ursula Wyndham compiled the family tree with her customary diligence and erudition. Others to whom I am deeply in debt include Alison McCann, Sir Philip Magnus-Allcroft, Tom Pierce, the Earl of Dunraven, Kiernan and Tamsy Guinness, Violet Wyndham, Lady Mary Lyon, Lady Dorothy Lygon, and the staffs of the London Library and the libraries of the British Museum and Trinity College, Dublin. Roger Fulford was kind enough to read the manuscript and make many valuable suggestions for its improvement. At Collins, Philip Ziegler always guided me with sympathy and admirable firmness. Despite all this, the mistakes and inadequacies of the book remain very much my own.

Introduction

George Wyndham, in his prime, was one of the most glittering figures of his age. Young, energetic, charming, sensitive and intelligent, there seemed, to the outward observer, to be nothing that could stand in the way of his triumphant progress. If politics failed him, literature was there as a consolation, and if literature provided a momentary setback, then politics could be pursued with even greater determination. A Chief Secretary for Ireland who read, and wrote about, Ronsard and Plutarch, and a poet who possessed a professional politician's knowledge of the ways of the world : this surely was, as his cousin Wilfrid Scawen Blunt remarked, 'the ultimate man'. In addition there were his looks – the looks of a romantic young guards officer, simultaneously strong and innocent, fashioned almost too perfectly for life's batterings and thus seeming to evince, in repose, an unstated longing for death. The young aristocrats killed in the First World War looked like George Wyndham; but they died younger and so were spared the mundane travails of failure and middle age.

Wilfrid Scawen Blunt lived longer than his cousin. Wyndham died in 1913, not yet fifty, already tired out by drink and disappointment. Blunt lived on until 1922, into his eighties, also suffering from a sense of despair as he remembered his crusades on behalf of the oppressed nationalities of the British Empire and contemplated their comparative uselessness. Less of the Establishment than Wyndham, he never carried with him the hopes of a great political party, but had entered politics with at least as great a degree of enthusiasm, going to prison at one stage for his beliefs. In literature too he was as active and as respected, and had as true a claim to the admiration of those attracted by the romance of action and adventure. Traveller, amorist, poet and revolutionary, Blunt espoused any cause or activity with all the enthusiasm at his command, and if the fervour often seemed too intense to be concentrated for long in one direction nobody could doubt that it was there.

Despite the difference in age (Blunt was some twenty years older) Wilfrid Blunt and George Wyndham were the closest of friends. Reinforced by ties of blood and a common love of literature, their friendship began in the 1880s and continued unabated until Wyndham's early death. Although George Wyndham was an ardent imperialist and supporter of Arthur Balfour at the Irish Office at the time when Blunt was arrested in Galway for campaigning for Home Rule, political disagreements were not allowed to come between them. Only occasionally were their politics compatible, but their affection for each other proved capable of riding out almost any storm.

The common background gave their friendship additional strength. In its heyday it was acted out against the easy opulence of late-Victorian and Edwardian society – the world of the Souls, the Crabbet Club and the great country houses where politicians of both parties mingled in benign sociability and amorous liaisons were conducted under the cloaks of discretion and romantic despair. Blunt and Wyndham may have been far apart politically, but they shared the ideals and customs of their class. Yet if each possessed the self-confidence of the Edwardian grandee, neither shared his conventionally philistine tastes, often preferring tennis to hunting or shooting and valuing, in a self-congratulatory way, good conversation and appreciation of the arts. Within their confines they were men of sensibility and taste.

At the end of the day they were men of achievement as well. Politically Wyndham has the edge. Although Wilfrid Scawen Blunt devoted forty years to campaigning against imperialism, his efforts never brought about the dramatic changes wrought by Wyndham's Irish land Act. Blunt may have gone to jail for his political activities but he was always essentially on the outside of politics. George Wyndham, as a minister and Member of Parliament, could bring about change as well as speak of it: his cousin, from the sidelines, had to shout especially loud to make himself heard at all. Encouragement Blunt could provide, and sympathy; but no matter how correct his prophecies might be, the immediacy of political power was never granted to him. In his last years this made him wonder if he had not shouted in vain.

I have not attempted to write complete biographies of George Wyndham and Wilfrid Scawen Blunt: that would be far beyond the scope of a book this size. What I have tried to do is to provide a picture of their friendship, their contrasting ideas and attainments, and the background to their lives. Inevitably, with two men who put so much into everything that they did, the story is tinged with sadness and failure. But there are moments of triumph and splendour as well.

Chapter 1
The Young George Wyndham

By the romantic, childhood and early youth are usually remembered with a wistful nostalgia that attains more force, and less attachment to reality, as the years pass. George Wyndham was a romantic of this type. Throughout his life he remained grateful for having been given a happy childhood, unhampered by poverty or the tribulations of family discontent; and in the future it was to give him reason to wonder, on several occasions, why the rest of life could not be more in tune with its beginnings.

George Wyndham was born on August 20th 1863, the second child and eldest son of the Honourable Percy and Madeline Wyndham. His father was a Wyndham of Petworth, the younger son of the first Lord Leconfield. The Wyndhams were originally a family of Norfolk squires who, by marrying money, progressed first to Somerset, to Orchard Wyndham at Williton, and then to the palace of Petworth in Sussex, constructed at the end of the seventeenth century by the sixth Duke of Somerset on land that he had inherited by marrying one of the richest women in Europe – Lady Elizabeth Percy, daughter of the last Earl of Northumberland and heiress to the vast Percy estates. After the Duke's death in 1748 he was succeeded by his son Algernon to whom George II granted, in addition to his other titles, the earldoms of Northumberland and Egremont. Then in 1750 Algernon himself died, without a son. The estates were divided, the Northumberland and Syon properties passing to his son-in-law Sir Hugh Smithson, who subsequently changed his name to Percy and was later created the first Duke of Northumberland; the Petworth and Cumberland estates to Charles Wyndham, the son of Algernon's sister Catherine who had been married to Sir William Wyndham of Orchard Wyndham. Sir William had been a Member of Parliament, friend and supporter of Bolingbroke in the reign of Queen Anne, and a putative Jacobite. In 1715 he was arrested and locked up in the Tower for his suspected allegiance to the King over the water.

For a Wyndham to pursue a political career was thus in keeping with the family's history. Sir William was a Tory; his son Charles was inclined towards the Whigs. He became Secretary of State for the South, succeeding the older Pitt in that office, and was embarrassed by the ghost of his father's extremism when John Wilkes, having been arrested after the publication of the forty-fifth number of the *North Briton*, told the two Secretaries of State who were interviewing him that he hoped he was to be given the same room in the Tower as that which had once been occupied by Sir William Wyndham. In 1763 Charles died, of apoplexy brought on by over-eating, at Egremont House in Piccadilly (now the Naval and Military Club) and was succeeded by his son George who reigned supreme at Petworth until 1837. Endlessly hospitable, a patron of Turner, discerning collector of pictures and sculpture, agricultural reformer and conscientious landlord, the third Earl of Egremont was a shining example of the kind of person a confident and secure aristocracy can, and should, produce.

Yet Egremont was a shy man who rarely found human relationships easy or rewarding. His benignity would conceal this; but his private life revealed the complications of his personality. He became engaged to Lady Maria Waldegrave, step-daughter of the Duke of Gloucester and great-granddaughter of Sir Robert Walpole; but later, embarrassed by society gossip, broke off the engagement. Henceforth he sought solace with a mistress called Miss Iliff, whom he kept upstairs at Petworth, siring six bastards by her before their marriage in July 1801. The marriage was not a success. In May 1803 they separated and Miss Iliff left Petworth never to return. Their one legitimate daughter died in infancy; and the oldest illegitimate child George, was George Wyndham's grandfather.

To father a series of illegitimate children was not regarded as particularly startling in early-nineteenth-century England; but with the third Earl a strain of eccentricity, which sometimes took a disagreeable form, entered the Wyndham family. Quarrels were pursued with an alarming relentlessness. After their father's death the two bastards, George and Henry (who became a Lieutenant-General on account of his service in the Peninsula and at Waterloo) hunted the same country in Sussex, each with his own private pack. There developed between them an extraordinary, almost maniacal rivalry, which only came to an end when, in order to rob Henry of his prey, George ordered all the foxes in his woods to be shot. George Wyndham married Miss Blunt, who came of an old Sussex family and was Wilfrid Scawen Blunt's aunt. Henry married a daughter of Lord Charles Seymour, only to desert her for a Mrs de la Beche with whom he lived in Sussex and, later, in Cockermouth Castle which his father had left to him for his life. Here he became Member of Parliament, first for Cockermouth, then for West Cumberland; but his mistress was never accepted in Cumberland society. After her death an ashamed member of the family went through her library at Cockermouth and, deciding that the books were worth keeping, solemnly cut out the piece of the fly-leaf in which she had inscribed her name.

Queen Victoria created George the first Lord Leconfield, recognizing, in spite of his ancestry, his territorial powers; and Percy Wyndham, George Wyndham's father, was born in 1835. At Petworth he must have suffered a peculiar upbringing. George Leconfield was deeply shy, agonized by the memory of his bastardy. All contact with the town was expressly forbidden, even though its shops and houses were clustered hard up against the imposing walls of the great house. His wife Mary would sweep through its narrow streets in a large black carriage and the children were not allowed to communicate with any of its inhabitants. Lady Leconfield fell a victim to strict evangelicism and became a virtual recluse. Once, after breaking her finger in the door of a London cab, she vowed never again to use so vile a method of transportation and ordered her carriage and horses to be put on the train with her on her journeys to the metropolis. At Victoria Station she would supervise their unloading, having travelled up first class from Petworth, filling the rest of the compartment with her servants because of her intense dislike of encountering strangers.

Percy Wyndham contrived to survive all this. He represented West Cumberland as a Conservative Member of Parliament from 1860 until the Reform Act of 1885 made him decide not to stand again; and was respected in the House of Commons for his independence and courage. Indeed if George Leconfield, with his bad temper and reckless quarrels, represents some of the less attractive sides of the aristocratic character his son demonstrates several of its possible virtues. On the occasion of his death in 1911, *The Times* obituary stated: 'He was remarkably cultivated and well read, spoke and wrote fluently and forcibly with a kindly vein of humour, was a thorough sportsman in the best sense of the word (he was master of the Tedworth Hounds from 1881 to 1885), and had a sense of his responsibilities and duties which was as humble as it was proud. For his ready sympathy, his wise and quiet helpfulness, and his courteous and upright life he was loved and respected not only by his friends but by everyone who knew him.'[1]

In politics he preserved his independence and never attained office. Coming from a landowning background, and himself acquiring a considerable estate in Wiltshire, he was always a protectionist and served on the council of the Fair Trade league. In foreign affairs he took the part of the Turks during

the Russo-Turkish war, and spoke strongly against Gladstone's 'Bulgarian atrocities' campaign. He also voted against
his party over the occupation of Egypt, opposing the principle
of undermining the Turkish Empire. Percy was out of sympathy
with the evangelical fervour of his mother. He attended
the Huxley-Wilberforce debate at Oxford and was an early
advocate of Darwinism, again voting against his party in a
minority of one or two, in the angry debates over the admission of the atheist F. C. Bradlaugh to the House of Commons
in 1880.

Like most Wyndhams Percy was shy: yet beneath the
forbidding exterior there was a man who was both sympathetic
and civilized. Educated at Eton, he managed to escape from
Petworth to go on a journey through Italy with a tutor,
before joining the Coldstream Guards in 1853. His early
aesthetic experiences, both at Petworth and on his Italian
tour, left a mark on his mind, and while still young he became
an enthusiastic amateur of the arts, buying pictures by Corot,
Daubigny and, before the Pre-Raphaelites became fashionable,
Rossetti. Philip Webb, who was later to build him a house at
East Knoyle in Wiltshire, Burne-Jones and Sargeant were
his friends.

Percy Wyndham possessed wide interests and sympathies.
In 1913 his son George was surprised to discover written at the
end of his father's copy of William Morris's *Signs of Change*:
'Pages 18 and 9. Splendid passage, I hope prophetic – wonderful and impossible as the change in condition, shadowed forth
on pages 20 and 21, appears from our present standpoint, it is
not more wonderful and impossible than our present standpoint would appear to those who lived thousands of years
ago.'[2] Thus the squire and retired Conservative politician sat in
the library of his Victorian country house, itself a supreme
expression of optimism and security, mulling over the cadences
of this English socialism; and seeing, amid Morris's celebration
of the workers ('The only producers') and his contempt for the
role that their age had forced upon them, the glimmering of a

new utopia. Morris was a friend of Percy's and his family. On hearing of his illness George Wyndham wrote to Wilfrid Scawen Blunt: 'Your account of Morris's health saddens me and makes me feel that we are all suddenly much older. For he was and is the leader of the world's return to its youth.'[3] When he died Wyndham simply observed: 'One by one the stars are extinguished.'[4]

For Percy, 1860 was the date that his life became free of the shackles that his upbringing had imposed upon him. Then, staying with his sister Lady Mayo in Ireland, he met Madeline Campbell and decided that he must make her his wife.

Madeline Campbell, George Wyndham's mother, had a romantic ancestry. She was the granddaughter of the ill-fated Lord Edward Fitzgerald and Pamela, reputed daughter of Philippe Egalité (Duc d'Orléans) and Madame de Genlis, the French novelist and educational theorist. Lord Edward met Pamela in France in 1792, when he was nearly thirty and she was only sixteen. He lost no time in becoming engaged to her, and his family were pleased, hoping that he would henceforth lead a more settled life. But if they thought that marriage would convert the impulsive Lord Edward to quiet domesticity, their illusions were to be shattered. As an early convert to Rousseau and the egalitarian ideas of Thomas Paine he became one of the leaders of the Irish Revolutionary movement which came to a head in the rebellion of 1798. Both he and his wife cut fine figures in Dublin, he with his plain brown suit and cropped hair style of a French Jacobin and she dressed entirely in Irish muslin. In 1798 it ended when he died in prison after being arrested by the English and his widow left, heartbroken, for Europe.

Pamela's eldest child, also called Pamela, was Madeline's mother. In 1820 she married Guy Campbell, the son of a distinguished Scottish soldier. Guy Campbell was also in the army, already a veteran of the Peninsula and Waterloo. They had eleven children, seven of which were daughters; and the youngest was born on June 20th 1835. Characteristically, Lady

Campbell wrote to her friend Emily Eden: 'I have really escaped with my life – I ain't dead yet, but such a big monster of a girl! A regular Megalonia of a female, that if you happened to find a loose joint of hers you would think it must belong to an antidiluvian ox. *Je vous demande un peu* what am I to do with a seventh girl of such dimensions? . . . I really believe she is harmless, for she would knock me down, but she is merciful! What shall we call her? I had some thoughts of Rhinocera (she was born the day the Rhinoceros landed) or Cuvier, because I was reading his life and works just before she was born, and took a passion for him . . . Might she not be called Eden? – Her other name is to be Madeline – her Godmother's name.'[5]

The daughter was christened Madeline Caroline Frances Eden and grew up in genteel poverty in Ireland and England, accompanying her parents from post to post until her father's death in 1849. She became a remarkable person, of great warmth and serenity. Wilfrid Scawen Blunt was to remain close to her for most of his life, even through its stormiest years, and for her son George she was 'Always generous – I want to say *generosa* in Latin – magnanimous, always a giver, a fountain of inexhaustible vitality.' In September 1895 he wrote of her to his friend Edward Clifford, who had been to Clouds for the first time: 'She is a *sursum corda*. Sometimes the bravest feel that they are shut in by doors closed fast for ever. Then her presence is an incantation which sings with the voice of the wind "lift up your heads, ye everlasting doors, that the King of Glory may enter in". God to her is, I think, pre-eminently the "King of Glory" and she has a peculiar gift for making this world glorious to all who meet her in it.'[6]

Two months after their first meeting in Ireland, Percy Wyndham became engaged to Madeline Campbell. Her mother wrote, somewhat apprehensively, to Lord Leconfield: 'I suppose you know Madeline has no fortune. I have had rather a struggling life of many trials. I became a widow ten years ago, and I have much to thank God for, in that He enabled me to bring up my many children upon less than six hundred a year, on my death the girls will have fifty pounds a year and that is all! So you must be content with Madeline's good qualities as her portion.'[7]

On October 16th 1860 they were married, and installed themselves in 44 Belgrave Square, the long lease of which Percy had acquired. Their five children were born here, and it was to remain their London house for the rest of their lives. In August 1860, Percy's uncle, General Sir Henry Wyndham of Cockermouth, died, thus vacating the parliamentary seat of West Cumberland; and Percy Wyndham was returned, without opposition, in his place, embarking upon a parliamentary career that was to last 25 years. Madeline settled easily into family life. Henceforth her serenity was to be ruffled only by the very deepest tragedies. At home she provided a shelter to which those in need could return and be sure of a welcome. Years later, in 1905, in a letter from Clouds, a guest provided a neat picture of Mrs Percy Wyndham at her most sympathetic. 'It was a delightful visit,' he wrote '. . . She has an exceptionally generous nature. Her largesse is unrestrained, and surpasses the imagination of the most clamative person. If there is a scent that is like her, it is the sweet briar – a delicious, homely fragrance. She is not (as some people have suggested) at all like a magnolia. It is much too luxurious, and overwhelming, and wealthy for her. She is never overwhelming. Her taste is perfect as to poetry, flowers, decoration, pictures, houses, garden. She is distinctly humble, and never realizes or thinks of her virtues. She is an admiring mother and an appreciative friend. I imagine all her servants rise up and call her blessed. The light of her penetrates in all directions.'[8]

Percy and Madeline embarked, without delay, upon the task of procreation. On August 29th 1863, their second child was born. The first had been a daughter, whom they had called Mary, perhaps in homage to Percy's mother; but the second was a boy, their eldest son. The parents were pleased, and decided to call him George.

George Wyndham's early years were divided between Cumberland, London, Sussex and Wiltshire. Belgrave Square was his parents' home; but, until Lord Leconfield died in 1869, the late summer and autumn were spent at Cockermouth Castle in Cumberland, which Percy's father had made available to him for the fulfilment of his constituency duties. This place, a small Georgian house built in the middle of a ruined castle that stands above the River Derwent, dominating the lakeland town of Cockermouth, left a profound impression on the young boy's romantic sensibilities. In 1912 he wrote to Wilfrid Blunt, after a visit to Cockermouth: 'I had not slept in that house since I was 6 years old, or seen it since I was 14 . . . I felt that I had dreamed for 43 years of the ruins, and the sound of the weir and of the wind through the trees of the courtyard.'[9] Wordsworth had been born in the town of Cockermouth. To him the castle had been 'a shattered monument of feudal sway', left in ruins after the civil war, yet when the Wyndhams came there the house had been lived in for some 20 years by General Wyndham, the skin of whose charger adorned one of the walls of the stone hall. After his father's death, the castle passed to Percy's older brother Henry and Percy rented Isel Hall, which was only some five miles further up the Derwent, from Sir Wilfrid Lawson for his Cumberland visits. The Cumbrian countryside always stayed with George Wyndham. To revisit it was to awake the contented ghosts of the past.

Madeline Wyndham's family expanded rapidly; Mary in 1861, George in 1863, Guy in 1865, Madeline in 1869 and Pamela in 1871. The oldest three formed a group of their own. They shared nannies, governesses and tutors. Among these were Mr Holland, the tutor, Mrs Horsenail (the nanny) and later Fräulein Schneider (governess). These people had no easy task. Fräulein Schneider's previous post had been with another family in Belgrave Square who had given her strict orders not to let her charges play with 'those wild Wyndham children'; and when George went to school for the first time Guy became so impossible to control on his own that he had to be sent a term later to join his brother.

In addition to Cockermouth, Isel and Belgrave Square the Wyndhams had other holiday haunts. There was Hyères in the south of France, where Mrs Ellis (one of Madeline Wyndham's sisters) had settled on account of Major Ellis's health. Here George Wyndham had his first experience of France and the Mediterranean. In 1885, on the voyage out to Egypt to fight with the Coldstream Guards, he wrote to his mother, after the ship had emerged from a storm: 'I retract all that I have said against the sea. Yesterday and last night were too wonderful. Bright blue sea all day just like Hyères . . .'[10] Then of course there was Petworth. This house, representing all the greatest aspirations and achievements of his Percy, Seymour and Wyndham ancestors, could not have failed to impress him. 'A visit to Petworth,' he told Wilfrid Blunt in 1898, 'always confirms my intention to get office.'[11]

These early visits to Petworth must have been curious experiences for the children. Despite the size of the house Nanny Horsenail and her charges were given two small rooms called the Chapel rooms, one of which they were supposed to use as a day nursery. In the other they would all sleep, huddled together amid the vastness that surrounded them. Family tensions, long a feature of Wyndham life, would make their parents uneasy, particularly after the death of old Lord Leconfield in 1869. The more intelligent, less awkward Percy had always been his parents' favourite son, and over the years this had come to be resented by his older brother, the more bucolic, less imaginative Henry. Percy had expected to be left Cockermouth, which would have suited him well, but his father had left all the Wyndham estates *en bloc* to Henry. After 1869, a meeting between the two brothers was potentially explosive, especially as Henry's temper became shorter as he slid not so silently, into middle age.

The wives, who were great friends, tried to prevent these clashes; but, unfortunately, prevention was more easily spoken of than obtained. Henry was his father's son, a fox-hunting landowner who had few outside interests. He constantly complained of the fact that, due to his father's illegitimacy, he was a mere baron; yet, typically, when Lord Salisbury offered him an Earldom in 1886 he refused it. Often in the evenings, after a hard day in the saddle, he would seek solace in a good dinner. Afterwards, over the port, the sight and sound of his brother, whose good example had been the bane of his youth, could become too much for him. Once Constance Leconfield, sister of the Prime Minister Lord Rosebery, wrote to her sister-in-law Madeline, after a particularly lively bout: 'I must here say that I do not at all know what was said, as Henry did not recollect enough afterwards to tell me, but he voluntarily that night said that he was sorry that he had been so angry, and he fully expected to see Percy the next morning.'[12]

On this occasion, however, Henry had gone too far and Percy left the house in a fury. In October 1874 Constance wrote sadly to Madeline: 'I have come round to thinking as you did in the summer (though at that time I thought you were wrong) that it would be wiser not to let Henry and Percy meet this winter. Henry's sores always take a long time in healing, and as long as anything rankles in his mind it is almost impossible for him not to lose his temper at times, so I should be frightened that if he saw much of Percy . . . there might be another outburst in an unguarded moment.'[13]

Madeline and Constance were drawn to each other by their pacific roles. In 1907 Constance wrote: 'I have always loved you so very much, for yourself first of all, and then because of the peculiar tie which binds one to a member of the family who has had the same experiences. You and I were both outsiders, and married Wyndhams . . . we went through a great deal . . . the long and frightful years when I was hardly allowed to see you, and there was the horrid cloud of suspicion and misunderstanding between our two houses.'[14]

Thus George Wyndham grew up, amid the lakes and mountains of Cumberland, the bustle of Victorian London, and family tradition and disputes at Petworth. Inevitably there was a dark side to all this. Even for a young child, death and violence are never far away. One afternoon in 1872, the Wyndham children were playing in the gardens of Belgrave Square. Suddenly they were summoned back into Number 44 to be told of the brutal murder of their uncle, Lord Mayo, who, as Viceroy of India, had been stabbed by a convict during a visit to a penal settlement on the Andaman Islands. In 1869 their grandmother died, and George's letter to his mother retains the immediacy of the family's grief when he says: 'We are so very sorry that dear Granny had to suffer so. You must be so unhappy poor dear Mamma. How we want to kiss and hug you and try to comfort you. We will both try to be as good to you as you were to Granny. I hope we shall soon see you.'[15]

In the autumn of 1874 the first stage of childhood came to an end; and George Wyndham was shipped off to boarding school. In this year too the Wyndhams acquired a new home for themselves. Breaking away from his family connections, Percy rented Wilbury, a house in Wiltshire, ten miles from Salisbury and owned by Sir Edward Malet. From here George set off for the Revd. C. G. Chittenden's preparatory school at the Grange, Hoddesdon in Hertfordshire where, some 20 years previously, Arthur Balfour had begun his schooldays. The Reverend Chittenden was a stern disciplinarian. Frequent use was made of a weapon known as 'the spatter' – a heavy leather horse strap which could clearly make a firm impression on the backside of a small boy.

Wyndham took the harshness of the Grange in his stride. The games were 'great fun', and there were always the headmaster's two charming daughters, Carrie and May, to console the younger pupils. Academic standards were high; and Wyndham's succession of competent governesses and tutors stood him in good stead. In 1877 the Reverend Chittenden's establishment showed its worth by enabling the boy to take Remove (a high form) at Eton. So in the Easter term of that year George Wyndham entered this training ground for those who aspired to rule late-Victorian England and her Empire.

Eton, with its vast medieval chapel, red-brick Tudor buildings surrounding the great school yard and slow river running through the small crowded town, must have seemed infinitely beautiful and bewildering to the young Wyndham, fresh from the more mundane atmosphere at the Grange at Hoddesdon. In his first letter home he told his mother : 'There seems to be nothing here but swans, boatmen, tuck shops, and boys in the whole place. There are only four boys come to the house as yet. When the train went away, four new boys, myself among them, were all left standing on the platform. It's a lovely place.'[16] Wyndham's housemaster came to the rescue of those four lonely figures. His name was R. H. A. Mitchell, and he was a kindly man, enthusiastic and adept at games but of no great intellect. The new boy found no difficulty in settling down, for, having enjoyed an open and easy upbringing full of affection and encouragement, he was not shy.

In George Wyndham's time, to become an Etonian was to join an extraordinary institution that maintained strong links with the past yet could also, through friendships and interests discovered during one's schooldays, foreshadow the future. That he was about to become part of a continuing tradition was immediately made apparent to him. When George took swimming lessons during his first summer there, the instructor remembered teaching both his father and his uncle; and on his arrival he was shown a room that twenty years previously had been Percy's. In addition it is not difficult to find, in the school career of any late-Victorian Old Etonian politician, auguries of the years to come. Arthur Balfour fagged for Lord Lansdowne, who later became his Foreign Secretary; and was sworn in as Chief Secretary for Ireland in 1887 by the Lord-Lieutenant Lord Londonderry who had once been his fag. St John Brodrick remembers unbending to congratulate the young George Curzon on winning the Prince Consort's French prize, although Curzon was junior to him in the school. Years later the one was Secretary of State for India when the other was Viceroy. Curzon was at Eton with George Wyndham, although several years senior to him. Politics had always been very much in the air at George Wyndham's home, with his father free enough in the not particularly onerous role of a Conservative country gentleman Member of Parliament to spend a good deal of time with the family, discoursing easily upon the major problem of the moment. At Eton Wyndham won a reputation as an agile debater.

Yet he was not a brilliantly successful Etonian. Perhaps this was fortunate. Glory, when it comes to one amid such glittering surroundings and at so early an age, is peculiarly intoxicating. L. E. Jones, in his wonderfully evocative memoir of Eton at the turn of the century, has described how 'my toy power, my miniature prestige, were so real to me, and represented so vividly in my eyes the full and final flowering of my ambitions, that I was cured once and for all, by my brief tenure of power and personal distinction alike, of any future wish for either'.[17] To be glorified at Eton was to receive as much tribute and deference as any youth could rightfully expect, unless he was either a monarch or hereditary head of a religious sect. George Wyndham never rose to such heights; but neither did he sink to the bottom of the Eton pile by becoming either a 'sap' or a 'scug', two well-worn terms of Etonian abuse.

The 'scug' (he who was a laggard at games) offended because there was no place for him in the sporting pantheon, and the 'sap' (he who became too preoccupied with his books) was objectionable because he went against the aristocratic maxim that achievements are only worthy of true admiration if they can be accomplished with effortless ease. In 1880 Wyndham was awarded his house football colours; and his academic performance was suitably unspectacular. In February 1880 he wrote to his mother : 'I'm afraid I shan't be high in school work

this half. I work much as usual, but I'm stupider than usual
and apparently can't do as good Latin prose and translation as
I could do last half.'[18]

It had been arranged that he would depart at the end of
1880, to go to a crammers where he would read for Oxford.
In September 1880 he wrote to his mother, at the beginning
of his last term: 'I feel such a swell. I am second in the House
and in the 3rd division in the school. It's so nice when you
come back finding lots of friends. I am already beginning to
feel melancholy about leaving.'[19] A final burst of football fury
was noted in October. 'This half, and this week particularly
has been a most fatal one for injuries. There are no less than
four in the school eleven who have had to stop playing, two
with their knees out, one with a broken ankle and another with
a sprained knee. Another boy and a master have both sprained
their ankles so much that they have to be strapped up and cannot play. And this afternoon a boy called Dickenson put his
elbow out, and Rawlins, a master, had his leg clean broken.'[20]
Then in December came the end; and Mr Mitchell and the
closely packed group of red-brick buildings were left for the
great world outside.

Percy Wyndham wished his son to go to Oxford, having always
regretted his own lack of a university education; but this was
not to be. The crammers in Surrey proved to be exceedingly
unpleasant; and, after the leisurely pace of Eton, the work
was as disagreeable as the company. 'The hours are horrid and
keep you about the place all day,'[21] George told his mother.
Percy saw that the establishment was not suited to his son. He
also agreed with George that, under the circumstances, it would
be better for the boy to leave out university and go straight
into the army. He seemed to be set on a military career and the
years spent at Oxford would only cause him to fall below
officers younger than himself who had joined from school.
Wyndham's intellectual tastes were not yet fully developed.

In addition his father, whom he greatly admired, had been an officer in the Crimea; and this was still the age when military glory was at least as great a prize as academic distinction. So at Easter he left the crammers to spend two months in Paris perfecting his French before setting about the business of the Sandhurst entrance examination.

At first his attitude to Paris was that of the ingenuous youth at large for the first time. French food and French culture perplexed him; but as time went by, matters improved. He boarded off the Champs-Elysées, in the Rue Marbeuf, with the Duplay family. He hired a large white horse and rode in the Bois, causing 'a sensation'. 'I met Mademoiselle Trubert,' he wrote to his sister Mary, 'and her mother and rode with them. I played tennis again today with them, and had a long conversation in French with the two Mlles d'Harcourt. Madame Trubert has asked me to a dance next Sunday. I will tell you how I got on amongst the Frenchies; here the proper thing is to take off your hat in your left hand, keep it off and shake hands with your right; it requires some practice to do this gracefully to everybody at a lawn tennis party, with a stick and gloves, after having been handed two raquets to choose from . . .'[22]

The two months passed quickly, not least because of the feminine company. He was good-looking and had self-confidence, so found little difficulty in making an impression. But the formality of grand French society successfully drove a wedge between him and any young girl of his own class. 'Here,' he complained, 'when you are introduced to mothers and their daughters at balls, you have to leave cards on them all! Fancy, how awful . . . They don't allow girls to go out to tea without their chaperones. I expect soon to find that you have to dance with one on each arm.'[23] In June Paris was exchanged for another crammers at Storrington in Sussex where he began to prepare for entry to Sandhurst and the British Army.

Mr Faithful, an army tutor of note, was George Wyndham's instructor at Storrington. The place was altogether preferable to the Surrey establishment; and there was time enough
for recreation as well. Hunting was a sport of which Wyndham had grown increasingly fond, thus once again following
his father's example. This flirtation with danger amid the
winter beauty of the English countryside was to have a lasting
appeal for him and he seldom missed an opportunity to indulge
in it. Hunting was good exercise, but for Wyndham it was
more than that. In the hunting field he found himself in a
situation which demanded only a strong horse, his own physical
courage and good scenting weather. This, although his body
became tired, was to be a constantly satisfying source of
relaxation. At Storrington there was a pack of harriers to
hunt with, and Wyndham would follow them with his cousin
Timmy Paulet, afterwards Marquess of Winchester. One day
he had a fall and broke his arm, but this was only part of the
game. Another way of escaping from his books was to visit his
uncle and aunt at Petworth. Here, despite the friction between
his father and Lord Leconfield, he succeeded in charming
everybody. 'The fledgling,' his Aunt Constance wrote to his
mother, 'is quite perfect, like sunshine in the house – we are all
quite devoted to him, and shall miss him dreadfully when he
goes away.'[24]

But he had been working as well, and passed the preliminary
army test easily, coming eighth in the list in the final examination in December 1881 and reaching Sandhurst without any
trouble. The next year was devoted to learning the art of
command at Sandhurst, where he managed to come fourth in
the riding competition, before joining the Coldstream Guards
as a subaltern in February 1883. It was from this position that
George Wyndham made his first foray into the glittering world
of late-nineteenth-century English society.

Henry James, observing London life with contemplative
New England detachment, wrote that 'nowhere so much as in
England was it fortunate to be fortunate'.[25] Certainly this was

true in the 1880s, when the season, still centring around a few hundred families of breeding and wealth, was never more splendid. The great houses, such as Devonshire House and Lansdowne House, were still in full swing. Hostesses could pride themselves that their entertainments provided, by giving men of influence a chance to meet each other informally, a useful service as well as pleasure. Yet during the course of the century a subtle change had taken place. The dominant forces were still the old aristocratic families, but the industrialization of England had widened the circle of wealth. Since the abolition of the Corn Laws, agriculture had lost its predominant position. The rent rolls were no longer so potent a force as the new factories, railways and mines of industrial Britain. Certain families, like the Londonderrys, began to rely more on the coal deposits on their land than on their farms; and those who had no alternative felt the challenge to the supremacy of old money offered by the new.

Most of the newcomers wanted to be accepted rather than to challenge; and, in true British style, society opened its gates to them, even if certain of its members didn't approve. Lady Dorothy Nevill, writing at the end of the nineteenth century, declared: 'Many years ago, when I first knew London society, it was more like a large family than anything else. Everyone knew exactly who everybody was, and it was extremely difficult – nay almost impossible – for a stranger to obtain a place until credentials had been carefully examined and discussed. Mere wealth was no passport.' But, as she went on to say, this was to change. 'Very soon the old social privileges of birth and breeding were swept aside by the mob of plebeian wealth which surged into the drawing rooms, the portals of which had up till then been so jealously guarded.' Lady Dorothy was curt in her dismissal of these interlopers. 'Such individuals have changed the whole standard of living, and imported the bustle of the Stock Exchange into the drawing rooms of Mayfair.'[26]

The secret of preserving social stratifications is elasticity, and it was through this that London society was able to assimilate these possessors of new wealth and shape their values according to its own. A welcome was naturally still assured for someone like George Wyndham, a young guards officer from a family of note. To him, as for Henry James, the doors of the city opened 'into light and warmth and cheer, into good and charming relations'.[27] We may imagine the stir that his looks and easy charm caused in the Mayfair drawing rooms, for all four of Percy Wyndham's children were notably good-looking. As he drifted from luncheon to garden party, to the races, from dining table to ballroom, rubbing shoulders with eminent men and beautiful women, the attractions of this new life, where one was so easily made to feel content, must have impressed themselves upon him. The fetters of his protected youth were thrown off, yet the responsibilities of manhood seemed far away. This was a hinterland where anything must have seemed possible, except the effort involved in achieving it, to those young people who made up its inhabitants.

Wyndham was always to find this curious world attractive, for his social attributes ensured that he could command attention and admiration within its confines. Its glitter would triumph temporarily over any failure or upset that he may have suffered, and there were patient listeners, usually women, who possessed the power to soothe. In middle age he would echo his cousin Wilfrid Scawen Blunt's words, from the sonnet sequence 'The Idler's Calendar'.

'I still love London in the month of May
By an old habit, spite of dust and din
I love the fair adulterous world, whose way
Is by the pleasant banks of Serpentine
I love the worshippers at fashion's shrine,
The flowers, the incense and the pageantry
Of generations which still ask a sign
Of that dear god, whose votary I am.

I love the "greetings in the market place",
The jargon of the clubs. I love to view
The "gilded youth" who at the window pass,
For ever smiling smiles for ever new.
I love these men and women at their task
Of hunting pleasure. Hope, mysterious too,
Touches my arm and points, and seems to ask
"And you, have you no Juliet in the masque?" '

But, like the hero of a Disraeli novel, George Wyndham, when he was not riding, hunting or dancing, was beginning to turn his attention to deeper matters. Percy Wyndham was a humane and intelligent man of an independent turn of mind who encouraged George's intellectual development. When the boy was seven he was taken to see *Hamlet* at the Crystal Palace. This was the beginning of a lifelong devotion to Shakespearian theatre which was later fostered by trips with his mother to Irving's productions at the Coliseum. Amateur dramatics were a feature of Wilbury life, with Madeline Wyndham, who was an accomplished amateur artist, designing and painting the scenery, and the children and governesses all taking part with great enthusiasm.

The true emergence of the littérateur came later. Eton seemed to do nothing for him here, perhaps because his literary sensibilities needed time to develop on their own, free from set books and approved texts. But towards the end of his school-days he was beginning to forage with profit in his father's library. Neither the army nor the season could stop this development. In August 1884 he wrote from a house party in Scotland to his mother: 'Please get a few books ready for me at Wilbury, as I think I feel rather inclined to read, and it would be a pity to throw away the advantage of such a "phase". I think I should like to read Voltaire's works and "Bolingbroke" the statesman.'[28] Still, Wyndham remained conscious of his military duties. In November 1884 he volunteered for the expedition that was being sent to relieve Khartoum but was unsuccessful as only a small number of men were taken from the Guards and the Cavalry. However, in January 1885 a telegram came to him while he was hunting at Brackley. Its message was that he was to return at once as his battalion was under orders to depart for Egypt in a matter of weeks. On February 19th his family watched him leave from Wellington Barracks to join his troopship, the S.S. *Manora*, at Gravesend. His father, the English reserve breaking down at last, gave him a letter.

'I wish,' Percy Wyndham declared, 'I could give you, dear boy, the best thing I have, I would part with it myself to do so, my assurance of the certainty of life after death, and that you will see your loved ones again whatever happens, and if, which God forbid, you pass from this plane I should not let it alter my life but think of you as my dear George still, whom I shall see again. God and all good spirits keep you, my darling boy. I cannot make you know what I think of you, but I feel to have had such a son is not to have lived in vain.'[29]

Percy Wyndham was watching his son go out to fight, and perhaps die, in a war that he himself had spoken out against. It was a painful moment for the two of them, scarcely made more bearable by the father's stoicism. George, however, appeared to be equally stoical. A soldier is trained for battle and the Egyptian business was an opportunity to put this training to test. Danger was hardly considered, for the young subaltern found difficulty in coupling courage with death. When the adventurer Colonel Fred Burnaby was killed in January 1885 at the battle of Abu Klea George wrote to Madeline Wyndham in tones of admiration and surprise. 'It seems odd,' he declared, 'that Burnaby should be killed, one had almost got to think that he could not be, but it shows that even very brave people who run many risks are killed in the long run.'[30]

As his father demonstrated, not everybody unquestioningly accepted the martial spirit of late-Victorian England. On January 22nd 1885, a cousin of George Wyndham sat down to write about Burnaby's death in his diary; and his entry sheds a different light upon this colourful aristocratic soldier. 'News of Abu Klea,' it runs. 'Burnaby killed and it serves him right for he was a mere butcher, and eight other officers, including young de Lisle. These English officers are mere butchers and I confess I would rather see them all to perdition than that a single Arab should die.'[31] Before Wyndham left for Egypt the writer, tall and erect, with a full dark beard and a voice 'sinisterly soft',[32] had spoken to him and arranged for Jemal-ed-Din, the Afghan reformer, to give his young relative a talisman to ensure his safety if he was taken prisoner by the Mahdi. This was Wilfrid Scawen Blunt – poet, supporter of nationalism, and the man who took on the British Empire at the height of its power.

Chapter 2
Youth of a Rebel

As one who went against the spirit of his time, Wilfrid Scawen Blunt aroused the strongest feelings amongst his contemporaries. His own daughter Judith, with whom he quarrelled bitterly towards the end of his long life, wrote of his political opinions; 'He was completely at the mercy of oriental deceit and Irish blarney and believed every woeful tale of oppression by the British government, however fantastic. A born agitator he became an ideal "bomb thrower" for every schemer who dared not throw his own explosives, and his house soon became famous as a hotbed of conspiracy for the scum of every nation.'[1] For English diplomats and civil servants he remained an increasingly irritating enigma, for he delighted in disturbing their most firmly held ideals. Yet even Judith, writing twenty years after her father's death with an acidity that demonstrates her inability to forget their old disputes, acknowledged that he possessed 'a magic so powerful that no one could overlook him or forget him'. Still these 'hypnotic glittering eyes – strange eyes, glowing and faceted with double lights which seemed to smoulder with fire' were with her and she realized that he had left a legacy too strong to be dismissed in a few angry sentences. 'Genius,' she wrote, 'he doubtless had, but it lay in literature and poetry and an inherent sense of beauty and good taste.'[2] It has been left to others to resurrect his politics, and few tributes would have pleased him more than that of Dr Syed Mahmud, a former Indian Minister of State for External Affairs who wrote to Blunt's grandson of this 'true interpreter of the deepest and wisest instincts of the Anglo-Saxon race . . . England's greatness will hereafter be remembered through Blunt's ideas and work, and not through Balfour, Curzon and suchlike. It will take a little time before Asia remembers him and thinks of his great sympathy and fight for her freedom. Asia is not yet settled down after centuries of her bondage.'[3]

The background of this rebel was impeccably establishmentarian. He was born on August 17th 1840, the second son of Francis Blunt, the scion of an old Sussex family who, after being educated with Byron at Harrow, served in the army in the Peninsula under Sir John Moore during the retreat from Corunna. The Blunts had estates at Crabbet near Horsham, but were staying that summer with Francis Blunt's sister (and George Wyndham's grandmother), the reclusive Lady Leconfield at Petworth. Thus Wilfrid Blunt was born at Petworth House, where George Wyndham spent part of his childhood. Blunt's early years were not to be so settled as those of his cousin. Within two years his father was dead and the family were forced to let Crabbet, moving to Petworth Rectory House. Here they stayed, living in the shadow of the great seat of the Wyndham family, and playing in its park with their relations, until Mrs Blunt took Wilfrid, his older brother Francis and his sister Alice off on a journey through France in 1846. Then in 1847 the boys were sent to a preparatory school at Twyford near Winchester. Here they remained in misery, until the winter of 1847 when their mother, realizing that the place did not suit them, led her offspring on another European journey. The memories of the Twyford year were not happy ones for the young Blunt. The bullying was brutal and the physical discomfort an agony. 'Morally,' he remembered, 'the school was a sink,'[4] and to find oneself trundling through Europe again in the family coach was a welcome relief.

There were to be more surprises. In 1850 Francis and Wilfrid were expecting to go to Harrow, their father's old school, when they were suddenly told that there was to be a change of plan. They were instead to travel in Italy with a tutor and thus set of once more for the Continent with their mother who broke the news to them at Boulogne that she had been received into the Roman Catholic Church at Easter. The means to her conversion had been Henry Edward Manning, himself recently, until his own conversion, rector of Lavington near Petworth. With him she had discussed the virtues of high Anglicanism, and Manning had encouraged her to take their shared ideas to what he believed was their logical conclusion.

The children, having been brought up by a stern Scottish Presbyterian nurse to abhor Rome, burst into tears; but before winter was out their conversion, with the aid of a tutor, was accomplished, though Wilfrid held out longer than the others. In 1852 at Aix-en-Provence the Roman Catholic Church received them. Its faith was to have a firm influence on Blunt, proving an alternate source of strength and bewilderment throughout his life. His Catholicism now sent him, in 1853, to the Jesuits at Stoneyhurst, and later to Oscott where he was taught by Dr Meynell, the most profound of his early mentors who introduced him to Shelley, Keats and literature. Side by side with his intellectual development came a spiritual awakening. He writes of himself before his encounters with the Jesuits as neither caring for nor understanding the things of the spirit, being 'by nature affectionate and truthful' but otherwise 'idle, greedy and selfish'. At Stoneyhurst there was a change which, as Blunt describes in a letter of 1876 to Dr Meynell, came largely through the good offices of Father Porter, a Jesuit who took a particular interest in him. 'To please him I became a good boy. I made a spiritual retreat, and I then discovered for the first time, as a reality, the scheme of God's government of the world. I learned that this life was only a preparation for another life, and, with the alternatives of heaven and hell before me, I was logical enough to see that the future was the only one worth living for. At that time I vividly felt God's presence as a reality in my daily occupations.

I did my best to please him . . . I was only six months at (Stoneyhurst); but I am convinced that, if I had remained there, the influence I have described would have lasted. Perhaps I might now have been a Jesuit.'⁵

With Oscott and Dr Meynell came a union of the spirit and the intellect. Hitherto Blunt had surrendered only to the emotional side of Christianity, for the Jesuits had been careful not to baffle their charges with too rational an approach. At first the religion at Oscott seemed unattractive. 'Its representatives among ourselves,' Blunt wrote to Meynell in 1876, '. . . were, for the most part, coarse and rampant . . . The president preached all his sermons on holiday afternoons and bored us accordingly . . . The soul cried out for more and at last more was provided . . . You gave us the spiritual food for which we longed . . . You taught us to think, to reason, to argue.'⁶ Dr Meynell, a brilliant Yorkshireman, awakened Blunt in a way that the Eton schoolmasters had failed to achieve with the young George Wyndham. The Jesuits had feared reason; but Dr Meynell took reason and used it to show the rationality that he believed to be inherent in the Christian faith. 'You showed us God in His works, in the necessities of the human mind, in the metaphysical contradictions involved by a denial of Him. At that time I believed, with the most implicit faith, that not only were the truths of religion reducible to absolute mathe-matical certainty, but that true reason could not do otherwise than fortify and illuminate our belief in them. I think I had no suspicion at that time that its sword could ever turn in my hand against myself. With these ideas, and a taste for discussion, but with no very profound knowledge either of theology or metaphysics, I went into the world.'⁷

The world was now a stranger place. In June 1853 Mrs Blunt had died. The daughter of the Reverend Chandler of Witley near Godalming, Manning described her as the wittiest woman he knew. Despite her capriciousness, she had provided one of the few solid features of her second son's peripatetic childhood. Henceforth he and his brother and sister were entrusted to the

care of two guardians: Mrs Wyndham (later Lady Leconfield) and Henry Currie, their mother's first cousin and a banker.
Both of these disapproved of Mrs Blunt's conversion, particularly the evangelical Lady Leconfield.

However 'Aunt Wyndham' as the young Blunts called her
was good to them. After Oscott Wilfrid continued with his
education, learning French in Lausanne and lodging in London
with the Walford family to visit tutors. Then, in 1858, one of
Mrs Wyndham's sons-in-law failed to pass the entrance examination for the diplomatic service and she suggested that her
nephew should stand in his place. He left for France to perfect
his French in Orléans, passed the examination that winter and
seemed set for a career as a diplomat when the Foreign Office
mysteriously declared that he was not suitable on account of his
unsatisfactory references. Mrs Wyndham immediately inter-
vened and, having dragged Wilfrid with her to Whitehall,
learnt from the minister, Lord Malmesbury, that the source
of the trouble was her nephew's former landlord Walford who
complained that Blunt had made a pass at his wife. On being
confronted with this the boy burst into tears. Malmesbury,
under the influence of Aunt Wyndham, was compassionate.
Blunt's nomination went forward, he was gazetted on the last
day of 1858 as an unpaid attaché, and all that remained of
the matter was some affectionate teasing from his new Foreign
Office associates.

In later life Blunt was to be contemptuously dismissive of his
early years in the diplomatic service, maintaining that the
only talents needed for an attaché or junior secretary were
sociability and ease of manner. Yet it was an agreeable milieu
within which a young man could take his time to grow up,
seeing the world as he did so. The first post was Athens where
he caused a stir with his feminine good looks, rode a horse
called Apocalypse, and travelled through the Morea, thinking
constantly of Byron, with his brother Francis who was now
an ensign in the 60th regiment. In the summer of 1860 he
was transferred to Germany and travelled across Europe to

his new post, working for a few weeks in Constantinople for the ambassador Sir Henry Bulwer before pressing on towards Frankfurt. Journeys then were longer and good travelling companions could make all the difference. On the boat from Constantinople Lord Stanley of Alderley, who had embraced the Moslem faith, amply filled this role, fascinating the boy with his profound knowledge of the Mohammedan world. In Vienna Blunt saw a young man of twenty-nine at work in the Chancery, with a distinguished face and curly hair 'writing with one hand busy with his work and his other caressing his black poodle's head'.[8] It was Robert Lytton, later Viceroy of India, who published verses under the name of Owen Meredith. Five years hence they were to embark upon a remarkable friendship that was to last until Lytton's death in 1890.

At Frankfurt Lady Malet, wife of the ambassador, was fascinated by the new creed of Darwinism. The embassy was full of discussions and arguments in which Blunt realized he could play no part, because his Catholicism prevented him from reading the necessary literature. Despite his confessor forbidding it, he read the books and found himself faced with a crisis of conscience. He could no longer accept unthinkingly the tenets of his youthful faith; and, to make matters worse, was in this condition when he heard the news that his sister Alice was thinking of entering a convent. Under his influence she reconsidered her intention; but the incident showed him the awesome power of religious fervour. Before transferring to Madrid in 1862 he went on a retreat at the Redemptionist Convent in Clapham to try to revive the feelings that the Jesuits and Dr Meynell had inculcated in him. These days were useless. The old ardour was gone. In Madrid he consoled himself with bullfighting and laughing at the Spanish royal family; but by the time his transfer to Paris came through in 1863 Blunt's moral anxieties and scruples were already weak enough to be washed aside by the rising tide of his hedonism.

Imperial Paris of the 1860s was a self-confident and exciting city. To a young man 'too beautiful to live', discovering the depths of his own sensuality, its pleasures were to prove all too enticing. At first, after the provincialism of Madrid and the earnestness of Frankfurt, Blunt seemed almost overcome by the new sophistication. This pursuit of pleasure, in its most obvious and sensual form, was surprising. Despite the failure of the Clapham retreat his Catholicism had not entirely left him. As he was to observe later :

' 'Tis no small matter to have lived in Rome,
In the Church's very bosom and abode,
Cloistered and cradled there, a child of God.'

But Lady Malet's doubts and this strange hedonistic city contrived to obscure his faith. Thus, here, amid the Paris of La Paiva, La Barucci and the great courtesans, Blunt experienced a love affair which, by fully awakening his senses, was to leave a mark on him for the rest of his life. There had been earlier infatuations, with girls and with older women; but, despite the Walford incident, at the time of his arrival in Napoleon III's Paris the young Blunt had not yet experienced physical love to the full. Here he was to associate with a woman who would guide him through its rituals with a hand as expert as any in Europe, and arouse his senses to a pitch that he would afterwards claim they never attained with any other partner throughout his long and active amatory career.

The story of Catherine Walters, or 'Skittles' as she came to be called, is one of the most fascinating of the Victorian era, if only as an example of the social mobility of a professional courtesan. Skittles, born in Liverpool in 1839 near the Toxteth docks, the daughter of an obscure customs official, and supposedly given her nickname on account of an early job in a skittles gallery, had arrived in Paris in 1863 with, although she was only 24, a string of legends attached to her name. Some said that she had been a bareback rider in her youth with a circus, others spoke of her unofficial engagement to the heir to one of England's greatest dukedoms; but what was sure was that she had captivated London with her beauty and daring and now seemed set to do the same to Paris. Horsemanship had been the key to her initial success. In Liverpool it is probable that she had early access to a livery stables where she had helped with the horses and taught herself to ride. Certainly on her arrival in London she launched herself on Rotten Row with great aplomb. Here she was first observed by the twenty-eight-year-old Marquis of Hartington, heir to the Duke of Devonshire and prominent Liberal politician, later to lead the exodus of Liberal Unionists from Gladstone's government. They rapidly, despite Hartington's dilatory nature, became lovers. For her there was no distant love nest in St John's Wood. The Marquis provided her with a house in Mayfair, several servants, horses in abundance, and a life settlement of £2000 a year. Yet it could not, and did not last. Hartington had his political career to think of and for a future Duchess of Devonshire to originate in Toxteth was unthinkable. The Marquis began to take an interest in the young German Duchess of Manchester, whom he was later to marry, and Skittles left, rejected, for Paris in 1863.

In Paris she found herself faced with formidable rivals. Nevertheless Skittles was soon turning heads in the Bois and received her first French patron in the form of Achille Fould the banker. He provided her with horses, and launched her into the *demimonde*. Yet her French was not good and to begin with she sought the company of the English community. It was here that she knew, amongst others, Lord Hubert de Burgh, later the Marquis of Clanricarde, and Wilfrid Scawen Blunt.

In later life Clanricarde and Blunt were to be bitterly opposed over the Irish question, but now they were colleagues in the embassy in Paris. De Burgh, as Clanricarde was then called, was some six years older, arrogant, rich and eccentric. Blunt was less certain of himself, recovering from a spiritual crisis and unhappy with the inconsequentiality of his life. He was turning towards literature for solace, writing 'poems not dispatches' and possessed all the romanticism of a young man

who had plenty of expectations but little experience. His youth
and his innocence appealed to Skittles who, despite the hardness of her world, still allowed herself the luxury of sentimentality. He was also extraordinarily handsome.

Initially Blunt was frightened. Skittles was not conventionally beautiful, although her large eyes and delicate features
were attractive. An affair with a courtesan was not this young
romantic's idea of first love. In his *Love-Sonnets of Proteus*,
in which Skittles is Manon, as she is the heroine of his sonnet
sequence *Esther*, he speaks to her thus:

> 'If I had chosen thee, thou shouldst have been
> A virgin proud, untamed, immaculate,
> Chaste as the morning star, a saint, a queen
> Scarred by no wars, no violence of hate.
> Thou shouldst have been of soul commensurate
> With thy fair body, brave and virtuous
> And kind and just; And, if of poor estate,
> At least an honest woman for my house.
> I would have had thee come of honoured blood
> And honourable nurture. Thou shouldst bear
> Sons to my pride and daughters to my heart,
> And men should hold thee happy, wise, and good.
> Lo, thou art none of this, but only fair.
> Yet I must love thee, read, as thou art.'

But she gave to Blunt at least as much as he was capable, at
this young age, of giving to her.

> 'Brave as a falcon and as merciless,
> With bright eyes watching still the world, thy prey'

She harnessed herself to him; and soon, as he writes in *Esther*,
he could scarcely conceive of himself before their partnership
and felt ashamed of his old innocence.

Although Skittles was only a year older than Blunt she was

infinitely more experienced. She was no mere prattling whore, but cultivated and well informed far beyond the terms of her upbringing. It was an extraordinary period of awakening for him, and one that conquered all restraint. He found himself raised to new heights of ecstasy, to be extending, almost daily, his field of experience and to be undergoing the transformation from an unknowing boy to a man. Nothing else seemed necessary to him at this time, save only this woman who appeared to have an almost superhuman power over his senses. In 1876 he was to write to Dr Meynell: 'As long as I was in love my love sufficed me, and I cannot say, as you do, that no human love ever satisfied the desires of my soul. I have on more than one occasion, seemed for days together to be walking some cubits high above the ground; and certainly during the whole of that time, some three years, I did not think of or regret the loss of religion.'[9]

Such an affair could not last. The nature of Skittles's profession dictated that she must not dally too long in the company of a young and poor diplomat with few prospects for the future. Other suitors began to take Blunt's place and his ecstasy was transformed into dejection. She who 'all hearts knew' seemed merely to have added him to her collection, and he spoke of himself disdainfully as 'her pensioner and bondsman . . . doing a fool's service for love of thee'. As they drifted apart dejection became anger and anger, in its turn, exhaustion. He was not able to fulfil his duties so preoccupied was his mind with her capriciousness. Later they were to become friends again, in England, where he would visit her, in common with the Prince of Wales, in her houses in Chesterfield Street and afterwards South Street, but a romantic disposition cannot turn love into friendship overnight. So he left Paris, 'banished by the paternal care' of Lord Hammond of the Foreign Office to Lisbon, temporarily a spent force, now acquainted with 'knowledge of life and love and suffering' who would, nevertheless, look back some thirty years later to observe 'this was my term of glory'.[10]

Wilfrid Scawen Blunt and Lady Anne shortly after their marriage in 1869.

George Wyndham in the Coldstream Guards 1885.

Blunt was to find a saviour during this 'terrible and un-deserved exile'.[11] On arriving at the Chancery on August 1863 in Lisbon he was told that everybody was away on leave except a young attaché by the name of Lytton who was living in the hills at Cintra. Tired and dispirited, he hired a ram-shackle carriage and embarked upon a journey through the dust and heat to find his new colleague. As he grew nearer his destination, he fell asleep under the inexorable Portuguese sun. When he awoke, at the top of a pass, the air was clear and it was as if he had emerged from some terrible stifling ordeal. Eventually, amid the mountain mist and sweet-smelling cork woods they stopped at the door of a little country inn kept by an ancient Welsh landlady and the young man whom he had briefly seen five years ago in Vienna came out to welcome him with all the abandon and sympathy of a long-lost friend. Lytton too was a poet. 'All that evening,' Blunt later wrote, 'and till late into the night we sat talking of things divine, poetry, philosophy, and sentiment, and many an evening afterwards, till the hours grew small and the candles burned low in their sockets and a new world of hope was opened to me by his sympathy, and wisdom, and encouragement.'[12]

These were days for restful discussions and mutual admira-tion. Sometimes they would ride together through the chang-ing landscape of the Cintra hills, or sit reading their own work to each other, Lytton often improvising verses, which he could do with great facility, or declaiming from Browning or Victor Hugo, his two favourite poets. Mornings were spent writing poetry, afternoons riding or walking, and evenings in reading and declamations. 'On diplomatic business,' Blunt wrote, 'I do not remember that we wasted a single word or a single thought.'[13] They were entirely alone as Lytton's wife was in England and there was no company to be had in this remote region. After three months spent in this way, Blunt's emotional wounds began slowly to heal. When he had stood 'at that parting of the ways in youth when a little sympathy, more or less, of a certain kind means a whole world of difference in its choice of a road – on this side to salvation, on that to perdition'[14] his friend had tipped the balance in favour of salvation. But the mournful introspection brought on by his break with Skittles could still return.

Luckily Blunt's next post proved to be enlivening. He was to return to Frankfurt, once more with the Malets. This was a different Blunt to the one who had been so perplexed by the discussions on Darwinism and the ridiculing of the Church that had occurred during his last stay in Frankfurt. Experience and Skittles had made him set less store by slavish adherence to the Catholicism of his youth. They had also hardened him. Henceforth the 'fair faced frightened boy with eyes of truth' became 'a pirate of the sea'. He would never allow himself to be enslaved by another as he had been enslaved by Catherine Walters; and in his final sonnet to Manon he declares, in angry lines evoked by the memory of an old humiliation :

> 'Let others suffer. I have suffered wrong.
> Let others love, and love as tenderly.
> Oh, Manon, there are women yet unborn
> Shall rue thy frailty, else am I foresworn.'

Lady Malet proved to be as helpful and congenial as Lytton had prophesied. At Frankfurt she introduced Blunt to Bismarck; but, despite his admiration for the Count, who left him with 'a feeling of the heroic', he did not care for Germans. It was therefore with a certain amount of relief that he left for South America in 1867, his spirit of adventure roused by this journey to one of the earth's remoter regions.

Here he gave way to the wilder side of his nature. Now with his Parisian traumas behind him, he took advantage of his great appeal to women. Yet philandering was not allowed to take up all his time. In Buenos Aires in 1868 he met the explorer Richard Burton, then Consul at Santos and drinking away his boredom. This meeting of two great travellers, the one already half-way through his restless life, the other still on the edge of his, provided the younger man with one of his strangest experiences to date. At this stage Burton 'seldom went to bed sober' and 'his dress and appearance were those suggesting a released convict' with 'a rusty black coat with a crumpled black silk stock, his throat destitute of collar, a costume which his muscular frame and immense chest made singularly and incongruously hideous, above it a countenance the most sinister I have ever seen, dark, cruel, treacherous, with eyes like a wild beast's'. He reminded Blunt of 'a black leopard, caged but unforgiving'. However their talks were 'of the most intimate kind, religion, philosophy, travel, politics', and Burton 'at the end of his second bottle, with a gaucho's navajo handy to his hand'[15] would ferociously relate an unexpurgated catalogue of his more spectacular exploits. This was the man who once boomed at a young curate: 'Sir, I'm proud to say that I have committed every sin in the Decalogue';[16] who delighted in shocking and knew very well how to; but this was also Frank Harris's Burton 'unbuttoned' and talking 'as only Burton could talk', the Burton 'of encyclopaedic reading', who 'knew English poetry and prose astonishingly . . . A magnificent story teller, with intermingled appeals of pathos and rollicking fun, campfire effects, jets of flame against the night.'[17] At this stage the East was still virtually unknown to Blunt and now, through the drunken tales of an inspired genius, he began to acquire something of its spirit.

To leave South America in 1869 for Switzerland was a considerable anti-climax. As if to make up for this, Wilfrid Blunt, at the age of twenty-nine, took a dramatic step. On June 18th 1869 he married Lady Anne Noel, the daughter of the Earl of Lovelace and granddaughter of Byron, and resigned from the diplomatic service.

Chapter 3
Egypt and Arabi

'I have always heard,' Constance Wyndham, later Leconfield, of Petworth wrote to Madeline Wyndham in 1869, 'that Lady Anne Noel . . . has a "good bit" of money. Her grandmother Lady Wentworth left it to her to make a home for her brother in London, but at one time she lived in lodgings by herself and practised the violin 6 hours a day. All the family are more or less cracked – the father was a vegetarian when I knew him, the eldest brother insisted upon earning his own livelihood as a mechanic, and to anyone who has seen the present Lord Wentworth any further remarks are unnecessary. However we will hope that this marriage may be all that we can wish.'[1]

Lady Anne's family history was remarkable. She was the daughter of Byron's Ada, only child of the poet and Annabelle Milbanke, and had been brought up chiefly by her grandmother Lady Byron. Her romantic ancestry must have appealed to Blunt, as well as her gentle good looks. Judith, their daughter, has described her mother, from childhood remembrance, in sympathetic terms. 'Young, ardent and vividly alive, her conversation was always interesting and amusing with the spontaneous originality which sometimes so charmingly accompanies unusual mental scope. She had an underlying magnetism which endeared her to everyone and a voice, Byron's voice, whose sweetness had an extraordinary attraction . . .'[2]

But there was more to Lady Anne than sweetness. She was also an artist of unusual talent who had studied drawing with

Ruskin and who was to paint a remarkable portrait of her husband – a huge unashamedly grandiose equestrian picture with the rider (Wilfrid) dressed in flowing Arabian robes. She was an accomplished linguist who spoke German, French, Latin, Italian, Spanish, and a Swiss patois and later was to master Arabic more comprehensively than Blunt himself, much to his fury. Yet she had not the flair that made her husband enliven whatever he chose to turn his hand to. Nowhere is this more obvious than in her books about their Arabian journeys, *The Pilgrimage to Nejd* and *Bedouin Tribes of the Euphrates*. These are methodical works, still of interest to Arabian scholars but, for the general reader, too heavy and inert. Despite Constance Leconfield's story of her practising her violin six hours a day in lodgings, she rarely attempted to play anything more demanding than the most lugubrious studies. Up to the end of her life scales formed the backbone of her repertoire; and this, when they were at home together, would drive Blunt almost beside himself with irritation.

Lady Anne had need of interests into which she could retire from the turbulence of their marriage. Blunt must have been an exceptionally difficult husband; and the demands put upon Lady Anne's patience and her pride were formidable. Yet as his philandering increased and his crusades became more vehement she grew more, rather than less, tolerant. Their house in Egypt became her real home where she could indulge her love and knowledge of the East and the Arabs. Battered by the world, she withdrew from it, becoming increasingly eccentric as she grew older. Arabic became her first language. She told her family that she thought in Arabic, even when in England, and, when away, always tried to keep in touch with Arabia.

Her clothes could be alarming. After her Eastern experience she thought it wrong to be without a hat or turban, even in her bedroom. Thus in bed she would wear a small Irish fishing hat and mackintosh, instead of a nightdress, to go with it, lying against her pillows, 'dressed', in the words of her son-in-law Neville Lytton, 'as though for a southwest gale in the channel'.[3]

But Lady Anne was a good wife. At first she must have seemed to fulfil all the worldly attributes that he could wish for. As Constance Leconfield observed she had 'a good bit' of money, which enabled him to retire from the diplomatic service and which, added to the inheritance that passed to him on the death of his brother Francis in 1872, allowed him to lead a life free from the necessity to earn his living. His daughter Judith castigates him for heartlessly taking advantage of the fortune while treating Lady Anne with disdain. It is undoubtedly true that her financial assistance enabled him to support the causes that he took up after their marriage, such as the legal defence of the Egyptian nationalist Arabi; but often her enthusiasm for these was scarcely less than his own. Her love for Egypt and the East was profounder and more informed than his. In Ireland she accompanied him to the Woodford meeting at which he was almost certain an attempt would be made to arrest him, and she fought an election in his name while he was in jail. Blunt in his quieter moments was forced to recognize how much she had contributed, materially and otherwise, to his life. Towards the end he advised his grandson to marry, as he had done, somebody with money. The advantages, he said, were outstanding, and he was even prepared to go to the extent of arranging a liaison between the young man and the child of someone he knew who possessed the necessary requirements. He acknowledged also her stoical goodness, which was often almost infuriating, and after her death, as his biographer notes, observed that she was 'of the salt of the earth. Nobody was ever so entirely and naturally good as she was.'[4]

She remained devoted to him. Even after their estrangement in 1907, a brief meeting was enough for her once again to fall into the power of his personality. His romantic outlook and bearing were to have a lasting hold on her, putting her in mind of her famous grandfather. When allowed, she became his enthusiastic partner in anything that he undertook, whether it was planning a journey, building a house or translating a poem from her precious Arabic. She may have felt that she had failed him in not producing a son, although one was born in 1870, only to live for four days, and perhaps tried to make up for this loss by assisting him in whatever way she could. In 1880 she was received into the Catholic Church by Cardinal Manning, thus adopting Blunt's religion, of which he was by this time an unenthusiastic follower. But in 1869 their life stretched before them. The bonds of his diplomatic service were broken; and Lady Anne was 'a virgin proud, untamed, immaculate', a young woman 'brave and virtuous and kind and just', 'of honoured blood and honourable nurture'. He could foresee her bearing 'sons to my pride and daughters to my heart', and the whole world should rejoice with this descendant of Byron and her Byronic lover.

The years after 1869 were to be exceptionally full. From 1869 to 70 the Blunts were living in Paris, he staying on to witness the fall of the city to the Prussians; and in 1870 they moved to the beautiful Charles II house of Newbuildings (a family property) near Horsham in Sussex. Then in 1872 a double disaster, in the form of the deaths of both Wilfrid's brother and sister, took them to Crabbet of which he was now the master by inheritance. In 1873, having made extensive architectural alterations to their new house, they left on a journey to Belgrade and Constantinople where Blunt developed consumption and was informed by doctors that he had only a short time left to live. In order to make the most profitable use of this time, and despite a collapsed lung, they wandered around Turkey, in the wilds of Scutari, gaining here an enthusiasm for out-of-the-way travel that was soon to develop into a passion. It was also the beginning of the formation of Blunt's political creed. Having 'spent six pleasant summer weeks wandering in the hills and through the poppy fields of

Asia Minor, away from beaten tracks and seeing as much of the Turkish peasant life as our entire ignorance of the language allowed . . . we were impressed, as all travellers have been, with the honest goodness of these people and the badness of their government'.[5]

In Scutari Wilfrid Blunt discovered a new freedom, that of a vast landscape unencumbered by the interfering paternalism of the West. 'I remember,' he wrote later, 'telling the peasants, who had complained to me through my Armenian dragoman of hardship in their lives at government hands, that there were countries in a still worse plight than their own, where if a poor man so much as lay down by the roadside at night and got together a few sticks to cook a meal he ran the risk of being brought before the Cadi and cast into prison; and I remember that my listeners refused to believe my tale or that such great tyranny existed anywhere in the world. My deduction from this incident is the earliest political reflection that I can remember making in regard to Eastern things.'[6] Thus began an obsession that was to last him for the rest of his life.

In the first months of 1874, the Blunts went to Algeria. Here Wilfrid's political education was carried a stage further, for this was 'an Eastern people in violent subjection to a Western', namely the French. The Franco-Prussian war had been followed by an uprising which had spread to the outskirts of the city of Algiers. Now the French were reasserting their power. Native property was being confiscated and redistributed to Europeans. The poverty in urban areas was intense and Blunt later observed that, despite his francophilism, he sympathized wholly with the Arabs. In the Sahara, amongst the wilder more remote tribes, the situation was better. They, with their pastoral life and traditions, were materially better off than the town dwellers, being largely unaffected by the vicissitudes of French colonial policy. In Jebel Amour the strange chanting and vigour of the nomads appealed to Blunt's sense of drama and pride. 'The contrast', he wrote, 'between their noble pastoral life on the one hand, with their camel herds and horses, a life of high tradition filled with the memory of heroic deeds, and on the other hand the ignoble squalor of the Frank settlers, with their wineshops and their swine, was one which could not escape us, or fail to rouse in us an angry sense of the incongruity which has made of these last the lords of the land and of those their servants. It was a new political lesson which I took to heart, though still regarding it as in no sense my personal affair.'⁷ Then in the winter of 1875-6 Wilfrid Blunt took his first step towards abandoning his detachment. He visited Egypt, which was to be the cause of his first great crusade.

The English involvement in Egypt, which the Blunts were to contest so enthusiastically, came to a head in the late 1870s and 1880s. The diplomatic cunning of Disraeli begins the story of its tortuous course. In 1875 he arranged for Britain his famous purchase of Suez Canal shares and thus the future of Egypt became a matter of acute interest for successive British governments. The country at this time was part of the Ottoman Empire, ruled by a Khedive or hereditary viceroy. In 1860 the Khedive Ismail had succeeded the prudent Said whose rule had led Egypt to a pinnacle of high material prosperity. At first much was expected of Ismail. He had been, before his succession, a rich landowner whose large estates in Upper Egypt were managed in an enlightened and efficient manner. Many European travellers had praised his shrewdness and ability.

However, power turned his head and his money-making talents came to be used not for his country but for himself. His judgement of people led him to listen to those who were unworthy of his trust. In April 1876 the Khedive's borrowing had become so out of control that he decided to suspend payment of his debts. France and Britain, particularly France, were anxious to protect their citizens who were bondholders of the Egyptian debt; and a commission was set up to examine the situation. Lord Derby was slow in nominating British representatives, and it was not until a Dual Control (with a Frenchman and an Englishman as controllers-general) was set up that, early in 1878, Sir C. Rivers Wilson and Major Evelyn Baring (later Earl of Cromer, British Consul-General in Cairo and effective ruler of Egypt for 23 years) went out as British representatives. Ismail, with obstinate cunning, stood out against all reforms, and thus, in 1878, the Sultan was obliged by the two European powers to replace him with his son Tewfik.

However in 1881 a new force entered the scene, riding on the back of Egyptian military discontent. In 1879 the Egyptian Army officers had mutinied over arrears of pay. Their demands were satisfied and the arrears were paid up but the potentially explosive situation remained. Anti-foreign sentiment grew in strength, fostered by the presence of the new European officials, who seemed to be dictating the policy of the country, and the Turks, Circassians and other Levantines who surrounded the Khedive. In 1881 this sentiment transformed itself into a movement of formidable popular appeal. Tewfik was compelled, as a result of a new wave of officer protest, to dismiss his war minister. Then on September 10th the officers struck again. The Khedive's palace was surrounded and demands were presented, including the removal of the present government, a new constitution and an increase of the army from 4000 to 18,000 men. Tewfik, holed up like a captive, was in no position to refuse. The leader of these rebels was Colonel Arabi Pasha, a native Egyptian, champion of the Fellahin, whose greatest ally in the West was to be Wilfrid Scawen Blunt.

Blunt, before the age of forty, had played no part in politics. Until 1880 he had, in his own words, 'never so much as made a speech to an audience or written an article for a review, or a letter to a newspaper'. At the beginning of Chapter IV of his *Secret History of Egypt* he gives some reasons for his long silence. 'Constitutionally shy in early life,' he declares, 'I had shrunk from publicity in any shape, and the diplomatic training I had had only aggravated my repugnance of being *en évidence*. Now, however, having persuaded myself that I had a mission in the Oriental world, however vague and ill-defined, I began to talk and write . . .'[8] Later in India he was to tell a Moslem schoolmaster that he took an interest in Mohammedan matters because 'in youth I had led a life of folly, and that I wished to do some good before I died'.[9] But the reasons for this break with his youthful hedonism were surely more complex than that.

Wilfrid Scawen Blunt was, by temperament, a romantic who had all the Byronic craving for action and adventure. A cause dear to him was a cause worthy of all that he could give it, and, if he was inclined to change his battlefields, while on them he would fight with all the fury at his command. Previously pleasure and poetry had been the twin pursuits of his adult life; and it was another poet, Lytton, who, on leaving to be Viceroy of India in 1876, wrote to him, almost enviously : 'We have chosen different paths in life – you pleasure, I duty – which doubtless others will mistake for ambition of which I have not a grain. I know not which of us two is the wisest or the least foolish in his choice. But probably we have both of us made a mistake for neither pleasure nor duty are any guarantee for happiness.'[10]

Blunt discovered that there was truth in his friend's words. No matter how ferociously pleasure might be pursued there was still a feeling of emptiness which grew as the years went by. To be young and amorous had been glorious for a while, with all the delights of conquest and admiration; but there can be no lasting satisfaction with such an existence. This did not mean that sensuality was to be spurned, but merely mixed with a more purposeful life. At the end of his *Love-Sonnets of Proteus* Blunt voiced this need :

> 'I would do service to my kind, contrive
> Something of good for men, some happiness
> For those who in the world still love and live,
> And as my fathers did, so end my days.
> I would earn praise I too, of honest men.'

To devote all his time to poetry would have been one solution, but there was nothing of the poetic recluse about Wilfrid
Blunt. His verses flowed from his life, and for them to flow
there must be a life full of sources of inspiration. Here again
action was the creed. As he wrote:

> 'The faith I held I hold, as when a boy
> I left my books for cricket bat and gun,
> The tales of poets are but scholars' themes.
> In my hot youth I held it that a man
> With heart to dare and stomach to enjoy
> Had better work to his hand in any plan
> Of any folly, so the thing were done,
> Than in the noblest dreaming of mere dreams.'

So it was that he espoused the cause of anti-imperialism. The
conversion was gradual. Despite his experiences in Algeria
he was still, during his first Egyptian winter of 1875-6, in his
own words, 'though not perhaps even then enthusiastically so,
a believer in the common English creed that England had a
providential mission in the East, and that our wars were only
waged there for honest and beneficent reasons'.[11] Fresh from
the Mediterranean, the Blunts struck out into the Egyptian
countryside.

The misrule of the Khedive Ismail and his profiteering clique
had led to mass starvation. The Fellahin, victims 'of monstrous
oppression', were observed by the Blunts with mounting horror;
and the travellers were shocked by the indifference to their
plight, exemplified by a banquet given for Steven Cave, an expert sent out from England to report on the state of the
country's finances, by the Khedive in the Viceregal lodge at the
Pyramids. Here the table was spread 'literally under the eyes of
a starving multitude of peasants, the very peasants Mr Cave
was there to save from ruin'.[12] In the spring of 1876 Blunt left
Cairo for Arabia convinced that there was a great deal wrong
with what he had seen.

The journeys he made in Arabia with Lady Anne further encouraged his sympathy for those who were obliged to live under a great empire. The first trip, in 1876, was foolhardy in the extreme. Despite their elementary Arabic and ignorance of the terrain they crossed the Suez Canal and made a long journey through the Sinai Peninsula and on by Aqaba to Jerusalem. However, after various mishaps they reached their objective and left for England, only to return in the winter of 1877-8 to visit Aleppo, Baghdad and the Euphrates valley where they came into contact with the great Bedouin tribes of Mesopotamia and the Syrian desert south of Palmyra. Their Arabic, particularly Lady Anne's, had improved and they began to make use of what they saw and heard. Here again Blunt came up against an imperial administration, and here again his sympathies lay with the governed Arabs rather than the governing Turks. 'The Turk in his own home in Asia Minor has a number of honest and manly virtues,' he later wrote, 'but as a master in a subject land he is too often a rapacious tyrant.'[13]

Wilfrid Blunt's travels excited official attention. After his return he was taken, on May 14th 1878, to see the Foreign Secretary Lord Salisbury by his cousin, Philip Currie of the Foreign Office, who was then Salisbury's private secretary. Salisbury listened courteously to the traveller's views but offered little comment on his remarks about the Ottoman Empire. This was scarcely surprising as he was, the next year, to guarantee to the Sultan the whole of his Asiatic dominions. Blunt grew increasingly depressed by the great power diplomacy of the time. He saw the Congress of Berlin and the Cyprus Convention of 1878 as a cynical carve-up of the world at which statesmen decided, in the course of an afternoon's bargaining, the fate of millions, who were thus robbed of control over their own and their children's future. It was a relief to return, in the autumn of that year, to Arabia. On their journey to Bagdad the previous winter the Blunts had purchased several Arab mares, which were to form the beginnings of the celebrated Crabbet Arabian stud. Now they were to embark on their most challenging trip to date; an expedition from Damascus into central Arabia – to Nejd, the original home of the Arabian horse.

Here they penetrated one of the most remote regions of the Arab world. The Emir Mohammed Ibn Rashid, ruler of independent Nejd, received them 'with all possible honour'. Blunt was delighted at the pride and independence of the Emir's subjects. He saw their sovereign's benevolent absolutism, in this simple pastoral setting, as a noble form of government. 'Here,' he observed, 'was a community living as our idealists have dreamed, without taxes, without police, without conscription, without compulsion of any kind, whose only law was public opinion, and whose only order a principle of honour. Here, too, was a people poor yet contented, and, according to their few wants, living in abundance, who to all questions I asked of them (and how many lands had I not put the same in vain) had answered me invariably, "Thank God we are not as other nations are. Here we have our own government. Here we are satisfied." '[14]

In 1879 they visited India where Lytton was now Viceroy, with Blunt hopeful at last, as 'a good Conservative and a member of the Carlton Club', of observing the virtues of British imperialism. Lytton opened the doors of his government to them. Sir John Strachey, his Finance Minister, led Blunt through the labyrinthine ways of Indian taxation and economics and Sir Alfred Lyall, his Foreign Minister, heard the traveller's views on the desirability of an Arabia free from the bondage of Ottoman rule.

Blunt's reactions were far from ecstatic. He wrote to a friend : 'I am disappointed with India, which seems just as ill-governed as the rest of Asia, only with good intentions instead of bad ones or none at all.'[15] What disturbed him was that the British gave to the Indian what they thought he ought to have rather than what he actually needed or wanted. Harry Brand, the radical Member of Parliament and friend of Blunt, was told this in another letter. 'I do not clearly understand why we English take their money from these starving Hindoos to make railroads for them which they don't want, and turnpike roads and jails and lunatic asylums and memorial buildings to Sir Bartle Frere, and why we insist on their feeding out of their wretched handfuls of rice immense armies of policemen and magistrates and engineers. They want none of these things and they want their rice very badly, as anybody can see by looking at their ribs.'[16]

Thus, through travel and enquiry, Blunt's reflections and observations began to take the form of a political creed. The East and the Arab cause were, he believed, objects worthy of passionate attention; yet still he felt the bonds of his own ignorance. In November of 1880 he once again departed for Arabia, this time to study the Mohammedan religion. Here, in Cairo and at Jidda, he listened while others discoursed. It was these conversations which provided the basis for his articles for the *Fortnightly Review*, published in the summer and autumn of 1881; and through them he became aware of a new liberal form of Mohammedanism, which wished to bring Islamic law abreast of modern knowledge and thus set in motion a political regeneration through the means of a religious revival. Naturally a reconstruction of the Caliphate was demanded, for religion had meant nothing to the successive Sultans for several centuries.

In his *Fortnightly Review* articles, Blunt tries to enlist England's support for this new Moslem liberalism and its proposed reforms before another nation takes advantage of the movement's discontent. He speaks with confidence of the coming to Islam of 'a man of justice' who may regenerate the Moslem world. On January 31st 1882, in Cairo, a *coup d'état* led Wilfrid Blunt to believe that, in the form of Arabi Pasha, such a man had at last arrived.

An unsuccessful political crusade can be an ennobling but desperately forlorn experience. When Blunt took up the cause of Arab liberty he was full of hope, seeing himself following in Byron's footsteps as a supporter of oppressed nationalities; yet by the end of his campaign for Arabi, in 1883, he was physically and mentally exhausted, and in a state of profound depression. His efforts had failed, his hero was in exile and the English were virtual occupiers of Egypt.

Initially there were foundations for hope. After Arabi had surrounded the Khedive Tewfik's palace and forced him to concede to his demands for a constitution and the dismissal of the old ruling clique, Lord Granville, the British Foreign Secretary, looked coldly upon Gambetta's idea of joint Franco-British intervention. But on January 8th 1882 Gambetta managed to agree with Britain on a joint note to Tewfik strongly supporting his continued rule. This angered the other great powers, who suspected British and French motives. Then on January 26th the Gambetta ministry was forced to resign over a domestic issue; and Arabi, who had been biding his time, staged his *coup d'état* in Cairo. The Prime Minister was ousted, a constitution was introduced and Arabi himself became Minister of War. The new French government was unwilling to oppose this new development and Gladstone was encumbered by the fact that many liberals, including himself, were sympathetic to the nationalist cause.

But *realpolitik* triumphed. For strategic reasons Egypt was too valuable to be entirely abandoned. Arabi and his supporters were unknown quantities, and the British and French fleets were dispatched to Alexandria to keep an eye on them. On June 11th there were nationalist riots in the city, with fifty Europeans dead and sixty others, including the British Consul, wounded. Khedivial troops restored order; but Arabi, still dominant, ordered his soldiers to fortify the harbour. The fleets in the bay regarded this as a hostile move and received authority to put a stop to it, which, on July 11th, after ten and a half hours of shelling, the British did. It was then that Gladstone decided to send troops who, under Sir Garnet Wolseley, routed Arabi's forces at Tel-el-Kebir. Thus the

Lady Sibell Lumley, daughter
of the Earl of Scarborough,
who married George Wyndham
in 1887.

Wilfrid Scawen Blunt
in Arabian dress,
painted by his wife.

Arthur Balfour outside the House of Commons.

country was saved for the Sultan and the bondholders. In September Sir Evelyn Baring arrived to take up his duties as British agent and Consul-General, a post he was to hold for over twenty-three years.

Throughout the Egyptian affair Wilfrid Blunt had worked tirelessly for Arabi. He visited Gladstone and was given the impression that armed intervention was out of the question; he wrote letters to *The Times* and lobbied in Parliament; and, when defeat finally came, arranged for a lawyer to go out to Cairo to defend Arabi at his trial, at considerable personal expense. Some friends, who were generally of an imperialist frame of mind, were shocked at his faith in the ability of an Eastern people to govern itself. Lytton wrote to say: 'Your letters in *The Times* have been extremely interesting and it would be a superfluous compliment on my part to say that I thought them exceedingly able'; but later, on receiving an invitation from Blunt to attend a meeting devoted to discussion of the Egyptian question, the former Viceroy pleaded a previous engagement, declaring: 'I don't care three straws about the Arabs. My only interest in the Egyptian question is an exclusively English one – about English interests and English policy in relation to that question.' He ended his letter with the admission: 'I should be a humbug if I concealed the repugnance and mistrust with which I contemplate the cause for which you are working.'[17]

When the battle was over Wilfrid Blunt left the field in a spirt of dejection. He sailed for Ceylon with Lady Anne but was laid low on the boat with a terrible fever. For three weeks he rested at Colombo, sick at first but steadily recovering. As he regained his strength, lying for part of the day in a beautiful garden overlooking a grove of bananas and surrounded by a wealth of tropical flowers and flitting butterflies, a hint of his old exuberance returned. The injustice of the Fellahin being sold into European bondage by the Khedive Ismail's extravagance rankled in his mind. Here too in Ceylon there was Arabi, now exiled from Egypt, who visited him daily, giving him a special token and recommending cures used by the Fellahin. It was this living evidence of his first great struggle that encouraged Blunt to set aside defeat and think again, amid the varied colours and shades of a Ceylonese garden, of what he might do to change the imperial order.

Chapter 4
Imperialism: For and Against

Sailing to Egypt with his regiment in 1885, George Wyndham felt himself to be on the edge of a new period in his life. Unlike his older cousin he did not wonder if this was a just or necessary war; and the voyage out inspired him to write with a new-found lyricism. Like Wilfrid Blunt, Wyndham found himself stirred by a journey towards a distant and unfamiliar objective. 'In the morning,' he wrote to his mother on February 27th, 'we went between Galoeta and Galatona, two rocky islands, the first about two miles long and 600 feet high, the other only a high rock. It looked like Monte Cristo's island, quite bare and desolate, till on turning a corner you could see a little house built against the side of the rock with a garden like a small pocket handkerchief and a few goats . . . The night was too wonderful; the moon nearly full with a great circle of light round it in the purple sky; the light horizon, as light as at dawn, all round and dark purple sea. I stayed up looking at it till past eleven o'clock; there were no ripples except the ones made by the ship; the reflection of the moon in this was much more bright and quite different from any I have seen before.'[1]

The expedition was not allowed to forget its purpose. 'We parade every day at ten,' wrote Wyndham, 'Timmy Myers our Surgeon Major has given us one or two lectures on "First Aid to the Injured"; we walk round the deck, practise with "Range-finders", read little military books about engineering, outposts, etcetera, laugh at Wolseley's *Soldier's Pocket-book*, abuse the

67

government, eat four square meals a day, smoke a great deal, and sleep ten hours at least out of the twenty-four.'[2] In March the soldiers disembarked off Suakin, prepared to bolster up the forces already fighting in the desert, and George Wyndham stepped ashore with Wilfrid Blunt's talisman in his knapsack.

During the two years between Arabi's defeat and this latest Egyptian campaign, Wilfrid Scawen Blunt's opinions had hardened. 'It cannot be too strongly insisted on,' he later wrote, 'that the great, the capital wrong committed by our English government in 1882 was less the destruction of the hopes of free government in Egypt as a nation, than the treacherous blow its armed intervention struck everywhere at the aspirations of liberal Islam.'[3] In August 1880, while in Portsmouth to welcome the imperialistic Lytton home from India at the end of his viceroyalty, he pondered upon the state of his country, in his eyes brought down to a mere shadow of her former greatness by jingoism and double dealing. 'For a hundred years,' he wrote, 'we did good in the world; for a hundred we shall have done evil, and then the world will hear of us no more.'[4]

A second visit to India, with Lady Anne, in 1883, merely reinforced his views. This time Lord Ripon, a Gladstonian Liberal with advanced views on imperial government, was the Viceroy, but Blunt believed at the end of his tour that 'in spite of all official announcements and statements of policy, and royal proclamation, the principle of Indian government remains what it always has been – that is to say, government in the interests of English trade and English adventure. The more liberal design has faded out of sight.'[5] The Indian Civil Service, much respected by his fellow countrymen, did not impress him. He saw it as 'a wholly conservative body – composed though it may be admitted to be in large part of excellent and honest men – men who do their duty – it has nevertheless the necessary vices of all corporations. Its first law is its own interests; its second only those of the Indian people.'[6] Some of its less distinguished members suffered particularly from his acerbic pen. In Madras there was the governor, Mr Grant Duff, 'a thin, sickly querulous man, out of temper with everything around him, yet paid ten thousand a year by Madras Indians for ruling them'; and at Lucknow Sir George Couper, 'the man most hated by the Mohammedans of Lucknow', in whose memory a ten-thousand-pound clock tower had recently been erected.

The lack of sympathy between the races shocked him. 'It is hateful to be here,' he wrote, 'as members of the alien ruling caste, reverenced and feared, yet secretly detested.'[7] He believed it to be absurd to talk of 'the Hindus as intellectually inferior to ourselves – indeed as anything but far our superiors' and was immensely impressed by some Indians that he met and by their thoughtful criticisms of British rule. In Madras an old Mahratta Brahmin Ragunath Rao's conversation 'might have been that of a Socrates' as he explained that 'under the East India Company, when communication with England was rare and difficult, the English officials and even the Governors and Governors-General were thrown to a large extent for their society on the Indians of rank and position, whose language they had been obliged to learn and with whom they lived on a footing of something like equality. Now they lived wholly amongst themselves, and were almost without intercourse with natives of any class, except perhaps the lowest, whom they treated at best with good-humoured contempt.'[8] This seemed to be borne out at the mixed Anglo-Indian social functions that he attended where 'conversation is all unreal, neither side speaking its real thoughts'.[9]

Blunt saw the English women as being largely responsible for this. With their rock-like gentility and refusal to meet any Indian on equal terms, he believed they were 'the cause of half the bitter feelings between race and race'.[10] He doubted if this English arrogance and short-sightedness could ever be put right. Therefore he advocated putting India on the same footing as Australia, giving to each province its English government, supported by English troops, but leaving the entire civil administration, legislation and finance in native hands. Blunt understood that, in practice, this would leave southern India governed by Hindus and northern India governed by Moslems; indeed it was precisely this uneasy mixture of races and religions that led him to maintain that some degree of imperial government did remain a necessity 'for none are more conscious than the Indians that they are not yet a nation, but an agglomeration of nations so mixed and interblended, and so divided by diversity of tongues and creeds, that they could not stand alone'.[11]

While in India the Blunts became friendly with the Viceroy and pressed on him a number of reforms, including the creation of a Moslem university. Here again they were to be disappointed. Lord Ripon's intentions were good, but his will was faltering. Blunt believed that the civil servants had succeeded in frustrating his attempts at reform. 'When I arrived in India,' he wrote, 'I found Lord Ripon like a schoolboy who has started in a race with his fellows and who has run loyally ahead, unaware as yet that these have stopped, and that all the world is laughing at his useless zeal.'[12]

All the world might well have also laughed at Wilfrid Scawen Blunt as he took up the cudgels against the imperialist spirit of late-nineteenth-century England. The Empire was at its zenith. In 1872, during a speech at the Crystal Palace, Disraeli had offered his fellow countrymen a choice. 'The issue,' he declared, 'is not a mean one. It is whether you will be content to be a comfortable England, modelled and moulded upon Continental principles and meeting in due course an inevitable fate, or whether you will be a great country, an imperial country, a country where your sons, when they rise, rise to paramount positions, and obtain not merely the esteem of their countrymen but command the respect of the world.' There was no doubt which alternative most preferred. The Empire became an immensely potent rallying point for popular opinion. Alongside the economic and strategic motives for imperial expansion there arose the notion of the civilizing mission and the romance, as expressed in Disraeli's *Tancred*, of holding 'the gorgeous East in fee'. The paternalistic idea of the Englishman's duty as that of imposing English government and law upon the uncivilized and thus civilizing them was widely accepted. As Lord Rosebery drily observed: 'An empire founded on trade alone must irresistibly crumble.'

Blunt's respect for the Oriental character and his desire to see British imperial power diminished rather than strengthened appeared strange against such a background. Naturally his ideas mystified most of his contemporaries, many of whom, particularly Lytton, found it difficult to take him seriously. At the Foreign Office, his cousin Philip Currie jokingly advised him to take up Arabi's cause as it would provide a suitable outlet for his romanticism. Lord Randolph Churchill, who flirted with Egyptian Nationalism in his search for a policy with which to oppose Gladstone, observed, while discussing India with Blunt in 1885, that the poet might make himself useful by writing a poem about the Conservative party for Sir Arthur Sullivan to set to music. Blunt was rather taken aback. 'I asked: "With something about the primrose in it?" He said: "Yes, if you like – but it does not matter so much what it is, so long as it is patriotic." I told him I would think about it, but feared I couldn't manage the primrose.'[13] Yet the authorities excluded him from Egypt for three years, commencing in March 1884, so as to prevent his campaigning on behalf of the exiled nationalists.

This merely excited him to greater efforts, as his recorded opinions of the great imperial heroes of the hour demonstrate. Of Wolseley, the victor of Egypt, whose 'ridiculous triumph down Pall Mall, with the Grand Old Man waving his handkerchief like a madman from a window', particularly offended him, he wrote: 'I should best of all like to see him hanged.'[14] Cromer, the new Consul-General, was similarly blasted, although Blunt had a certain amount of personal affection for him. His defect was that he had little or no idea of

71

Egyptian native opinion. 'Lord Cromer,' writes Blunt, 'never seems to have taken the trouble to consult any native authority, or to have gone further afield than the Blue Books for his knowledge of events unconnected with his own special work. Even about these he is occasionally inaccurate, and seldom quite sincere.'[15]

British victories now moved him almost to fury. When Sir Herbert Stewart, on his way to relieve Gordon at Khartoum, defeated the Mahdi's forces at Abu Klea, Blunt received the news in a spirit of lonely desperation, isolated from the revelling of the rest of England. He saw the two armies in sharply contrasting terms. 'A mongrel scum of thieves from Whitechapel and Seven Dials, commanded by young fellows whose ideal is the green room of the Gaiety – without beliefs, without traditions, without other principles of action than just to get their promotion and have a little fun. On the other side men with the memory of a thousand years of freedom, with chivalry inherited from the Saracens, the noblest of ancestors, with a creed the purest the world ever knew, worshipping God and serving him with arms like the heroes of the ancient world they are. It is over the death of these that we rejoice. No, I desire to see their blood avenged, and every man of Stewart's butchering host butchered in their turn and sent to hell.'[16]

The death of Gordon, a contributor to Arabi's defence fund and a man whom Blunt termed 'the most chivalric figure among Englishmen of our generation', was not allowed to stand in the way of Blunt's delight at the English reverse brought about by his defeat. 'If ever right triumphed in the world,' the indefatiguable diarist recorded, 'it was at the fall of Khartoum', and, journeying from London to Crabbet on that day 'I could not help singing all the way down in the train'.[12] It was little wonder that Charles Hardinge, a young diplomat who was staying with Blunt for the hunting and who later became Viceroy of India, remarks in his memoirs that his host 'displayed such unmistakable signs of gladness that I left by the first train next morning without saying goodbye'.[18] This must indeed have seemed shocking, particularly as national sympathy for the beleaguered garrison rose to such a height that it practically brought down Gladstone's government.

It was the Mahdi and the death of General Gordon that took George Wyndham to Egypt to be one of Blunt's despised 'young fellows'. When the Mahdi's dervishes had risen against the misgovernment of their Egyptian overlords, a force was sent from Egypt under Hicks Pasha to subdue them. On November 5th 1883 this was cut to pieces and the Mahdi, a former slave trader, led his followers on to force the evacuation of the whole Sudan south of Wadi Halfa. Thus in February 1884 General Charles Gordon arrived in Khartoum as Governor-General to evacuate all Egyptians and Christians. His plan was to appoint Zobeir Pasha, another slave trader whom he had once fought against, as Governor-General in his place to hold Khartoum and the Nile valley against the Mahdi; but the English government felt that they could not make use of such a man. Slowly the dervishes closed in on Khartoum and Gordon, hero of campaigns in China and the Sudan itself, was trapped. A relief force under Wolseley embarked too late to save him, despite Sir Herbert Stewart's victory at Abu Klea. On January 21st 1885 contact was made with Gordon's garrison by means of four steamboats sent by him from Khartoum; but the rescuers fatally delayed going further upstream for three days. On January 26th Khartoum was stormed and General Gordon killed. Two days later the rescuers arrived, too late to do anything but mourn.

For George Wyndham, arriving at Suakin, the enemy was Osman Digna, another slave trader who had espoused the Mahdi's cause. Suakin was a flat plain of sand with hills in the distance. The enemy's scouts could be seen through glasses, and their camels were visible to the naked eye. The position was dangerous. 'They sometimes come to within 600 yards,' Wyndham wrote to his father on March 10th. 'Osman Digna's strong position is at Tamai where they say he will have 15,000.

He has sent to call on the English general to surrender as he intends to shoot half our soldiers and spear the rest.' The Arabs would creep into the camp at night, singly or in twos and threes, and stab the sleeping soldiers. Yet to Wyndham it was exciting, even beautiful. 'When we were near the shore,' he told his father, 'three hoopoes fluttered round the ship. On shore I have seen vultures, kites, small birds rather like larks, and little black and white birds the size of a bullfinch; several flights of wild geese have flown over. I am perfectly well in every way and do not even feel tired after yesterday's work.'[19]

At first he was rather bemused by the Egyptians. 'The natives,' he told his sister Madeline, 'are of all colours, some quite black, much blacker than niggers, with hair and much better looking than niggers. They are Nubians I believe, they remind me of penwipers and ornaments for holding stamps and sealing wax etcetera, etcetera. Others are brown.' He was not entirely sure what to expect in this remote corner of the world; but action was not long in coming. The troops were ordered to occupy a hilly position at Hasheen; and came under fire. Wyndham's training stood him in good stead when the danger became real. 'Croppy Ewart's horse was shot under him,' he told his father. 'The enemy then almost ceased fire and were shelled by the artillery and they retired. The Bengal Lancers and mounted infantry came into our square to dismount, the former are splendid fellows. I saw one with his spear dripping with blood sitting up looking as proud as Lucifer and very pleased with himself although the back of his right hand was cut open to the knuckles. They lost a good many horses and some men.' The bullets did not alarm him. 'Being under fire,' he wrote, 'is very much like not being under fire and the "whit-ping whit-ping" of the bullets and little puffs of dust sound and look very harmless.' At the end he observed : 'All the men were quite fit today; I have never been better in my life; I like campaigning quite as much as I expected, which is saying a good deal. I slept like a log last night.'

The next task was to escort a convoy to Hasheen, to the very position they had already taken and garrisoned. The journey was hard. 'The whole country,' he wrote, 'is strewn and reeks of dead camels and bodies; my stomach heaved a good deal but now we are perfectly hardened to any stench.' The fighting became rougher. The Arabs attacked, the English formed squares, and the rallying cry was: 'Stand then, Englishmen, stand!' At the end of one encounter there were over 100 dead Arabs in Wyndham's square and 240 round it. Of another assault he wrote: 'They came straight at my half company, only one reached the bayonets, about fifteen got to within seven yards. I have got the shield of the leader of the charge who rolled over in front of me first just as I was going to use my revolver.' At the end of all this Wyndham clearly felt that his family were in need of reassurance. 'I think of you all a great deal,' he declared, 'and am sure I feel quite plainly that you are thinking of me. I do not feel at all far away or separated from you in any way and have long talks with you in imagination.'

The natives brought back memories of his last meeting with Blunt. 'I can quite understand Wilfrid being so fond of them, they are always smiling. Their "deportment" is more dignified and fascinating than anything I have ever seen and it is a great pity that all the beautiful ladies in England cannot carry their heads and shoulders like these boys and young men do.' On Monday May 3rd, after Wyndham had taken part in an exhausting march with the camel corps, Lord Wolseley himself appeared on a tour of inspection. It may be imagined that the young subaltern's reaction to the Field Marshal was a good deal more respectful than that of his cousin.

His service in Egypt was a chastening experience. Previously he had led a life of the utmost ease, surrounded by a benevolent and understanding family. When he writes from the desert to say 'I live entirely on soup with vegetables in it, macaroni, rice, bread and marmalade with lots of coffee and cocoa; have not eaten meat "pure et simple" for three days', he is speaking as someone who is used to most of the comforts that late-Victorian England could provide. To hear of men shooting their officers in the back took the glitter off the 'romance' of battle. However the enemy, in true chivalric tradition, were respected, for their courage and also for their fervour. Wilfrid Blunt, who was shown Wyndham's letters by George's father Percy, was able to derive satisfaction from this, noting in his diary on April 23rd 1885: 'George Wyndham has written home accounts of the enormous numbers of Hadendowas who have been killed. Some of these Hadendowas had shaved their heads and wore the Mahdi's uniform – a wonderful instance of fanaticism.'[20] Blunt, typically, went on to jump to the conclusion that 'they [the English officers] are all sick, however, of the war'. But on May 5th Wyndham wrote to his father: 'I have never been so well and in such spirits before, I wake every morning fit to buck out of my skin.'

On May 19th Blunt noted: 'George Wyndham, I am glad to say, is ordered home again from Suakin, and there is every reason to believe nothing will be done against the Arabs.'[21] At Remleh camp in Alexandria he awaited his departure, reading the Shakespeare that his father had given him and contemplating the beauty of this Egyptian port. Life at last was easy again. 'We bathe every morning before breakfast,' he wrote to his mother on June 14th . . . 'Some of the gardens round here are lovely. I never knew what Oleanders meant . . . having only seen them in pots, till I came out here where they are twenty feet high, one mass of flowers, most of them pink, but some carnation or white. There are also lots of magnolias and bamboos which spread over your head.' Meanwhile he was, like so many soldiers before and after, angered by the way the war was regarded by some at home. Wilfrid Blunt had claimed, as part of his campaign against British intervention, that money was being paid to soldiers for dead Arabs' hands to encourage their slaughter; and this provoked a strong letter of denial to Percy Wyndham from his son. 'Luncheon in Belgrave Square,' Blunt noted on June 6th. 'George Wyndham has written from Suakin, very angry with me for saying in *The Times* that money has been paid for dead Arabs' hands. Only one hand had been brought in, and it was not of a dead but of a live Arab whom they had gone out and brought in alive to camp, and nothing was paid for the hand.'[22]

Living amid such idyllic conditions it is scarcely surprising that Wyndham was sad when, at the beginning of July, he embarked for Cyprus on the way back to England. Here, he was given, at the age of twenty-two, command of a company. But, after months of action, he became bored. On August 22nd he told his sister Mary: 'At last!! We are going home. I had no hope of this, and had got in to such a plodding way of going on, bored to death, that I could not imagine what getting orders for home would be like; then all at once they came and I am dazed like the "Prisoner of the Bastille" and no doubt when I get to London I shall cry out, "Take me away from this noisy vicious town and send me back to my peaceful isle." '[23]

Chapter 5
A Stormy Courtship

In December 1883 George Curzon, recent graduate of Balliol and Fellow of All Souls, wrote to a young married woman some years his senior, who was later to marry George Wyndham:

'Sibell, God sent child. May I write you a word now my darling. I can't see you Sibell, though my whole soul is straining after you. What am I to do Sibell? All this week I have done nothing but dream about you the whole night long and then when I wake up so great is the disappointment that my morning is one of unhappiness. This last night just over I have been dreaming that you came of your own accord and sat many times on my knee and many times cast your arms about my neck and kissed me many times ah many times my Sibell. And now I am here alone and though you have been loving me all night you are a hundred and fifty miles away by day and I am wretched.

Angel love me in a letter do. You can make me happy by loving me and you would not surely make a human creature, a fellow creature, unhappy. You take all I have; you know you do: you must give me a little in return. Other people ask me to love them and I cannot because you have taken it. You have it all. There is nothing on earth I desire in comparison thee. Sibell have compassion on my fainting soul . . .

God bless you my own darling, bless you and protect you.

May you be happy at this Christmas. I shall be so lonely without you.'[1]

From Kedlestone on Christmas Eve, he wrote again.

'My beautiful love . . . I have got home and found your beautiful letter which cheers and inspires me, love, and seems to bring you before me in all your surpassing charm and loveliness.

You angel. God be blessed for having placed you on the Earth. And thank you oh my love for that sweet little case. Already the photograph is in it and ever shall remain there without a rival. I am so pleased with it and with the dear words, "our" words, that you have written outside.

It is a darling little Christmas present and fills me with Christmas thoughts of my darling . . . Sweet woman I pray for you this night that no thorns or briars may hinder your path through this thorny world but that your simple pure and Godlike nature may fill all that it meets or touches with its own sweetness and purity – as it does me – aye and fills me too with a longing that grows weary and that is beyond the power of words.

Duck, I meant to get you a little Christmas present this morning in London but had not time. It will come for the New Year instead. But though "nothing in my hand I bring" yet on my tongue are words of love and prayer for you that others may perchance be breathing, but none I swear with such intensity.'[2]

The object of Curzon's admiration was Sibell Grosvenor, daughter of the Earl of Scarborough and wife of Earl Grosvenor, son of the first Duke of Westminster. She was beautiful and much admired, for her gentleness as well as her beauty. Mary Gladstone said of her: 'She is a sweet little soul and the key-note is unselfishness';[3] and later, as George Wyndham's wife in Ireland, she provoked a similar reaction in a cottager on the island of Achill who said: 'We have seen many ladies but you are the first that has been kind to us.'[4] The effect of her charms on men could be startling. Her brother, Osric Lumley, once calculated that, after Grosvenor's early death, there were over eighty people in love with her, including the curates – for she was of a religious disposition.[5] Lord Hartington was later to tell Margot Asquith that 'Lady Grosvenor was by far the most dangerous siren in London and that he would not answer for any man keeping his head or his heart when with her',[6] to which Margot entirely agreed.

In 1883 her husband, Earl Grosvenor, was an invalid, deteriorating fast. She shared her distress with Curzon who, on January 2nd 1884, wrote:

'My darling angel . . . Have just come in not having been in the house since twelve o'clock and found your letter and telegram. The former pulls down my hopes: the latter raises them again, not that I fear terribly after what you say. Oh Sibell, I pray it may not be so. The Great God spared him last Thursday at the awful crisis: surely he will do the same again. I join you in fervent prayer my Sibell. May all your toil and watching be rewarded. Would I could do anything to relieve you, to lighten the anxiety. It must weigh you down almost to the ground. Dear boy, I am so rejoiced that he is at peace and resigned in case the worst should befall.

I sent some violets yesterday for his room. I hope they have reached you. They come from France. Little woman cheer up: raise your spirits: hope for the best. Let me encourage you my darling. I am so grateful to you for writing to me these daily reports. You don't know how eagerly I look forward to them – and then I pass them on to others . . . I think of him lying there in the very bed where I was. I cannot bear to fancy that room a room of death. No Sibell he shall live. He shall laugh and play with us again as before: and we will call you his saviour and guardian angel. All the love and sympathy I have in my nature goes out to you sweet Sib in this hour of your tribulation.'[7]

On January 22nd Lord Grosvenor died, leaving his young wife a widow with two daughters and a son. Henceforth Curzon was free to pursue her with even greater ardour, and also to think of marriage.

After his return to England in September 1885, George Wyndham resumed the life that he had enjoyed before the army had taken him to Egypt. Yet he was, in a sense, a different person. The old pleasures appeared empty and ceremonial duties a waste of time when compared with the war in the desert. Parties began to pall. Thus he wrote to his father of having 'capital fun at Stanway' (the home of his sister Mary who had recently married Lord Elcho) at a hunt with 'the best show of foxes I have ever seen', but Mary Elcho was told he was suffering from 'restlessness which deprives me of ideas, and compulsory inaction which deprives me of news'.[8] 'I am not at all sure,' he declared of his Egyptian service, 'that it was not a preferable life to this of frowzing on guard and wasting one's time and money without amusing oneself or doing good to anyone else.'

Reading was a potent consolation. 'I have been rather plodding away,' he told Mary Elcho, 'at my books about Voltaire, Rousseau and Diderot, and the middle of the last century generally, and have just finished Ockley's *Saracens;* they were fascinating people : like all people thoroughly in earnest, their lives give great pleasure to those who have nothing to be earnest about. At least I think this is the great charm about the early Jews, Christians, Saracens, Turks, Buddhists, etc., and all the other early religious or political people, that they knew they were right and everyone else wrong; whilst we only know we are wrong and think everyone else is too.'[9] Clearly he was searching for some form of stimulation; and even nature came under the lash of this new melancholia. 'There is a good deal of consolation,' he wrote, 'to be got out of spring, when it is there; when it is not, whether in nature or the inner man, it is impossible to realize it through a medium of black skies and biting winds; and even although the spring does come back in a general way, still the individual flowers never come again, never.'[10] But through the 'black skies and biting winds' some sunlight was beginning to emerge. At about this time Wyndham wrote: 'I have been seeing a good deal of Sibell Grosvenor who is very nice to me and nice altogether.'[11]

The friendship developed fast; and by the middle of April he was writing:

'Dearest S.S. I loved getting your little line the other night, it was such a quick answer to my letter, that I hope this one will bring another. I have been thinking of you a great deal and feel as if I had written several times, but know that this was only in imagination. These letters are like the conversations that I have with you (without your knowledge) walking along the line of large pots of oleanders in the marble colonnade of the Palace of consolation, where your soft white dress looks even cooler and more refreshing than the marble on which we stand.'[12]

By June Wyndham was in love.

'Darling Sibell,' he wrote on June 23rd, 'you cannot imagine how stale, flat and unprofitable everything is to me after my Midsummernight's Dream! If only I could get Puck's "Love in Idleness" and squeeze the juice in your dear sapphire eyes:

"The juice of it on sleeping eyelids laid
Will make a man or woman madly dote
Upon the next live creature that it sees."

My head was so full of thoughts as I was whirled away from you through the night that I sat up wide awake, without reading, and saw the sun rise; yet now I cannot write all I thought, but only bless you and long to see you again.'[13]

Sibell Grosvenor made Wyndham's military duties seem even more commonplace. From St James's Palace he wrote to her on June 24th: 'I do thank you, darling Sibell, for having written to me. I like to think of you waking in the Rose Room at six for I know what a dear you look and it is nice to have something delightful to think about in this guard room. I suppose it is a heavenly day, the little circle of sky I can see out of this window above the squalid leads, slate roofs and disgusting yellow bricks of the guard room is lovely; quite sapphire blue with a beautiful pyramid of fleecy clouds almost insulting by its loveliness to me caged up in this place so ugly as to be melancholy and so commonplace with everybody talking about things that bore me and the sentries looking so coarse and fond of beer. I have been watching this cloud thinking of it as you, you dear, and the squalor and dirt and commonplace of the guard room as my life . . .'[14]

Wyndham was more tentative when he discussed his feelings with his mother in August. He wondered if he could ever make Sibell Grosvenor love him and he explained that, through her, he hoped to gain that impetus which he felt was lacking at present in his sedentary life. 'You know how I have been very hopeless, hopeless of everything. I am hopeless now of doing any great or useful thing but I have one tiny ray that by devotion I may make one other than myself a little happier without neglecting my duties too much and thus live a life instead of dawdling altogether through a useless existence.'[15] But Wyndham had to contend with strong opposition. Sibell Grosvenor was some ten years older than her prospective suitor and it was barely two years since the death of her first husband. Her parents were worried by Wyndham's youth and inexperience. Furthermore she had promised her father-in-law, the Duke of Westminster, that she would not remarry without first obtaining his consent.

The first Duke of Westminster was the archetypal Victorian aristocratic grandee. Vastly rich from his huge estates, which included virtually the whole of Belgravia, a philanthropist and deeply religious, he was also the owner of Eaton Hall, Victorian England's most substantial essay in country house building. George Wyndham had visited this in 1885, and had not cared for it. 'I'm quite sure I don't like Gothic architecture,' he had told his mother; and he found Westminster's notion of ducal grandeur similarly unappealing. 'There is a big chapel and clock-tower like the Houses of Parliament,' he had continued, 'with clock, value twenty thousand guineas, that plays forty-eight tunes, the same tune every hour for a whole day (Maddening!); today we had "Jenny Jones", yesterday "Home Sweet Home".'[16]

Westminster had been created a Duke by Gladstone in 1874 as a reward for his public service and adherence to Liberal principles, even though, as a Member of Parliament, he had opposed the Liberal party's Reform Bill of 1886 and consistently refused ministerial office. His charitable commitments were numerous, leading him to be president of several metropolitan hospitals, the Gardeners' Royal Beneficent Institution, the Metropolitan Drinking Fountain and Cattle Trough Association and the United Committee for the Prevention of Demoralization of Native Races by the Liquor Traffic. Despite his affection for the Turf (he was probably the most successful racehorse breeder of his generation and won the Derby five times) Westminster was a prudent man who never bet, not even on one of his own horses. He believed sternly in the creed of duty and was austerely correct in all that he did. He married two impeccably aristocratic wives, having fifteen children by them. Despite the fifty indoor servants and forty gardeners at Eaton, when there was not a house party the Duke lived in a state of quiet domesticity in a few rooms. He mistrusted quick decisions and revered experience. Neither George Wyndham's youthful charm nor rapid courtship appealed to him and he set his face against granting his daughter-in-law, of whom he was exceedingly fond, permission to marry this romantic young guards officer.

Wyndham was distraught. His parents realized that something should be done to lessen the blow of this disappointment. Thus when he suggested that he might go to India as
ADC to his cousin Robert Bourke, later Lord Connemara,
Governor of Madras, his father agreed. The idea came to
nothing. So he settled down once more to English life, half content to be still near Sibell Grosvenor yet half miserable at the
immensity of the obstacles that stood in their way. By this
stage she had become equally fond of him, as another suitor
felt obliged to remark in September of the same year.

Since Grosvenor's death, George Curzon had admired the
widow as steadfastly as he had the wife. As late as September
3rd 1886 he was still writing, after they had made an expedition together to Oxford, in tones of gratified affection.

'My darling, what a day yesterday was! beautiful and to
be remembered. You shone like a sun ray upon Oxford,
idealizing the ideal, and irradiating the radiant. These tran-
quil interludes amid the shocks of life were possibly fore-
tastes of what is to come. They certainly give one a sense of
calmness and happiness beyond compare. I hope you did not
regret having come all that way and submitted to all that
fatigue. Few but you would have done it. You made me very
happy if that is any reward: and I fancy that you were
not altogether without a similar sensation yourself.'[17]

But on September 19th he felt obliged to hit out at his competitor. 'I should like to have seen you again on Friday but
others – other and nearer Georges made such a victim of you
that I could scarcely get in a word or a look edgeways, and at
times it made me quite mortified and sad.'[18]

However for Curzon the battle was already lost. Wyndham's letter of September 11th, from Victoria Barracks,
Windsor, shows who was receiving more attention. 'You
darling you have spoilt me today with that lovely letter and
then another little one – I must write down now to you as you

did to me "I am happy" Darling Sibell (I write your name because it is lovely like you) the sun streaming in through my windows this morning at 5.45 woke me with a happy state of consciousness of the delight of loving you, lovely lady; and I could not stay in bed but ran around the room and read Shelley.'[19] They decided to marry, despite the Duke's opposition. On November 11th Wyndham wrote to Sibell Grosvenor's mother, Lady Scarborough, to appraise her of the situation. 'Sibell has told me,' he said, 'that she has written to you about me; and I must write to say how wonderful it all seems, that I should have won so great a prize . . . I know quite well how unworthy I am, but will try to make up as much as I can by devoting myself utterly to her happiness. Nothing is settled and the Duke of Westminster sees many objections. I hope you will not mind me writing to declare myself in this way.'[20] Lady Scarborough had no objections and looked upon her prospective son-in-law with great favour. But not even she could dent the stern armour of ducal resistance.

A confrontation seemed to be the only way of settling the matter. On a cold December day Wyndham left his barracks at Windsor for Maidenhead, to visit the Duke of Westminster's southern residence of Cliveden, built by Sir Charles Barry and acquired by the Duke from his first mother-in-law, the Duchess of Sutherland. Here in the great house on a hill beside the banks of the Thames, he attempted to plead his case before the Duke and his second wife Catherine. He did not meet with much success. 'I will tell you,' he wrote to Sibell Grosvenor on the evening of December 4th, after he had returned from his ordeal, 'exactly what happened today. It was as everything always is – quite different from what I expected. D (the Duke) does not consider it at all (he takes the ground that I am young and that nothing will make me older) . . . I gave up my day and toiled all the way to Cliveden and was only fifty minutes in the house altogether! I don't know how it happened . . . I was shown into a room, D came in after a little and was kind. I plunged into the matter after a little and pleaded and was very gentle. I was surprised at his not trying to consider it. The only thing he said with any interest as far as I can make out was to go on saying "you had formally promised" and repeated your promise again lately in a letter! Have you? This surprised me so that I could hardly go on. Well I should have gone on I daresay and said lots more, but he got up and said "won't you see Katie?" I was rather upset at the time but said yes, so he went away (we were about ¼ hour together) then I saw Katie. D said he would not ask me to lunch and seemed anxious for me to go so I went . . .'[21]

A promise made rashly and then renewed in an effort to please her father-in-law had erected a terrible barrier. 'You had no right,' wrote Wyndham in desperation, 'to put yourself in his power when you loved me and I loved you and if it goes on I shall tell him that he had no right, that even if he were your own father, he had no right to accept such a promise from a grown-up person. It is monstrous to make such a slave of you. And what right can he have to tell me not to marry you – None. He admits this, because he said "it is not as if my consent was necessary" but repeats that you volunteered to promise . . . It is because you tried to please him, by submitting so, that we are punished.' The Duke must be asked to give Sibell Grosvenor back her promise. 'This is the only thing to be done,' Wyndham wrote, 'you cannot force D to tell a lie by saying he approves of a thing he does not – But I am sure you give him more pain by being in sorrow than would be the case if you married and all went well. Everyone has said this to me of their own accord; first my father . . . and now today Katie, who says that D says "that if he felt sure it was for your happiness he would not mind".'[22]

Then, just when all seemed lost, the Duke of Westminster, on December 12th, wrote to Mrs Percy Wyndham. She told George that when she had seen the letter she feared that the Duke was going to appeal to her to dissuade her son from pressing his suit. But she had been wrong. The Duke began: 'My dear friend, so the die is cast and all is settled' and went on to say that he would no longer oppose the marriage, despite his continuing reservations. Wyndham, in Victoria Barracks, erupted in ecstatic triumph. He celebrated, and commented on his celebrations, in a typically romantic fashion. 'I have been very triumphantly happy today,' he told his mother, 'alone in my castle. I send one song of triumph [it has not survived] written after reading your letter, in it remembering the sunrise at Gibraltar, as the most lovely thing I have seen, and mix it up with the happiest moment of life, winning the most lovely living thing. Since dinner I have written another wild "whoop" of triumph – which I reserve and I think it probably gives me more pleasure now than it will and I doubt if it ever would please anyone else. Only I had to have a shout and as I have been alone all day I wrote my shout.'[23]

He also wrote to the Duke of Westminster, and received the following rather daunting reply.

Eaton December 14th

'My dear George,
Thanks for your note.

I hope that all will go well, tho' you cannot expect that I give my "consent" – all that I can do is to say that I will not stand in the way of Sibell's and your happiness any longer.

It will be for you to do all you can, in the coming year, to remove all the objections that we all see and feel to exist – and on you the responsibility – and it is no light one – must lie – may God grant you grace and strength to do your part honestly and well for her sake and for yours.

Yours sincerely
Westminster.'[24]

The engagement was announced, and the wedding fixed for the private chapel at Eaton Hall on February 7th 1887. On December 9th, from Southport, where earlier in the year he had been

elected a Member of Parliament, George Curzon wrote to Sibell
Grosvenor about his loss.

'My darling Sibell,

And so the end has come and you have done what I always
felt and said you would some day do viz : take the happiness
out of my life. You have a right to do this of course : you
gave and you can take away. I make no complaint : but I
realize more fully I think than you do that all is at an end
between me and you : and that that connection which has
been the light of my days for seven years is broken for ever-
more . . . I cannot write this without emotion : my tears are
falling now on the blotting paper as I write. The taking out
of a man's life of that which he has grown to regard as a
treasure and core of his being is not accomplished without a
pang. And yet I would not make you sad in what I hope and
presume is your gladness. I do not want my last letter to you
to be one of bitterness or reproach. Let me therefore say on
this last time that I bless you for all the marvellous and most
beautiful happiness which you have given me. For nearly
eight years you have been more to me than anyone else. You
have given me thoughts and feelings and emotions – aye –
and hours and hours of life which I can never forget till I
die. For all this I praise and bless you. I thank you for having so much as deigned to look on me, still more for having
given me a faint portion of your affection. Now for the last
time, as I have done scores and scores of times before, I say
God bless you and keep you . . . Goodbye my own love, my
lost love, goodbye. Forgive me if I have ever done you any
harm : and let me sign myself just for this last time

Your ever loving George.'[25]

Despite his disappointment, Curzon and Sibell Grosvenor remained friends. Wyndham too, as he became enmeshed in
politics, became close to his former rival. Indeed in 1891, when

they were both rising young Tory Members of Parliament, Curzon became involved with a woman who was blackmailing him and Wyndham acted as an intermediary. The circumstances of the case are still rather mysterious; but the involvement of George Lewis, a solicitor whose speciality was extracting prominent figures from situations that were potentially disastrous, showed that Curzon believed himself to be in trouble. The woman lived in Westbourne Terrace, which rivalled St John's Wood as a suitably discreet area in which to house a mistress, and a man called Pemberton appeared to be acting as her evil genius. A trip to Switzerland, with a nurse, was arranged for her and this perhaps demonstrates that the liaison had gone further than Curzon had originally planned. Certainly he was horrified by its consequences, particularly as it had, at one moment, threatened to jeopardize his political career when she had tried to send telegrams to Lord Salisbury and other ministers denouncing him. But these had all been stopped and destroyed.

Disgust came when the woman made a final confession. 'Finally,' Curzon said, 'I heard from her own lips a story at which I am still tingling with black anger and shame. On the night that I left England, according to her own confession, she went on to the street and took a man. I was nearly beside myself with horror and loathing: and even now, six hours later, I can scarcely sit still and write about it. I have felt that more than all. No horror that I have gone through equalled that. It will be a long time before I recover from it: and I say before God that I never want to set eyes upon her again: never. Treachery, betrayal, anger, abuse, revenge – all I have forgiven but coarse and vulgar sin never – no, not till I die. I desire you please never to write to her again . . . All I can say is God have mercy on me and save me from such a fate again. Forgive my wrath but it is stirred to the foundations.'[26]

The matter was settled, and never heard of afterwards. Curzon was grateful to Wyndham; and their friendship, and the sadness felt by him at Wyndham's early death, is shown by a letter sent to Sibell in 1917, after the publication of *Recognita*, an appreciation of her husband by Charles Gatty. 'What happy memories,' the Lord President of the Council wrote, 'of our unforgotten past are revived by reading the reviews in the papers of Charles Gatty's book . . . The personality of dear old George stands out . . . and history will recognize him as one of the rare spirits of our time.'[27]

The first part of the honeymoon was spent at Halkyn Castle, and it was from here that Wyndham wrote of their 'perfect wedding'. The Duke had been markedly genial; and this was the beginning of a relationship which, despite past difficulties, was to develop into mutual admiration. On the occasion of Westminster's death in 1899, Wyndham wrote from the War Office, where he was under-secretary, of 'the kindest man I knew' and how 'his loss is a great one to many'. To Wilfrid Ward he simply described the Duke as 'that kind and chivalrous gentleman'.[28]

Messages of congratulation and good wishes flowed in. One had a particular significance. Mary Elcho, Wyndham's eldest sister, wrote to him after his departure from Eaton : 'I got a letter from Arthur Balfour about two o'clock in which he desired me to be the bearer of all his good wishes.'[29] Later, in Rome, where the couple were continuing their honeymoon, these good wishes took a more practical form. Arthur Balfour, then Chief Secretary for Ireland, wrote to the young guards officer to ask him to be his private secretary. Wyndham saw that this was an opportunity of a political career. Initially he had doubts, although these were soon overcome. 'I should be sorry,' he wrote to Mary Elcho, 'to leave the army and then find little to do, owing to Government going out etcetera : but "nothing ventured, nothing have"; and I am quite prepared to send in my papers and throw my lot into the political boat.'[30]

In Easter week of 1887 the couple were back in England. Henceforth they divided their time between a house at 35 Park Lane in London and Saighton Grange in Cheshire, near

Eaton, which had been given to his daughter-in-law by the Duke of Westminster. Wyndham was to grow increasingly fond of Saighton. There were still the remains of the old medieval fortress that had stood on its site, and the outlook was wonderful, stretching out across the Cheshire plains towards the Welsh hills. The house soon became as much a part of his life as Clouds, and it was from this calm domestic base, in a new home with his wife and his three step-children, that he began the association with Ireland and the Irish that was to lead to his greatest triumph and also to his ruin.

Chapter 6
Ireland: Adoption of a Cause

The Irish question dominated the late-Victorian political scene. Indeed, Henry James formed a peculiar detestation for Ireland, which dared to disturb the calm of his vision of the Old World. When a friend wrote, in the mid-1880s, describing the Irish as 'a great people', the novelist retorted, 'I see no greatness, nor any kind of superiority in them, and they seem to me an inferior and third rate race, whose virtues are of the cheapest and commonest and shallowest order, while their vices are peculiarly cowardly and ferocious. They have been abominably treated in the past – but their wrongs appear to me, in our time, to have occupied the conscience of England only too much to the exclusion of other things.'[1] But, even for James, there was fascination amid the chaos. He told another friend : 'If I had nothing else to do I think I should run over to Ireland : which may seem strange to you on the part of one satiated in his youth with the Celtic genius. The reason is that I should like to see a country in a state of revolution.'[2]

Erstwhile revolutionaries shared this view. On April 27th 1885, Wilfrid Scawen Blunt called on the Irish Nationalist Member of Parliament, Justin McCarthy, at McCarthy's lodgings in Ebury Street. The Nationalists had always spoken up for Arabi in the House of Commons. Blunt's object now was to propose himself as an ally for their cause. McCarthy was cordial but cautious. He explained that their experience of English allies had not been good, at the same time acknowledging that both Arabi and the Mahdi, Blunt's heroes, were also

regarded as heroes in Ireland. McCarthy, who was with his son
Huntley, asked if his visitor owned land in Ireland and was glad
to hear that he did not. Lest they doubt the degree of his
dedication, Blunt then emphasized that he would follow Parnell's lead on all Irish questions, 'short of dynamite'. He was
sure of his own suitability. 'As a Nationalist,' he wrote, 'I could
take up the cause of Ireland with my heart in it. Also I was a
Catholic and opposed to the present government.'[3] The
McCarthys seemed satisfied. They told him that his past
actions had demonstrated that he possessed the courage of his
convictions; but first, however, he must see Parnell. An
appointment was then set up for May 16th at the House of
Commons; and it was here that he met the leader of his new
cause.

The condition of Ireland was one of the great disgraces of the
nineteenth century. Land was the key to the Irishman's position, for land was his livelihood. Since the Union, Irish industry
had been stifled by heavy duties and the free import of English
goods, so there was nothing else to which he could turn. His
plot was invariably small. In the 1841 census it was estimated
that fifty per cent of all holdings were under five acres. Naturally there was ample historical reason for this. During the
Napoleonic wars corn prices had soared. Farms had been
divided into even smaller units and, at wartime prices, it was
possible for the tenant to make a living out of such a unit. Rents
were also raised, along with the new prices, and for a while
it was possible to pay these; but then, after the wars, prices
fell. The rents, however, stayed the same. As trading in cattle
developed landlords began to convert their land from arable
into pasture. This, coupled with the sharp increase in population (from 5 million to 8,175,000 during the period of 1800 to
1841), led to the continuance of the subdivision of land.
Tenants had no security of tenure. Their rent was totally at the
mercy of the landlord's whim, who was at liberty to raise it to

whatever level he thought the tenant might be able to pay. The great famine of the late 1840s emphasized the Irishman's dependence upon the land. In the summer of 1847 3 million people were existing on public works or charity. From 1845 to 1848 the population fell, either by death or emigration, from over 8 million to 6 and a half. The famine changed the face of Ireland. Emigration became part of the pattern of life. In 1852 there were 220,000 emigrants to America; and others sought work and refuge in the miserable slums of industrial England. Some of those who stayed behind sought a violent solution to their problems. In 1848 the Young Ireland movement attempted to play its part in the year of revolution, but the insurgents were easily crushed by the British.

In 1858 James Stephens arrived in Dublin from Paris to found the Fenian brotherhood. Fenian revolutionary tactics, demonstrated by the Clerkenwell prison explosion, drew the British public's attention to the Irish question. Gladstone, also influenced by European liberal distaste for the ways of British rule in Ireland, turned his mind to its solution after his first great electoral victory in 1868. In 1869 he brought about the disestablishment of the Irish Church, and in 1870 passed an Irish land Act which gave compensation to evicted tenants and enabled them to borrow from the State two-thirds of the purchase price of their land. This brought land to the forefront of Irish politics, where it was to remain for the next four decades. It also, by legislating against the landlords, turned them into the Aunt Sallys of the Irish question. Henceforth the land became the symbol of Irish aspirations and distress; and its owners the representatives of oppression, worthy of any insult or outrage the Nationalists might care to throw at them.

This became apparent as the Irish cause grew in strength during the 1870s and 1880s. In 1875, when Charles Stewart Parnell was elected Member of Parliament for Meath, the necessary leader was found. Hard, uncompromising, the possessor of a strong dislike of the English – nurtured by his American mother and the rigours of an English aristocratic education – Parnell was prepared to go to almost Fenian lengths to promote the cause. But in the late 1870s a severe agricultural depression created all the suffering and discontent that a revolutionary could desire.

In 1879 the Land League was formed, under Parnell's presidency, and in 1880 he was elected chairman of the Irish Nationalist group in the House of Commons. Henceforth a two-pronged campaign was conducted, in Ireland and at Westminster. The tactics were rough. Outrages multiplied, with murder, rick-burning and boycotting becoming part of the hazards of Irish life. It was against such a background that W. E. Forster, Gladstone's Chief Secretary for Ireland, introduced a coercion bill in February 1881, accompanying it with another land act in April which provided fixity of tenure, fair rent and the freedom for the tenant to sell his right of occupancy to the highest bidder. The agitation continued, and in October 1881 the British government arrested Parnell under the terms of the coercion Act and imprisoned him in Kilmainham jail.

The move failed. Agrarian outrages increased and the Land League attempted to institute a campaign involving the non-payment of rents. Gladstone saw the necessity for a bargain. Therefore in the early months of 1882 the famous Kilmainham treaty was arranged under the terms of which Parnell was released, coercion was relaxed, and the land Act amended to give protection to those tenants who owed arrears of rent, of which there were estimated to be some 100,000. In return Parnell would calm the country. On May 2nd he was released with an immensely enhanced reputation. Lord Cowper, the Viceroy of Ireland, and Forster resigned. Their successors, appointed by Gladstone, were Earl Spencer, as Viceroy, and Lord Frederick Cavendish, younger brother of the Marquis of Hartington, as Chief Secretary. On May 6th, after Spencer's ceremonial arrival in Dublin, Lord Frederick, walking in Phoenix Park near the Viceregal Lodge with Mr Burke, the under-secretary, was, with his companion, ambushed by a band of assassins and hacked to death with surgical knives. Parnell was horrified. Together with Michael Davitt and John Dillon, two other prominent Nationalists, he signed a note condemning the murders, the work of a group known as 'The Invincibles'. In Ireland the violence continued. The year 1882 established a record of 26 murders and 58 attempted murders. Then in 1883 The Invincibles were brought to trial, and the rule of law began slowly to reassert itself, stiffened be a new coercion Act. Parnell, at the height of his influence, worked for a temporary appeasement and, despite a series of bomb explosions in London, the Irish turmoil descended into one of those vaguely disquieting lulls that resemble an unexpected burst of sunlight in the midst of a dour and remorseless winter. In the next two years the franchise and redistribution Acts greatly strengthened the Nationalist hand, by extending the franchise to Ireland on the same terms as in England, yet allowing the Irish, despite their drop in population, to retain the same number of seats. In June 1885, as a consequence of Tory hints that the party might adopt a more conciliatory attitude to Ireland if it returned to power, Parnell indulged in the first of his switches in electoral allegiance. He joined with the Conservatives to defeat the Liberals in an amendment to the Budget, and thus prepared the way for the Irish to assist Lord Salisbury in the 1885 General Election which had had to be postponed until November because the franchise redistribution was not yet complete.

When Wilfrid Scawen Blunt arrived to see Parnell at the House of Commons on May 6th 1885, he had set his heart on entering Parliament. Primarily it was Lord Randolph Churchill, as leader of the Fourth Party (a Conservative ginger group which specialized in needling Gladstone) who had attracted his allegiance, on account of the interest he had shown in Blunt's Egyptian crusade. But Lord Randolph was proving and erratic ally. On April 14th Blunt had had a perplexing interview with him. 'I said,' wrote the indefatigable diarist afterwards, 'I was going to consult him about getting into Parliament; I wanted to push my ideas but hardly knew how to set about it. He said: "Oh! I can do that for you whenever you like. If you will, come forward as my supporter you can't do better, and I am asked almost every day to recommend candidates." I said: "What will this bind me to? You know my foreign politics, but at home I am a Catholic and a Tory as regards the land question and education, and in Ireland I am a Nationalist." He made a face at the word "Nationalist". He said: "You could not come forward as an avowed Nationalist, but you need not say much about that. If you say you have wide opinions on the Irish question it will be enough, and when you are once in Parliament you can take your own line." '4

Blunt wished to know the nature of 'Tory Democracy', a slogan which had recently been associated with Lord Randolph. Churchill was disconcertingly honest. 'He said: "That is a question I am always in a fright lest someone should put it to me publicly. To tell the truth I don't know myself what Tory Democracy is. But I believe it is principally opportunism. But say you are a Tory Democrat and that will do." I said: "You know me well enough to be sure that I would not be paid to be in Parliament if I was not free to take my own line. I had thought of standing as an Irish Home Ruler with Parnell, but I was in doubt and thought I would consult you." He said: "You would lose your influence if you did this. Parnell would require you to join his policy of obstruction and you would be discredited . . . But you should write me out a programme of your ideas and I will see if there is a constituency that will accept them." I said: "I will think it over and let you know." '5

Blunt observed: 'I think that perhaps, after all, I shall be freer with Randolph; and certainly his conversation binds me to nothing.' Neither his visit to the McCarthys nor his appointment with Parnell accorded ill with his affection for Churchill who was, at this moment, angling for Irish support for the Conservative party. Parnell was encouraging, as the two of them walked up and down the central lobby of Westminster. The Irish leader said he could not nominate him for an Irish constituency as an Englishman would be regarded as an interloper. 'Besides,' Blunt records him as remarking, 'we have always been betrayed by all the Englishmen who have gone with us – every one. Sometimes by our own people, but always by the English.'[6] However he did say that if Blunt chose an English constituency he would promise him the solid Irish vote. Blunt was struck by Parnell's presence and his straightforwardness. He took his advice and threw in his lot with Churchill.

The manifesto that was drawn up for Lord Randolph was entitled 'Am I a Tory Democrat?' and was published in *The Times*. Churchill, although still worried by the blatant advocacy of Home Rule, approved of it. Eventually on July 16th a deputation from Camberwell came to sound out Blunt's views and, despite his Irish opinions, offered him the seat. Huntley McCarthy promised to fix the Irish vote (there were under a thousand in the constituency) and Lord Randolph, now Secretary of State for India, agreed to send a letter of support to the adoption meeting. This he failed to do, taking last-minute fright at Blunt's uncompromising views on Ireland. However, despite the fact that two other Conservatives had put themselves up, Blunt was adopted, the committee deciding in his favour by sixteen to one. On Ireland he had declared his policy to be 'one of ascertaining Irish wishes and giving Home Rule as far as possible in accordance with them'.

Wilfrid Scawen Blunt found himself depressed by the mundanity of English electioneering. Previously his political experiences had been confined to the more exalted heights of Eastern intrigue, public meetings of protest, after-dinner discussions with great statesmen and letters to *The Times*. The dreariness was further exacerbated by the fact that, at this time, he had the Moslem reformer Sheykh Jemal-ed-Din stay-

ing with him in James Street. Together they had visited the
India Office to talk with Lord Randolph; and the memories
of the flamboyance of his old Egyptian and Sudanese campaigns
coupled with this easy contact with a Cabinet Minister made
the dingy halls and streets of Camberwell seem exceptionally
grey. On July 27th he noted in his diary : 'There is something
exceedingly absurd in this electioneering business; one hundred
frowsy fellows in a stuffy schoolroom talking nonsense to each
other about things they none of them understand or care about
a straw. It is an experience, however, like any other, and we
must go through it if we are to achieve anything of large
importance in the world. Yet it is a terrible come-down after
the politics of the golden East, or even of an Arab tribe.'[7]

Blunt had a low opinion of the electorate, finding his chief
supporters to be 'men of no position, character, or intelligence'.
He began his campaign 'with very small meetings to very
degraded audiences, sometimes in rooms obtained for the
purpose, but oftener mounted on a wagon in the streets, where
I found that nothing much short of pure socialism would be
listened to'.[8] Considerable efforts were made to liven it up. At
one meeting the speakers harangued an amazed and uncomprehending audience in Arabic and Persian, but received little
reaction. Distractions abounded. Lord Dufferin, Viceroy of
India, decided to invade Burma and depose King Thebaw in
October. Blunt immediately protested vigorously to the
Foreign Office and The Times about this latest piece of imperial
expansion.

Yet the East could encroach upon his goodwill as well. In
James Street Jemal-ed-Din, having been there for three months,
was beginning to outstay his welcome. The final straw was
when, after a fiery discussion about religion and politics, the
Afghan and some Oriental friends began to belabour each other
with umbrellas. Blunt asked the friends to leave and suggested
to his old mentor that he might be happier lodging elsewhere.
A disagreement followed and Jemal-ed-Din left England for
Moscow a few days later 'in anger against everything

English'. From Russia he went to Persia and Afghanistan, eventually arriving at Constantinople where, many years later, Blunt found him living in the precincts of the Yildiz Palace, half-pensioner half-prisoner of the Sultan. Blunt acknowledged the deep influence that this man had had on him and was saddened by their quarrel. However he recognized the difficulty of transplanting such a figure from the world of Moslem custom and scholarship into a London drawing room. 'Jemal-ed-Din,' he wrote, 'was a man of genius whose teaching exercised an influence hardly to be overrated on the Mohammedan reform movement of the last thirty years. I feel highly honoured at his having lived three months under my roof in England; but he was a wild man, wholly Asiatic and not easily tamed to European ways.'[9]

After this unpleasant incident Blunt threw himself with greater vigour into the Camberwell campaign. He refused to stick to any party line; but shamelessly promoted his own causes. In November a large meeting was held to press for the recall of Arabi to Egypt, hardly a popular cry in Camberwell, and on November 12th the candidate declared for Home Rule 'in its full sense', supporting Parnell in his demands for an Irish parliament. He had several devoted helpers, including Lady Anne and her maid Cowie, but he was too advanced for his electorate. He lost the election by one hundred and sixty-two votes out of the six thousand one hundred and twelve polled; and was thus thwarted in his first attempt to enter the inner circle of British political life.

Chapter 7
Ireland: The Plan of Campaign

Before the General Election of November 1885 the Conservative party appeared benevolent towards Irish aspirations. But on December 17th, soon after Lord Salisbury's election victory, Herbert Gladstone leaked the news of his father's conversion to the cause of Home Rule. The position of the two parties immediately changed, the Liberals becoming, after the exit of the Liberal Unionists, the natural allies of Irish Nationalism and the Conservatives taking a stand as the defenders of the law against agrarian outrages and Irish violence. The Irish joined with Gladstone to vote the Salisbury government out of office. On April 8th 1886 the Liberal Prime Minister, in a three-and-a-half-hour speech, introduced his first Home Rule Bill. After a long debate, in which the Conservatives brought Ulster to the forefront of British politics, it was defeated in the House of Commons. In the July election Lord Salisbury was voted into office with a composite majority of 118. For the next twenty years, except for a brief interregnum from 1892 to 1895, the Conservatives were in power. Throughout that time Ireland never allowed them to forget its discontent.

For the moment Parnell, fatally distracted by his love affair with Mrs O'Shea, was in the background. Other leaders took the extra-parliamentary campaign in hand. John Dillon and William O'Brien were two Irish Members of Parliament who recognized the force of the land issue. On October 23rd 1886 they published in the Nationalist newspaper *United Ireland* the details of their new programme of agrarian protest. They termed it the Plan of Campaign; and its principal theme was the banding together of tenants to resist unreasonable or impossible demands of rent.

While the Plan of Campaign was not a major upheaval like the land war of 1879-1882 the comparative sophistication of its organization caused the Conservative government, and the Irish Secretary Sir Michael Hicks Beach, considerable concern. The courts were quick to declare it illegal but attempts to imprison Dillon and the other leaders failed. The landlords were further demoralized by the disorder. At Dublin Castle, centre of the British government in Ireland, morale was equally low. In January 1887 the Cabinet finally decided on a special coercion Act. Arthur Balfour, Scottish Secretary and nephew of Lord Salisbury, was called upon to administer it. On March 5th 1887 he took up his post as the new Chief Secretary for Ireland, amid cries of derision; and called upon the newly married George Wyndham to be his private secretary.

It was in the spring of 1886, in March, that Wilfrid Scawen Blunt embarked upon a tour of Ireland, for the purpose of political observation. After his defeat at Camberwell in 1885, he had become increasingly disillusioned with the Conservative party. Lord Randolph Churchill, he felt, had let him down by not writing to support his candidature. Blunt had then seen the leader of Tory Democracy drift further away from Home Rule, a cause to which he had hoped to convert Churchill. After Gladstone's conversion Lord Randolph saw that he must desist in his flirtations with the Irish. He also may have felt that Blunt was now more likely to be a liability than an asset. In December he told his erstwhile ally: 'It is out of the question. If you want Home Rule you must go to Mr Gladstone. We cannot touch it.'[1] This was precisely what Blunt did.

Before leaving for Ireland Blunt had asked Morley, Gladstone's Irish Secretary, not to have him imprisoned. Morley replied that he would try to avoid doing so, but, if it became necessary, a most luxurious dungeon would be placed at his disposal. Blunt went on his own, without Lady Anne. Soon he was in the thick of things. The Irish Nationalists, including Dillon and Davitt, afforded him all the assistance they could, and he had little trouble in getting people to talk about their problems. He believed that this facility was due to his unique position as both revolutionary and English landlord, observing that 'there is no country in the world where social position carries more weight with it than in Ireland';[2] but the Irish were ready to co-operate with anyone who took their part.

His tour was conducted in a typically abrasive style. He travelled all over the country, from Dublin to the west, Roscommon, Donegal, Sligo and Galway, soon realizing that he had found a cause that would become as dear to him as any in the East. At the town of Gweedore in Donegal, in the terrible winter weather of the west coast, he came upon a priest, Father McFadden, holding a religious retreat. Almost a hundred people were packed into the small house, receiving communion among cows, hens and the Father's horse. 'It was,' wrote Blunt, 'a very curious and impressive sight, which I am glad to have seen. I have witnessed no such faith anywhere – no, not in Arabia!'[3] Through dispatches which he sent back to the *Pall Mall Gazette* he quickly fell out with several landlords. He had some memorable encounters, not the least of which was in April with Dr Duggan, Bishop of Clonfert, on the Clanricarde estates in Galway.

Michael Davitt had furnished Blunt with a letter of introduction to this remarkable priest, who was to be the subject of his long poem 'The Canon of Aughrim' and who seemed to him to epitomize all that was noble, fierce and tragic about Victorian Ireland. Soon the visitor realized that he was in the presence of a revolutionary. Here, amid the soft green fields and broken-down hovels of the west, they spoke of Ireland's problems. 'The landlords have ruined the land,' the Bishop told Blunt. 'Look out yonder! All that grass land I can remember tilled – and look there at the Poor House; twenty-eight thousand paupers lie buried in that field. When people ask me what England has given to Ireland, I answer "The Poor House". Yet they often choose to die in the road rather than go to it. I remember six thousand people in this town with shops, and trades, and prosperity, now there are only three thousand. Lord Clanricarde will not give another lease or renew it when one falls in. I have £3000 in the bank to build a church with; he will not lease me a site for it. You ask me what I would do with Lord Clanricarde if I had the settling of him. First I would put him in a glass bottle, and not let him out till he came to an agreement. Then we would appoint three persons to value his land, farm by farm, holding by holding. All should be taken into consideration, the tenant's necessary expense, his living, his farm capital. Then he should be obliged to sell. He must be got rid of anyhow. The land must be the peasants'. He should go away with what remained after all fair deductions had been made. It would not be much.'[4]

This story was given additional spice by the fact that Blunt remembered Clanricarde as Lord Hubert de Burgh, his old comrade in the Paris embassy. He had memories of the 'penurious habits and certain oddities' that had contrived to make de Burgh a mysterious and unattractive figure. Now that de Burgh had succeeded to his vast estates these characteristics had developed almost to the point of mania. There were few more eccentric or parsimonious individuals to be found than the Marquis of Clanricarde. The Marquis would boast that he never visited Galway, although he received a large annual income from his 50,000 acres there. It was said that not even when his mother died there did he take the trouble to cross the Irish Sea for her funeral. Letters to him from distraught or discontented tenants were never answered. All appeals from Irish charities went straight into the wastepaper basket.

Despite all this, he was a cultivated man who was well read and a considerable collector of pictures. He cut a peculiar figure, dressed in ludicrously shabby clothes and endlessly fussing about domestic economies. T. P. O'Connor, the Irish Member of Parliament, remembers him in 'an extraordinary old-fashioned and rusty hat' and 'a frock coat a good deal too large for him'.[5] But, when one considers the state of the villagers and tenants around Portumna, Woodford and Loughrea, the ultimate irony came when he complained to his own landlord in Albany about the condition of his rooms and demanded a reduction in rent. It was scarcely surprising that his agent Blake, testifying before the Bessborough Commission in 1880, said, in answer to a question whether there was any ill feeling between agents, landlords and tenants: 'I think there is. They look upon us as a different set of people.'[6]

They did indeed, and acted accordingly. The Clanricarde estates, because of their size and condition, were in as great a turmoil as any in Ireland. The tenants organized themselves against their landlord with determination and militancy. His unfortunate agents went in fear of their lives. One, indeed, was assassinated as he was driving to church with his wife, thus causing his master to send his famous message: 'If you think you can intimidate me by shooting my agent, you are mistaken.' The successor had to be guarded 'as abundantly as the Tsar of Russia'.[7] Evictions, naturally, were commonplace and, with the help of the Land League, tenaciously resisted. One house, known as 'Saunder's Fort', held out for days; and Hicks Beach, in London, was put in a terrible quandary. He had little sympathy for Clanricarde and was reluctant to use the army or the police to evict a tenant whom everybody knew was incapable of paying a ridiculous rent. In addition the whole exercise made the authorities look absurd. At one stage the Clanricarde evictions required the presence of two Resident Magistrates and five hundred officers and men of the Royal Irish Constabulary, in addition to the landlord's own bailiffs. The operations resembled a medieval seige and cost Dublin Castle something in the region of £3000.

It was almost a relief for Blunt to drive with the Bishop to the site of Aughrim, the last battle fought by the Irish against William of Orange. As they stood together on a hill, looking out over the plain, Dr Duggan was passionately moved. 'They call it the last battle,' he told Blunt, ' . . . but this is not true, for the battle has gone on ever since. Look at those great grass fields, empty for miles and miles away; every one of them contained once its little house, its potato ground, and its patch of oats. I remember many of them myself, with the happy souls who lived in them : and where are they now? O England, England! They are engulfed in your great cities, Liverpool, London, New York. They would have lived here happy, and died, and saved their Christian souls, and they have been driven out to live like devils and die like dogs, and be damned to eternity, and all for the sake of making a few English landlords rich. O England, England! If I was not a priest here . . . do you know what I should be doing? I should be going about in your dockyards and ports, blowing up your ironclads with dynamite.'[8]

To leave Dr Duggan and his Fenian determination was a sadness for Blunt. The Bishop blessed his visitor who openly wept and continued weeping for most of the way to Carrick. Here Blunt found police constables bound for Arigna in Roscommon, where evictions were to take place on the estate of the Earl of Kingston. What he saw there gave him an almost comfortable assurance as to the justness of his cause. Two hundred and fifty armed bailiffs and constables evicted a series of tenants, ransacking the cottages, throwing out the furniture and turning the inhabitants 'adrift upon the world'. The sight made him positively ill with rage. One of the men who had been turned out was a small farmer whose father had been a self-taught scholar, and all that he was left with was a copy of Horace's *Satires*. 'Though I am ill,' Blunt wrote, 'I am glad that I came. No one can understand what the Irish land question is till he has seen an eviction.'[9] Eventually the proceedings were stopped and the bailiffs and constables left. They had, Blunt estimated, collected £20 for the landlord at a cost to the government of £1000. He and the local priest had organized the opposition and as they departed the government forces took off their helmets and shouted 'three cheers for the other side'. Blunt believed that the constables' hearts were not in their job, as was shown by the fact that they collected over £5 amongst themselves for the evicted families.

After this he felt that he, as a property owner, should speak to the landlord. The Earl of Kingston was a weak young man, deeply in debt and entirely in the hands of his agent Tatlow. He lived in an impressive house surrounded by a large park on whose wall he had once sat with a shotgun, confronting an angry mob of his tenants. Kingston had written a strong letter of protest to the *Pall Mall Gazette* about Blunt's articles. Now he wrote to the author himself asking him to come to discuss the matter. They talked for the best part of two hours. At first Lord Kingston wanted to bring Tatlow in to justify his actions but Blunt refused to see the man, saying: 'We had better speak as gentleman to gentleman.' Kingston accused Blunt of accepting too easily the lies of the peasants. He said it was impossible for him to live on his present rents, and if he reduced them even further he would be destitute. Blunt told Kingston he must hear the grievances of the tenants for himself, but this the Earl refused to do, saying that if he went into a single cottage it would only encourage the rebels. Blunt said that he could not agree and must fight such a system with all his power. Lord Kingston observed: 'At least let us fight as gentlemen,' to which Blunt replied, 'I am sure we will do this.'[10] Three days later he returned to England.

By participating in the land agitation on the side of the tenants, Blunt had succeeded in annoying many of his friends. Some of these believed that, as a landowner himself, such behaviour was tantamount to class treachery and therefore unforgivable. Lord Pembroke, an old friend, was particularly upset as he had large estates in Ireland. Colonel King Harman, a large landowner in County Roscommon, proprietor of the vast Rockingham Castle and a Member of Parliament who professed to support Home Rule, was said to be so angry at the remarks about him in one of the *Pall Mall Gazette* articles that

he was thirsting for its author's blood. Blunt considered proposing a duel, but was dissuaded. Lady Gregory, later to become
a leader of the Irish literary renaissance, also chided him. At
this stage she, coming from a Protestant landowning background, was no friend to the cause of Home Rule.

After reducing his rents at Crabbet to make sure that his own
situation could not be used against him, Blunt, undeterred,
continued his frantic activity. For the remainder of 1886 and
most of 1887 he was scarcely still for a moment. There were
more visits to Ireland, an attempt to capture Kidderminster for
the Liberals in the election of the summer of 1886 – after the
defeat of Gladstone's first Home Rule bill – and a trip to Rome
with Lady Anne in October. Egypt then claimed his attention,
and he and Lady Anne went on to rest at Sheykh Obeyd. Sir
Evelyn Baring, who had previously banned this old supporter
of Arabi from the country, had no objection to the visit, but
they found Cairo in a melancholy state, full of its British
occupiers. When the Drummond-Wolff Turkish Convention,
set up to find some satisfactory solution to the Egyptian
problem, broke down, Blunt saw that his cause here was
virtually without hope. He decided to turn his full attention
towards Ireland, and returned to England forthwith.

Here the activity continued with speeches at Oxford and
Cambridge, and on Easter Monday 1887, a great demonstration
in Hyde Park against Irish coercion. Blunt drove along
Northumberland Avenue, St James's Street and Piccadilly in a
brake behind two magnificent Arab horses and, having encouraged the marchers to boo at the Carlton Club and Brooks's,
took the chair at the meeting which followed. From its begin-
ing the Plan of Campaign had had his full support. By now
the Irish Nationalists appeared to have entirely accepted
Blunt, despite his English origins, and on his trip to Ireland in
July of 1887 they warmly welcomed him as one of their
own.

Yet Blunt still managed to combine the satisfactions of his
aristocratic way of life with support for causes which went

against the opinions of those with whom he shared his pleasures. In Rome he occupied his leisure in fox hunting and stayed with the Duke and Duchess of Sermoneta at Fogliano near the Pontine Marshes, shooting duck at five in the morning on the ducal ponds. In Scotland there was grouse with the Wagrams; and in September 1887 he accepted with delight what was, for him, a particularly beguiling invitation – to spend a weekend at Clouds in Wiltshire with the Wyndham family.

Percy and Madeline Wyndham were one of the few dependable features of Wilfrid Blunt's life. When he was young, his family dead and his peregrinations estranging him from his own country, they had provided, with their affection, a degree of warmth that always proved immensely comforting. Since his marriage this had grown no less true. Both Wyndhams admired Lady Anne, and a visit to Wilbury, and later Clouds, was to be, for the Blunts, like returning to a second home. Wilfrid felt the family ties strongly. Percy, his first cousin, was almost the only close member of his family left. His sense of kinship provided an anchor, offering stability amid the fury of his political and literary activity. This feeling was heightened by Percy Wyndham's tolerance of his cousin's opinions. Like Blunt he strongly disapproved of the British intervention in Egypt, and encouraged him to stand for Parliament in support of Randolph Churchill. 'You two,' Wyndham said one evening in the Travellers Club, 'if you stick to your principle of telling the truth at all costs, may yet save England.'[11] When Percy Wyndham left the House of Commons in 1885, protesting against the extension of the franchise, Wilfrid Blunt felt that his courage and independent mind would be a great loss.

But it was to Madeline Wyndham that Blunt gave his unbounded affection. Throughout his early journeys in Arabia he would send her long letters, painting in her mind, which was occupied with family matters in Wiltshire, a vivid picture of his life at that particular moment. His descriptions appealed to

Madeline Wyndham's romantic nature. In the same way that she, by creating, with her houses, family life and generous character, an atmosphere of sublime rest and ease into which Blunt could retire from the turmoil brought upon him by his crusading spirit, so he could lead her, for an instant, out of the humdrum contented domesticity of her life into a stranger less predictable world. Each, in fact, had something to offer the other. In addition Madeline Wyndham was a strongly maternal person, adored by her children, and, in her turn, adoring them. She may at times have thought of Wilfrid Blunt, with all his restlessness, as a wayward child in need of affection. Certainly she delighted in his visits and when, in 1885, the Wyndhams' country house at Clouds was ready for occupation he was one of the most regular guests.

Clouds was situated at East Knoyle, a village eighteen miles west of Salisbury; and was described by Wilfrid Blunt as being 'the most interesting of our modern dwellings'.[12] Built by Philip Webb, the friend and associate of William Morris, to replace another house on the same site (originally called Clowdes after some former occupier but since changed to Clouds), it was intended by the Wyndhams to be their family home for generations. Endless trouble was taken over its building and decoration. Percy Wyndham told Webb it was 'the house of the age'.[13] With it came some two thousand acres of land and, in this corner of Wiltshire, bordering on Fonthill where Beckford had once acted out his dreams of Gothic grandeur, the Wyndhams settled down to establish a home worthy of their own aesthetic aspirations and the traditions of their family.

Material for the house had been gathered for years, both in England and abroad. Madeline Wyndham's enthusiasm for decoration was immense. She and her husband were friends of the Morrises and Burne-Jones, and the tone was Victorian leavened by 'a riot of unexpected colour'.[14] The gardens were created against the green sandstone background of the house with imagination and horticultural skill. In 1887 it must have seemed that Clouds would, as they hoped, last forever, passing from father to son with ease, secure against the unchanging solidity of England's prosperity and contentment. The weeks went by slowly, with Percy Wyndham, now free of his parliamentary duties, settling easily into the life of an English country squire, and Madeline attending to the problems of the family and the servants. Contained within the house was an entire social system, with a hierarchy, carefully graded from the lowliest scullery maid to the master, to support it. Country houses were, in those days, like small kingdoms and, once inside one, it was possible to become almost oblivious of the rest of the world. At weekends, however, this contented isolation would be broken and the Wyndhams' friends would come to stay. In September 1887 it was decided that Wilfrid Blunt should be asked, despite his eccentric Irish opinions, so that he could meet George, to whom he had recently given some valuable literary advice and encouragement, and George's master, their old friend, Arthur Balfour.

Chapter 8
Ireland: The Politics of Coercion

Arthur Balfour in 1887, the year of his appointment to the Irish Office, was something of an enigma. Tall and thin, his etiolated figure was not thought to be one of the more formidable presences on the Conservative benches; and the fact that he was the Prime Minister's nephew led, inevitably, to the customary jeers. The Irish reaction was a mixture of delight, because they believed that they had now been offered their weakest opponent to date and amused contempt. T. P. O'Connor a Nationalist Member of Parliament, aptly describing the new Chief Secretary's appearance, said that 'Mr Balfour is a tall and very slight man. The neck is long, narrow and thin as that of a delicate girl. On the whole the impression he would give to a stranger, who saw him for the first time and did not know him, would be that he was a more than usually mild member of the mild race of curates.'[1] One Parnellite was even more forceful, remarking: 'We have killed Forster, blinded Beach and smashed up Trevelyan; what shall we not do with this weakling?'[2]

Arthur Balfour's career to date offered little to refute this view. The eldest son of a prosperous Scottish border landowner, he had enjoyed every advantage that money and good connections could bring. His father had died eight years after Arthur's birth and it was his mother, Lady Blanche Balfour, sister of Lord Salisbury, who was the most potent influence on his early life. After an undistinguished time at Eton he went to Cambridge where he discovered a talent for philosophy and, almost alone amongst his patrician contemporaries, science. For a time he even considered giving up his inheritance to devote his life to philosophical study, but Lady Blanche was having none of this. She, in true Cecilian style, reminded him of his responsibilities and so, at the age of twenty-six, he became Member of Parliament for Hertford, a constituency that contained Hatfield, the residence of his uncle, within its bounds. Immediately after his election he set off on a slow leisurely trip around the world, waiting two and a half years before making his maiden speech, on the subject of Indian silver currency.

Lord Salisbury took his nephew under his wing, making him his parliamentary private secretary when he was at the Foreign Office. After a period in Opposition, during which he became a rather unenthusiastic member of Lord Randolph Churchill's rebellious Fourth Party, he received office from his uncle who was now Prime Minister, as Scottish Secretary. Here his most onerous duty was to deal with a wave of land agitation which was sweeping the Western Islands. Some thought that this brief experience of agrarian disorder was hardly sufficient preparation for Balfour's appointment in March 1887 to the Irish Office to administer the new coercion Act.

Balfour himself realized the weight of his new burden. 'The history of Irish Secretaries,' he wrote, 'since Mr Gladstone came into office in 1880, was not wholly encouraging. Mr Forster had never concealed the fact that if he had known what the office involved he would never have taken it. His successor (Cavendish) was murdered. Sir George Trevelyan, who followed, temporarily broke down under the strain.'[3] Yet he was confident and felt prepared for the coming crisis. Underneath the frippery and social ease there was a resilient toughness that could resist almost every assault.

Philosophic detachment was perhaps the main source of Arthur Balfour's strength. His famous remark to John Morley ('when I am at work on politics, I long to be in literature and vice versa'[4]) has often been thought of as evidence of his lack of serious concern for either whereas it in fact denotes a remarkable ability to escape from the turmoil of both. This ability to retire into a calm inner solitude, gave him an elevated disdain for passionate involvement. He never, he once told a friend, thought about politics in bed. Such serenity of mind came to infuriate his opponents. Balfour appeared sometimes to see politics merely as an intellectual exercise, seldom allowing himself any display of passion when pursuing his policies. 'What made Irish government so difficult,' he later observed, 'was English sentimentality.'[5] In the end it was this cold façade which proved his undoing with the English electorate and was one of the reasons for the Conservatives ditching him in 1912. H. G. Wells once observed: 'Balfour might perhaps have been a very great man indeed if his passions had been hotter and his affections more vivid.'[6]

Even his friends were occasionally disconcerted by this dispassionate approach. George Wyndham wrote to Charles Gatty, after the latter had observed that he believed Balfour's attitude to politics to be too detached for the average Tory voter, 'The truth about Arthur Balfour is this; he knows there's been one ice-age; and he thinks there's going to be another.'[7] Extended to human relationships such a view led to an absence of emotional involvement which was sometimes the despair of others. Margot Asquith, while speaking with him about his close friend Lady Desborough and his niece Blanche, suddenly blurted out: 'You're fond of me and of Ettie and of Baffy; but you don't really care – you wouldn't mind if we all died,'[8] to which Balfour replied: 'I should mind if you all died on the same day.' Yet the quality of his mind and his intense intellectual curiosity made him a delightful companion and a sympathetic listener. Once, in the 1920s, he was sitting next to a young girl at lunch and she, terrified lest she should bore this distinguished elder statesman, began wondering whether she should ask him about the League of Nations or the Versailles Treaty or the Irish question. She was rapidly put at her ease by his turning to her and remarking: 'I understand that you know the Sitwells. I do wish that you would tell me all about them.' Astonished, she did, and he listened enraptured, interjecting appropriate and encouraging questions, for the rest of the meal.[9]

Ireland was the first considerable challenge that politics had offered to Balfour. Initially it appeared as if his uncle had severely misjudged his capacity for handling the situation. On March 28th he introduced the Crimes Act, which set up the 'proclaimed' districts in which those who took part in subversive meetings, organizations or conspiracies could be convicted without a jury trial. It was a poor début. 'Arthur Balfour,' wrote Randolph Churchill to Hicks Beach, 'fills your place very badly. He made a terrible fiasco introducing the bill on Monday – want of knowledge, the most elementary want of tact and judgement coupled with an excited manner and a raised voice. Of course the Irish interrupted brutally and he was unable to cope with them.'[10] However the jeering soon changed to admiration. The new Chief Secretary's coldly courteous style infuriated the Irish Members and his resolve proved to be stronger than even his friends had dared to hope. By the end of the session (September 1887) Cranbrook was writing to Salisbury: 'They (the Parnellites) cannot make much of Balfour who foils them by his skill and coolness and indeed leaves no just opening for their rancour';[11] and Salisbury himself remarked, in a letter to Lady John Manners, 'The Treasury bench is infected with the spirit of Arthur Balfour and very much disposed to vigorous measures.'[21] Indeed vigour, not a quality many would have previously associated with him, had been the keynote of Balfour's first months at the Irish Office. Coercion was back; the National League (organizer of the Plan of Campaign) was declared a 'proclaimed' or illegal organization; and Sir Joseph Ridgeway, a firm ex-Indian Army soldier, had taken over from Sir Redvers Buller, whose confidence and reputation had been badly damaged by the failures of the past as permanent under-secretary in Dublin. Gladstonian appeasement was clearly at an end.

Wyndham found his new job exhilarating. In August he had crossed with Balfour to Ireland, on one of the many official visits they were to make to that country, and wrote to his wife: 'I must tell you that we crossed with John Dillon and O'Brien! Arthur and I sat down to a little supper, cheek by jowl with the former. We both felt inclined to burst out laughing, it was so absurd after pounding away, he and Dillon, at each other all through the Session.'[13]

Balfour proved to be an easy and stimulating taskmaster. He had known the Wyndhams since 1879 or 1880, when he had met them in Sir Frederick Leighton's studio while admiring pictures, and delighted in their company. Clouds soon became one of his favourite houses and its owners welcomed him, as often as he wished, as their guest. George Wyndham's cultivated tastes also pleased him and provided a welcome diversion from the problems of Dublin Castle. He encouraged the young man to enter politics himself. However on Conservative policies, even those of his chief, Wyndham kept a reasonably open mind. In August 1887, just after the proclamation of the National League, Blunt and he had met in the lobby of the House of Commons, where Wyndham seemed doubtful whether Balfour's measures would have the desired effect. 'He does not seem,' wrote Blunt, 'to have much hope of his party succeeding in their desperate idea of stopping Home Rule; and the proclaiming of the League, he said, would have little more effect than to put an end to open boycotting, tearing down of placards etcetera . . . George is a charming boy, and is still young enough to talk without reserve . . . He is to be at Clouds when we go there next month.'[14]

Blunt was opposed to what Balfour was attempting to do, although he found the man himself sympathetic enough despite 'that philosophical hardness of view which is at the bottom of his estimate of political things." Blunt believed that Balfour, because of his scientific interest, espoused the Darwinian theory of the survival of the fittest. This he detested. He believed it represented 'the world of life no longer as an ordered harmony, but as in its essence a struggle for existence where whatever right there was was on the side of might, and where it was a waste of pity to deplore the extinction of the less capable races either of beast or man before the competition of their more capable rivals'.[16]

Blunt suspected that Darwinism had given added impetus to imperialism and that its adherents could have little or no sympathy with the Catholic Irish peasantry. He also believed that it was impossible for so urbane and metropolitan a figure as Balfour to understand that these people were 'a happier people far than our English peasantry . . . social, joyous and dignified by their religion . . . better fitted for the land in which they lived and which they passionately loved, than could be any new band of immigrants which could take their place from Scotland or England'.[17] It was not so much their poverty that Blunt pitied as their subjection to the unnatural laws imposed upon them by the English government which 'were driving them from these happy homes' to a 'grim fate as outcasts in our English and American cities'. 'On all these matters,' Blunt wrote, 'Balfour and I stood a whole world apart.'[18] In September 1887, he went to Clouds determined to discover exactly how great this distance might be.

Wilfrid Blunt arrived at Clouds some days before Arthur Balfour. He occupied the time with talking to his cousins, partridge shooting on the Wiltshire Downs and playing the after-dinner games that were then so great a feature of country house life. Moving amongst the large rooms, decorated with Morris materials and full of light, and walking across the stubble in the clear downland air, he felt entirely at ease. The conversations ranged over literature (George Wyndham was beginning to write verses), family matters and recollections of their shared past. Then, on the afternoon of September 3rd, Arthur Balfour arrived with the novelist Henry James, and Blunt was given his opportunity of observing the Chief Secretary at play.

It must have been an intriguing party. James, the New England assimilator of the Old World's customs and foibles, Balfour, the philosopher statesman, and Blunt, poet and revolutionary, were three of the most remarkable figures of their time, whose opinions on any matter would have been worth having. This autumn, however, it was impossible to avoid Ireland. The Chief Secretary, fresh from administering the Crimes Act, was aware that this very weekend a proclaimed meeting of the National League at Ballycoreen was to test its viability. Wilfrid Blunt had lately been vociferously campaigning, in the Press and on political platforms, for Home Rule; and Henry James found the Irish question 'thrilling' and of 'throbbing interest'.[19]

Blunt had met Balfour before, at social gatherings, but this was their first encounter since the Chief Secretary had taken office. He found him gracious enough, but was shocked by his cool, almost surgical approach. At dinner, the Irish Nationalist Member of Parliament, John Dillon, whom Blunt knew and admired, came up for discussion. Dillon was an ardent Home Ruler who worked tirelessly for his cause, despite chronic ill health. 'I am sorry for Dillon,' Blunt records Balfour as saying, 'as if he gets into prison it is likely to kill him. He will have hard labour, and it will be a different thing from Forster's ridiculous imprisonments at Kilmainham. There is something almost interesting about Dillon; but it is a pity he lies so.'[20] After dinner a game called Reversi was played, at which the Chief Secretary excelled. In the course of it he made a mistake, but observed to his partner that there was no more vain or foolish feeling than remorse. That evening Blunt recorded in his diary: 'Balfour is clever and light in hand, but with a certain hardness and cynicism which are not altogether pleasant.' He was forced to admit, however, that he was 'a man of considerable capacity and more backbone than what his "lackadaisical" appearance would suggest'.

The next day was the day of the Ballycoreen meeting. At Clouds the atmosphere was calm. In the afternoon some of the guests played lawn tennis. The match consisted of Balfour and Guy Wyndham (George's younger brother) against Wilfrid Blunt and George Wyndham; and Blunt was delighted that he and George gave the others a 'thorough good beating for the honour of Home Rule'. He thought it 'rather absurd my being here playing tennis with the Chief Secretary on the very day and at the very hour of the Ballycoreen meeting, where he evidently expects bloodshed'. At tea Balfour observed to George Wyndham that he supposed it was all over by now, yet there was no way for them to find out what turn events had taken as the Irish Office had been ordered not to disturb their Chief's Sunday with telegrams.

Later that evening Blunt and Balfour finally 'had it out about Ireland'. Balfour appeared reasonable, even being prepared to admit the ultimate inevitability of Home Rule, but coldly firm. He appeared to believe that the imprisonment of Dillon, O'Brien and half a dozen others would take the wind out of the Nationalist movement. Blunt told him that he was wrong, declaring that 'the Nationalists had nothing to do now but to sit still and win; at the next elections in England the Liberals would come back into office and then, Home Rule being their chief plank, Home Rule was a certainty'. With this Balfour agreed, but said Home Rule would not come for some years yet, particularly if Gladstone died or retired and no competent successor was found. 'After all,' he declared, 'when it comes I shall not be sorry. Only let us have separation as well as Home Rule; England cannot afford to go on with Irishmen in her Parliament. She must govern herself too.' The next day Balfour left for London, having heard by telegram that all had passed off quietly at Ballycoreen; and Blunt stayed on for another day, to shoot more partridges and discuss more poetry.

The quiet passing of the Ballycoreen meeting was soon demonstrated to be a moment of unnatural calm in the Irish storm. On September 9th a mass meeting was held at Mitchelstown in County Cork, on an estate of the Kingston family, to protest against a summons that had been served upon William O'Brien for inciting Kingston tenants to resist eviction. O'Brien himself remained in Dublin; but Dillon was there, accompanied by Henry Labouchère, the radical MP and several other supporters. Violence erupted, stones were thrown and the police fired on the crowd. Three rioters were killed and fifty-four policemen were injured. In the debate in the House of Commons on September 12th Balfour found himself the centre of an uproar. He stated his case with chilly rationality, despite an impassioned display of anger by Labouchère. But it was Gladstone who first uttered the phrase 'Remember Mitchelstown', and made it the cry of all those who opposed Balfour's Irish policies.

On September 10th, Wilfrid Scawen Blunt was staying at Naworth Castle in Cumberland with the Howard family when he heard the news of the Mitchelstown meeting. He concluded that it was his duty to return to Ireland. 'There are so many,' he wrote, 'who have shirked committing themselves that, now that it is a case of a real fight with the government, it would be mean to hold back. I have so often resolved to wait for the first blood, and now it has been shed.'[21] On September 14th he arrived in Dublin and embarked upon another of his forays into the troubled countryside. Dr Duggan, he was pleased to see, was 'more Fenian than ever'. Blunt attended O'Brien's trial at Mitchelstown, performed under the regulations of the new Crimes Act. The Nationalist was given three months imprisonment, a sentence which Blunt felt had been dictated by Dublin Castle. 'The whole trial,' he wrote, 'was a farce, and so, too, will be the punishment, for O'Brien will be out on bail tonight and attending meetings of the League during the whole of the following month.'[22] On September 26th he arrived back in England, to visit Knebworth with his wife and his daughter Judith, and to introduce George Wyndham to Lytton.

Blunt never allowed his political convictions to interfere with friendship; and it is a measure of the affection with which his friends regarded him that they did not allow these convictions to rob them of his company. Naturally a shared pleasure in literature contributed to this. 'In relation to many matters,' Lytton had written to him on August 23rd 1887, 'about which we both feel strongly, we have necessarily separated. But it is not, I firmly believe, that the old ties between us are broken, it is only that new ones have not grown out of new interests.'[23] The visit to Knebworth was a great success. 'There was,' wrote Blunt, 'a tacit understanding between me and Lytton that politics should be avoided when we met, and we had enough to interest us in our common love of poetry, and the higher things of the spirit, without troubling each other with matters where we knew we differed.'[24] However, Lytton's hospitality did not dampen Blunt's revolutionary ardour. On October 13th he went to London, to the office of the Home Rule Union. Here he was commissioned by the Union to test the validity, in Ireland, of the new Crimes Act, particularly the rules pertaining to 'proclaimed' meetings. As an Englishman it was thought that his arrest would put the British government in an awkward dilemma, for such meetings were still perfectly legal in England. At the same time a letter arrived from O'Brien, welcoming Blunt's new commission and suggesting that he and Lady Anne should be present at a protest meeting which was to be held on the Clanricarde estates at Woodford in Galway. This letter was followed by a telegram from John Dillon urging Blunt to return to Dublin at once; and on the morning of Saturday September 15th he arrived there with Lady Anne and her maid Cowie.

Lady Anne and Cowie were tired by their journey but Blunt, leaving them to rest in the Imperial Hotel, departed immediately with William O'Brien in search of action. O'Brien, at this stage on bail, was anxious to reach Woodford without alerting the police, so they went first to Limerick, then to Bodyke, where evictions were in progress, and later on to Tomgreany. At Tomgreany a meeting was improvised and O'Brien spoke on the village green. Later, by night, having given the police the slip, the party proceeded to Woodford. Blunt was impressed by the assistance given to O'Brien in his efforts to reach the Galway village unnoticed. 'In that day,' he wrote, 'O'Brien's popularity in the west of Ireland was such that nearly everyone was in complicity with him against the Government, down to the smallest employee on the railways, and the prison warders.'[25]

On the way to Woodford they passed several groups of police but were not challenged. The night was cold, and the twenty-mile journey an agony. Blunt observed later: 'I was never more pleased than when at last we met a man on horseback come from Woodford to meet us, who told us the end of our journey was close at hand.'[26] An enthusiastic crowd came out to meet them and their carts were escorted into the centre of the village. The meeting began almost immediately, although by now it was midnight. O'Brien addressed the crowd from the upper window of a shopkeeper's house. He ended his speech by burning the Lord-Lieutenant's proclamation which forbade all public meetings in the district. Blunt and an English Member of Parliament, James Rowlands, also made speeches. Then all retired to bed to be woken at daybreak by a detachment of British troops who had come to occupy the village. 'It was a case,' wrote Blunt, 'for them of "too late for the fair" and the laugh in the streets next day was very much against them.'[27]

On October 21st Blunt heard that the evictions had been renewed at Woodford and that a girl's head had been brutally battered in a struggle with the police. 'It occurred to me,' he wrote, 'that the moment was now come for me to take action as delegate of the Home Rule Union, and after consulting Dillon and O'Brien on the point of its opportuneness, I decided to return at once to Woodford and hold, not a secret meeting such as the last had been, but a public one.'[28] The idea was to throw out an open challenge to the authorities. Blunt knew that, if the letter of the new law was obeyed, his arrest must surely follow. He took Lady Anne with him and the Rowlands, so that the instigators of this plot should be entirely English. Rowlands, as a Member of Parliament, was worried. He was not prepared to have his name on the handbills advertising the meeting but agreed to sit on the platform. Blunt had no such qualms, and when the bills were distributed in Woodford and Loughrea on October 22nd he was clearly advertised as the chairman. That night a telegram arrived from O'Brien in Dublin saying that the meeting had been proclaimed and that copies of the Lord-Lieutenant's proclamation had been dispatched by the mail train to Woodford. Some sort of clash was inevitable.

On Sunday October 23rd the Blunts woke, in the house of John Roche, a Nationalist miller, to find that during the night one hundred and fifty policemen had moved in, together with a company of Scots Guards. Copies of the proclamation, signed by Arthur Balfour and Lord Londonderry, were in evidence everywhere. 'This was,' Blunt wrote, 'indeed doing us honour beyond all we could have hoped, and placed our little meeting on an almost heroic footing.'[29] He wrote an answer to the proclamation, to establish the reasons for his presence, beginning:

'Sir,

It having been announced to me that the meeting of the Home Rule Union advertised for this afternoon has been proclaimed at Dublin Castle, this is to inform you that I do not recognize the right of the Lord Lieutenant causelessly to interfere with a meeting convened by orderly Englishmen, loyal subjects of Her Majesty, for orderly and loyal purpose. As chairman of the meeting I shall appear in my place at the hour named and shall use my full authority to make matters pass quietly and with decorum. I guarantee the moderate language of the speakers, who are to be all Englishmen, and if uninterfered with by the police, the good conduct of the audience. On the other hand, I give you fair warning that on you and on your men will rest the full responsibility of any breach of the peace, should you seek any forcible means to disperse the meeting. I hold you personally responsible for any wanton attack on the unarmed crowd, and I warn you, in dealing with the speakers, that there will be ladies as well as gentlemen present on the platform.'[30]

Having thus advertised himself, Blunt attended Mass on the morning of the meeting. At the service the priest exhorted the congregation to attend the meeting despite the proclamation. At two o'clock a ragged procession consisting of Blunt, Lady Anne, the Reverend Fagan (a radical Norfolk clergyman), the local Nationalist MP, other sympathizers and two hundred villagers set off for the field where the gathering was to be held. Byrne, the Divisional Magistrate, tried to stop them, only to be swept aside and accused of trespassing by the farmer who owned the field. This surprised the magistrate so much that he allowed them to pass, following into the field with his constables. Blunt and his associates mounted the platform, and the chairman opened the proceedings with a loud shout of 'Men of Galway!'

Immediately Byrne, who was by this time also on the platform, signalled to his men to rush the speaker. Chaos followed, during which Blunt managed, briefly, to resume his speech. But by this time a full-scale fight was in progress and the audience was in no mood to listen. Byrne pulled at Blunt, and Lady Anne who clung to her husband, and with the help of seven or eight men got them off the platform, seizing Lady Anne by the throat in an effort to prise her apart from the villain of the piece. Blunt, fearing that his gesture would be in vain, jumped up from the grass and shouted at the constables: 'Are you all such damned cowards that not one of you dares to arrest me?' Whereupon one of them, Sergeant Wade, laid his hand on the agitator's arm and arrested him. Blunt then whispered to Lady Anne: 'It is all right now. Come along.' And Balfour's new prisoner was led off the field of battle, amid a hail of stones aimed at his captors. Outside the courthouse the police had to charge the unruly crowd with their batons;

and Roche the miller was arrested for defending himself with his blackthorn stick. At the police station the prisoners were locked up for the rest of the afternoon before being brought before a local JP on a charge of resisting the police. Blunt was offered conditional bail, providing he did not hold another meeting that night. This he refused, on the grounds that the proclamation was not true law, and was sent, with Roche, to Loughrea to spend the night in jail.

Chapter 9

Ireland: The Prisoner

The night journey to Loughrea was long. On the road they were met with moving demonstrations of sympathy. In every village there was a bonfire, and people standing with torches to cheer their new hero. Stones were rolled in front of the brougham to slow down its progress, so that they did not reach their destination until after midnight. In Loughrea a throng of well-wishers had to be beaten back by the batons of the escorting constables. Just before they entered the doors of the prison a man leapt on to the driver's seat and dealt the constable holding the reins a blow with a dagger before disappearing into the night. But the driver was protected by his thick coat, and they were conveyed into the gloom of the jail where the jailer, an avowed Nationalist who kept a portrait of Gladstone on the wall of his private room, treated them with consideration.

The next day Wilfrid Scawen Blunt was brought before two magistrates and sentenced to two months in prison. Later he was to express his opinion of his judges. 'It will exemplify,' he wrote, 'the extremely low level of the justice at that time administered in Ireland when I record that these two persons entrusted with summary powers were neither of them possessed of any legal knowledge or even of social fitness, one of them being a Limerick grocer, the other a decayed racing man, who, on the very day on which he was sentencing me, was having judgement delivered against himself for debt in the court of the Queen's Bench. Yet the case they were set to try was one of extreme constitutional complexity, needing high magisterial ability.'¹ They refused Blunt's attempts to bring cross summonses against Byrne, the police and Balfour. He was sentenced subject to an appeal to Quarter sessions, and, availing himself of this appeal, was released on bail.

After visiting Dr Duggan, who shed tears over Blunt's martyrdom, the prisoner returned to England. Here the Liberals welcomed him as a worthy victim of Conservative tyranny. He went on a speaking tour of the north with Sir William Harcourt and was prevailed upon to stand as anti-coercionist candidate for Deptford. The first days of the new year saw him once again in Galway, to surrender his bail at Portumna. The trial, before Mr Justice Henn, lasted a week. Appearing for Blunt were The Macdermott and Tim Harrington, both of whom gave their services free; and prosecuting were 'two of the Castle Bloodhounds', Atkinson and Edward Carson, later to become a leading Unionist Member of Parliament.

Wandering, when the court was not in session, in the grounds of Portumna Castle – the Clanricarde family residence now shuttered and deserted in the absence of its owner – Blunt found himself a prey to conflicting emotions. On the one hand there was pride in his act of defiance; on the other the realization, brought on by the great desolate castle and its ancestral park, of how far he had gone against the dictates of his upbringing and his class. His father, some sixty years before, had been acquainted with the Clanricarde of the day and had visited this part of Galway to shoot and fish with his friend. Blunt tried to imagine 'what my high Tory father's feelings would have been, as ex-officer of the Guards, squire, and Justice of the Peace, could he have foreseen that his son's first and only visit to the place . . . would be in the character of law-breaker and accomplice of its owner's rebel tenantry'.²

Soon there was to be ample time for such speculation. The sentence was confirmed. The prisoner was then conveyed, in the company of his wife, to Galway by train, for incarceration in Galway jail. At each station there were crowds to cheer them on their way. 'Once more,' wrote Blunt, 'the thought surged strongly in me of how noble a thing it was that I should have been called to suffer something, however little, of ignominy and pain in expiation of my country's crime.'[3] A peasant girl reached out and grasped his hand, calling out her blessings upon him, and he felt, for the first time, a fear of the loneliness which was about to engulf him. In the carriage, with the two escorting constables, he and Lady Anne spoke in Arabic in order that they should be able to give the freest expression to their thoughts. At Galway he said goodbye to her and entered the cell assigned to him. She remained for some days in the town, outside the prison walls, content merely to be near him; then, aware that there was nothing she could do, returned to England.

The reaction in England to Wilfrid Scawen Blunt's Irish escapades varied from admiration to extreme horror. The Liberals welcomed him as a valuable ally. Asquith, Sir Charles Russell (later Lord Chief Justice), Robert Reid (later, as Lord Loreburn, Lord Chancellor) and W. S. Robson (afterwards Attorney-General) signed a paper in which they stated that both the dispersal of the Woodford meeting and Blunt's sub-sequent arrest and conviction were, in their opinions, illegal. His friend W. J. Evelyn, a Tory MP and Home Ruler, declared he would vacate his seat at Deptford in order that Blunt should be able to stand as an anti-coercionist candidate in his place.

Other Tories, and his friends who were of their way of thinking, were not so enthusiastic. On September 13th 1887 Lytton had written to Lady Francis Balfour, the Chief Secretary's sister-in-law, about the introduction of the Crimes Act. 'What a comfort it is,' he had exclaimed, 'to see any English Minister behaving like a man who is not frightened by cant! I really believe that, if the present Parliament does not perish prematurely, Arthur Balfour has now a great chance of pul-

verizing the League, pacifying Ireland, and achieving for himself a great place in English history.'[4] Now he remained silent.
Some did not feel the need for restraint. Lord Salisbury wrote
to his nephew: 'I was delighted to see that you had run
Wilfrid Blunt in'; and this sentiment was certainly echoed
by most Conservative politicians. Lord Cranbrook called Blunt
'a conceited ass'; and Salisbury also observed, with approba-
tion: 'The great heart of the people always chuckles when a
gentleman gets into the law.'[5] Only Lord Randolph said some
words in his favour, and they were of a personal rather than
a political nature.

The Wyndhams were particularly perplexed. Previously
they had regarded their cousin's crusading spirit as leading, on
occasions, to eccentric statements and behaviour; but now to see
him locked up, a prisoner on the orders of Arthur Balfour,
one of their closest and most admired friends and George
Wyndham's master, stretched their tolerance to its uttermost
limits. The prison sentence was especially painful for George
Wyndham. On December 8th, after the arrest, Blunt had written to congratulate him on the birth of his child Percy, and had
asked Wyndham to be his literary executor. Wyndham had
answered: 'I am much honoured by your charge and will, of
course, readily undertake it; at the same time I sincerely trust
that I may not be called upon to fulfill it. But if it should unfortunately be so, I can promise you to spare no pains in
putting your work before the public.'[6] Yet in January Wyndham was writing to his father declaring that 'Wilfrid is
apparently temporarily out of his senses, but I can hardly
believe all that is attributed to him'.[7]

Wyndham's anger was understandable; and the events that
had led him to believe that his friend was 'temporarily out of
his senses' demonstrated the zeal with which Blunt carried on
his campaign, even when behind bars. At first he found prison
life tolerable. Soon, however, boredom set in. He had no writing
materials and only a small badly printed Bible to read. The sole
labour imposed upon him was oakum-picking. The nights

were difficult and it was these 'with their terrible thirteen hours of unlighted darkness' and himself 'insufficiently clothed and covered' which steadily destroyed his peaceful acquiescence. The discomfort of the miserable plank bed was a further agony.

One of his few solaces was his own greatcoat which, in addition to providing warmth, came to represent a tenuous link with his old world outside the walls. However, according to the prison rules he was not even allowed to hold on to this. On January 11th he managed to smuggle out a letter, written on tissue paper, to Lady Anne. 'I am not unkindly treated,' he observed, 'only I am never allowed to leave my cell, and the Governor worries me from time to time about my greatcoat. They sent me one from Dublin yesterday, but it was too small, a miserable skimpy thing, without pockets, and I shall cling to my own as I do to my life, for it is "my plumage by day and my bed by night". My chief misery is that I have nothing to do. The Bible they have given me is of microscopic print, and except when the sun comes into a corner of my cell in the afternoon I cannot read a word of it. So push on the application for writing materials and books.'[8]

Fortunately Blunt had friends, both inside and outside the jail. The warders' attitude was generally respectful. His own, Danby, assured him: 'We are obliged to distinguish between case and case, and it is not often we have a gentleman like you here, but when we do we know how to consider him. Why sir, it was only last year we had just such another case as your own, a gentleman from Dublin who had had a misfortune like yours – he had signed another gentleman's name thinking it was his own, and he was here with us for some months. How was he to be sweeping out his own cell? We could not let him do it any more than I can you; a case, sir, just like yours.'[9] This, on its own, would have been cold comfort; but the chief warder often passed him *The Freeman's Journal* and the Governor would, on his daily visit, deliver a brief digest of the news from outside the walls. The Bishop of the diocese, Dr McCormack, saw that he was eventually furnished with a good quarto copy of the Bible.

Meanwhile, outside, other admirers did what they could. Jane Morris, wife of William, wrote to Jane Cobden, daughter of Richard: 'I want you to help me about Mr Blunt. He is most desirous to be allowed writing materials so that he may edit a new volume of poems while in prison. He says in a letter to me "it would make all the difference between a blank misery and a profitable retirement". What he asks me to do is to interest all the poets and literary people I know, and get them to get up a correspondence in *The Times* on the subject; then he thinks the police would support him. Naturally I asked my husband first, but he says *The Times* would not insert anything of his. Swinburne is a violent unionist and would certainly refuse to write a line on the right side. Oscar Wilde is the only other poet I know personally, and his unsupported letter would have little weight I fancy . . . Can you think of any others who seem likely to help? I can scarcely think of anything myself, my brain is whirling – How badly British matters are going! It is heartrending.'[10]

It was the overcoat that led to trouble. The Governor was informed by the prisons board in Dublin that the prisoner must give up his overcoat for the regulation garment. He should also, the board insisted, be made to surrender his travelling carpet that he had brought with him. Blunt refused to consider these demands; and on January 13th the coat was removed by force. Instantly he demanded to see the prison visiting justices. 'I declared,' Blunt wrote later, 'I would not put on again any of my prison clothes till attention had been paid me.' He also decided to repeat to the visitors the conversation that he had had with Balfour at Clouds some four months before. Having heard that William O'Brien and John Roche had been arrested, he believed that these revelations might assist them by attracting public sympathy towards political prisoners.

Blunt cut a strange figure before the Justices. Frail from the cold and lack of sleep, wearing only the prison blanket from his plank bed, he firmly enunciated his objections to his treatment. The listeners were sympathetic. Lord Clanricarde was not popular, even amongst the landlord class (to which the Justices belonged) who felt that his parsimony and neglect of his property were befouling their already tarnished reputation. In addition Lady Gregory, whose family were local magnates, had appealed for understanding on Blunt's behalf; and his own personal charm was not without effect, even in circumstances as bizarre as these. The result was that he was given an overcoat exactly like his own, but made of regulation prison material; and the following day his statement about the conversations at Clouds was widely taken up by the Press.

On January 15th George Wyndham wrote to his wife from the Chief Secretary's Lodge in Phoenix Park : 'We had all sorts of things to do today, some of them tiresome, rows with police, and Wilfrid's overcoat and lies by Harcourt and I say "Pooh!" to them all . . .'[12] The Nationalists, however, were very far from saying 'Pooh!' The Clouds conversations were a gift to their cause and their newspaper *The Freeman's Journal* carried Blunt's statement in its entirety. After accusing Balfour of saying that he was intent on imposing severe sentences on the ringleaders of Irish agitation in order that they should die miserably in their jails, the rebel referred to the dangers inherent in his own situation. 'I feel unsafe in Mr Balfour's hands,' he declared and he feared 'that unless protected by those responsible for the direction of prison discipline I should incur considerable risk of ill-treatment or perhaps worse'.[13] The Chief Secretary's response to his prisoner's accusation was to telegraph : 'Ridiculous lie. I do not believe Mr Blunt ever made the assertion. Balfour.'

Later Blunt was to claim that his declaration to the visiting justices had had a lasting and beneficial effect. 'It is certain that my action,' he wrote, 'whether justified or not, was among the causes, perhaps the strongest, of his having to mitigate his plan of treating his political prisoners with the full measure of his intended severity, and as a fact they were soon after accorded exceptional privileges; and when John Dillon fell eventually into his hands, Balfour was careful that no evil of the kind he had predicted would befall him.'[14] But Blunt's behaviour shocked many of his close friends. In Conservative households throughout England people wondered how a gentleman and a landowner could degenerate into a meddlesome political agitator; and even many Liberals regarded the forging of a political weapon out of a private conversation as 'hitting below the belt'. George Wyndham might charitably conclude that 'Wilfrid is temporarily out of his senses'; yet there were others who believed the man was not only calculatingly sane but dangerous as well. Percy Wyndham was particularly angry and came close to vowing that he would never speak to his cousin again.

Echoes of this penetrated through the prison wall. Now, amid the cold, damp gloom of his cell, Blunt found that he had offended some of his closest friends. He wondered if he could ever return to his old life in England, with its easy pleasures and comforts. He realized that the lives of others, whose cause he believed to be unjust, were unaltered by his suffering. In Dublin George Wyndham wrote to his father, describing a lunch at the law courts as being 'prodigious' with 'oysters, woodcock, pâté-de-foie-gras, etcetera';[15] while in Galway boiled mutton, milk and bread were being served to the jail's only 'gentleman' inmate. In his sonnet 'At the Gate', composed at this time, Blunt records his sense of deepening gloom.

> 'Naked came I into the world of pleasure,
> And naked come I to this house of pain.
> Here at the gate I lay down my life's treasure,
> My pride, my garments and my name with men.
> The world and I henceforth shall be as twain,
> No sound of me shall pierce for good or ill
> These walls of grief. Nor shall I hear the vain
> Laughter and tears of those who love me still.

Within, what new life waits me! Little ease,
Cold lying, hunger, nights of wakefulness,
Harsh orders given, no voice to soothe or please,
Poor thieves for friends, for books rules meaningless;
This is the grave – nay, hell. Yet, Lord of might,
Still in thy light my spirit shall see light.'

But although neither Parnell nor Gladstone spoke up forcefully in his favour, Blunt need not have felt deserted. After their sybaritic visit to the law courts, Wyndham recorded how 'Arthur and I drove away on a car and came in for a "hostile demonstration" driving off amid yells of "Balfour the liar!" It amused me very much.' Further demonstrations took place on the occasion of Blunt's transfer from Galway to Kilmainham jail at the beginning of February. There must have been pleasure for the prisoner too in the news that his cousin George Shaw-Lefevre, later Lord Eversley, had held a meeting on his behalf at Woodford which the police had not dared to break up.

The reason for Blunt's transfer to Dublin was that the Irish National League had brought an action, in his name, against Inspector Byrne for assault at Woodford. This was due to be held at the Four Courts and was regarded by the League as a chance to thwart Balfour and the entire policy of coercion. A jury was to decide upon the verdict, unlike Portumna, but a unanimous decision was required. The judge was Chief Baron Palles, already notorious as a condemner of the Plan of Campaign, and the prosecuting counsel was Peter O'Brien, the Attorney-General of Ireland, known as 'Peter the Packer' for his skill at 'packing' juries in order to gain the verdict that the authorities desired. Blunt again had The Macdermott and Tim Healy on his side. The odds were stacked against him and the League. Palles summed up in a moderate manner but with force behind his words. 'He treated me,' Blunt later remembered, 'as a well-meaning but ignorant Englishman, who had blundered into an illegal position without understanding that he was breaking the law, but who nevertheless must take the consequences of his mistake.'[16] However Blunt felt sure that if Peter the Packer had not lived up to his name and manipulated the selection of jurors the League would have won their case. As it was eleven out of the twelve were for the League, but the twelfth, a Quaker, could not be moved. There was not a unanimous verdict, so the case was dismissed. Afterwards the prisoner returned to Kilmainham, amid the cheers of the crowds. Nationalist interest and enthusiasm had been aroused by the trial; but Balfour had successfully ridden the storm.

Dublin was even more dispiriting for Blunt than Galway. Here he encountered a deeper sense of isolation. The prison 'with its Dublin thieves and pickpockets, and its stony-visaged warders' held no consolations. 'The solitude,' he wrote, 'encompassed me once more like a nightmare and with redoubled importunity.'[17] Particularly irritating was the proximity of the Chief Secretary's Lodge where the imagined conviviality was as mournful to Blunt as the sound of laughter in the next room. 'At the very moment of my reincarceration,' he observed, 'and during the weeks that followed . . . Balfour was holding high revel at the Chief Secretary's Lodge outside, entertaining there a party of my especial friends, including my Wyndham cousins, with George Wyndham as his private secretary.'[18] At other such gatherings in England he had been a voluble and appreciative guest. Now he wondered if he had not cheated himself of this life, and its friendships, forever. In addition, there was the bad news of his Deptford candidature. Despite having been unable to campaign in the constituency, Blunt had gone ahead, allowing Lady Anne to take its full burden on her shoulders. Now he heard that the by-election had resulted in a Conservative victory.

Blunt claimed to have received a strange foreboding of this. 'I had gone to sleep,' he wrote, 'full of confidence in the result.

In the middle of the night however, I awoke, and, while I lay thinking of other things, suddenly the whole prison was shaken by a wind, which filled it with a noise like the roaring of a crowd, and I started up exclaiming: "It is the Conservatives cheering our defeat." I waited awhile, some twenty minutes till the clock struck twelve. From that moment I felt certain things had gone wrong, and my confidence vanished.' Later he heard that the election result had been announced in Pall Mall at that very hour, to be greeted with cheers in the Carlton Club. This was to be his last attempt to enter Parliament and its failure contributed further to his low spirits. 'The last twenty days of my imprisonment,' he wrote, 'were like a whole year to me of mental suffering, which, if they had been prolonged, would, I believe, have driven me mad.'[20] The chaplain had given him Victor Hugo's *Notre Dame de Paris* to read, in which he found no relief. He whiled away the time partly with this and partly by making anagrams out of Balfour's name on a slate.

His jailers, however, were satisfied with his condition. He was quiet at last, and there was insufficient evidence of physical deterioration to give the Nationalists another martyr. On February 28th a member of the Kilmainham visiting committee called on him. 'I visited the gaol this day,' the member recorded in the visiting committee minute book, 'and saw Mr Blunt and enquired as to his state of health. I was glad to find he was so much better in health than when I saw him here previously and expressed himself so, and also stated that he had no complaint to make as he was satisfied that every official in the gaol that he came in contact with treated him respectfully and kindly.' The chairman of the prisons board had a copy made of this entry, writing on it, 'Immediate. Submitted for the information of the Chief Secretary, having regard to the reports in the Press as to the alleged ill-treatment of this prisoner while he had been in Kilmainham.'[21] Balfour's signature at the bottom records that he saw the report.

On the morning of March 6th Blunt's sentence had run its

full course. The Governor bade him farewell, saying that, in honour of his visit, he and his wife had decided to christen their son, born that night, Wilfrid Blunt. Surprised, yet seeing that this was curiously in keeping with the topsy-turvy nature of his Irish experiences, Blunt left Kilmainham and joined, in the street outside, Lady Anne and a waiting group of friends. The period of his martyrdom, as he had once termed it, was over.

On their return to London the Blunts went to pay a call on Gladstone. They were grateful to him, despite what they regarded as his past duplicity over Egypt, for his encouragement during this low period of their lives. The old man had written to Blunt in prison, and Mrs Gladstone had assisted Lady Anne throughout the rigours of the Deptford campaign. Gladstone immediately assumed that Blunt had come to demand some favour; and he began to apologize for not having done more to further his visitor's progress in the Liberal party. Once Blunt assured him that this was not the purpose of the visit he was sufficiently relieved to invite them both to lunch. Gladstone then advised Blunt to write about his prison experiences, remembering the success of his own pamphlet on the prisons of Naples and how it had caught the imagination of the British public. He also encouraged him to renew his charges against Balfour with regard to the conversation at Clouds, and spoke of the Chief Secretary with extreme bitterness.

Blunt, still smarting from his defeat, took Gladstone's advice. Again he pressed his charges and once again the newspapers, for whom the activities of the aristocratic agitator were always good copy, carried their readers back into Percy Wyndham's drawing room. On March 23rd *The Times* printed a long detailed letter, repeating the details of Balfour's supposed thirst for Irish rebel blood. 'In conclusion,' Blunt wrote, 'let me say that the conversation was entirely serious; that the portion I have quoted took place between ourselves alone; that the precise date was Sunday, September 4th 1887, the hour about 5 p.m. . . . Once more I challenge Mr Balfour to say whether or not we met at Clouds, whether or not we discussed his Irish policy, and whether or not my account of the conversation is accurate. His answer as it now stands is a flat denial of everything.'[22]

Balfour felt obliged to reply in public. In a speech at Stalybridge he termed Blunt's accusation 'malignant and stupid'. After this statement *The Times* noted that 'such a denial ought really to settle the dispute. The question of what Mr Balfour actually said to Mr Blunt is one of interpretation quite as much as of recollection, and Mr Blunt's record is not such as to forbid the possibility that he had either forgotten or misunderstood, or both.'[23]

Gladstone, who had believed that Blunt's revelations would be more damaging, did not intervene, perhaps thinking that, unless the disclosures were of a very startling nature, it was undignified to make use of the conversational sweepings of a Tory drawing room. Blunt was saddened by the lack of interest. This was the ultimate disappointment of his Irish activities. Particularly disheartening had been the violently personal nature of some people's reactions. Both Conservatives and Liberals were shocked that 'a gentleman' should make such unscrupulous use of a private conversation. The Chief Secretary's aloof, almost amused, denials had given the impression that he was not prepared to descend to the level of his adversary's tactics. In short, the person who had been most damaged by the whole affair was Blunt himself. 'The issue,' he later wrote, 'confirmed me in my resolve to have nothing more to do with English public life.'[24]

One letter, however, provided comfort, demonstrating the power of friendship to rise above temporary disagreements. It was written on March 18th by George Wyndham from Saighton. 'You will easily guess,' he said, 'that the whole matter is a painful one to me, and particularly so because it had annoyed my father very much . . . When anything of this kind occurs, I think it is always best for a man to lay open his mind to his friends, for, even if the opinion he holds is distasteful . . . their friendship is less endangered by its free communication than by the sense that it is, in some way, concealed . . . Personally I should never quarrel with any man for his opinions . . . It is your opinion that the conclusion you have drawn from the words spoken at Clouds is a legitimate conclusion. Again, it is your opinion that you are justified, by the nature of the case, in making public a conclusion arrived at under such circumstances . . . I think it only right to say, frankly, that on these two points my opinion is opposed to yours . . . We have so many grounds for friendship, our common love of Sport and of Poetry, and especially our common blood, and I think it would be very foolish to allow differences of Politics and of Opinion to interfere with it in any way . . . I sincerely hope that you think so too.'[25]

On March 19th Blunt replied to his cousin from Crabbet. 'I accept your letter,' he wrote, 'in the spirit in which it is written. In cases of this sort, it is better not to argue, and I say nothing except that the whole matter has given me more pain than any incident connected with my public life. I am trying to go back to my resolution of last summer and be quit of politics, but one is not always one's own master and I may not succeed. But when the present political bitterness is over, I hope we may see each other again. I often thought of you and your father and was immensely vexed at his name being dragged into the quarrel. Let us not quarrel permanently whatever happens.'[26] They did not quarrel permanently; although there were to be occasions when, again, the ties of their friendship were to be subject to strain.

Chapter 10
Ireland : Kicks and Ha'pence

Throughout the turbulence the Chief Secretary was calm. At Dublin Castle the administration was greatly encouraged by its master's determination. Previously morale had been sinking, now the civil servants believed they had a workable policy at last. Balfour was prepared to stand by them, even when they made mistakes. After Mitchelstown a verdict of wilful murder was passed against the police by the coroner's jury, but Balfour had this quashed. Naturally the officials were delighted.

He also had an eye for ability. Finding, on his arrival at the Irish Office, a particularly cowed and despondent collection of law officers, he rectified this by appointing the vigorous 'Peter the Packer' O'Brien Attorney-General and Edward Carson, a formidable and dour Protestant, one of his assistant prosecutors. The keystone of Balfour's policy was coercion accompanied by relief, or 'kicks and ha'pence' as Carson termed it. If the agitators were stifled and their most obvious grievances removed, it was thought that the Home Rule movement could be killed by kindness. Balfour's approach was ruthless. By August 1888 some 21 Members of Parliament from Parnell's party, including John Dillon, had been given prison sentences. Another method of attack was to utilize the force of religious feeling. In 1887 an English Roman Catholic mission, led by the Duke of Norfolk, visited Rome to confer with Pope Leo XIII; and in April 1888 the Papal Rescript was issued in which Leo condemned boycotting and the Plan of Campaign. Wilfrid Blunt, as a Catholic, was incensed by this, seeing it as a piece of diplomatic chicanery unworthy of the head of the Church. But its effects were limited. The Nationalist priests and bishops did not change their ways, and Parnell dismissed the Rescript as 'a document from a distant country'.

The decline and fall of Parnell greatly aided the cause of the Union. The process was as rapid as it was dramatic. In 1889 the Irish leader stood at a new peak in public esteem. Preoccupied with his involvement with Mrs O'Shea, he had stayed aloof from the Plan of Campaign, believing that English opinion would be enraged by its brutal methods. The letters that had appeared in *The Times* purporting to show that he had been a party to the Phoenix Park murders had been demonstrated, in front of a special commission of enquiry, to be forgeries. Later that year Parnell visited Gladstone at Hawarden. The Conservative government was losing by-elections. A drift of opinion towards Home Rule could be perceived, particularly as Balfour's 'kicks' seemed so far to have manifested themselves without much evidence of the 'ha'pence'. Then, on November 17th 1890, a divorce was granted to Captain O'Shea in which Parnell was cited as the co-respondent.

The end of the story is well known. The flight of the nonconformists from his cause, leading to Gladstone's famous letter which was, in effect, a demand that the Irish party either dismiss Parnell or lose their connection with the English Liberals; the condemnation of Parnell by the Irish Bishops; the defeat of his candidate in the Kilkenny by-election on December 22nd despite Parnell's personal intervention, coming after the celebrated deliberations in Committee Room 15 in which the Irish MPs had voted to jettison him as their leader by 44 votes to 26; the emergence of Dillon and O'Brien as anti-Parnellites; additional by-election defeats and then, on September 27th, his fatal decision to address an outdoor meeting in the rain while suffering from rheumatism. Gravely ill, he returned to be with Mrs O'Shea, whom he had married in June, at Brighton. Here, on October 6th, he died and was later buried in Glasnevin cemetery, the Irish briefly coming together to recognize that they had lost the greatest promoter of their cause since Daniel O'Connell.

Parnell's reputation had towered over his party. The regard of the Irish for his memory grew with the years, but the immediate result of his passing was disastrous. The Nationalists degenerated into factionalism, brought on by the quarrels of his last months. It was at this opportune moment that Balfour brought in his 'ha'pence' in the form of a land bill and the Congested Districts Board, set up to help the poorer parts of the west. By June 1891 the operation of the Crimes Act was suspended in virtually every part of Ireland. With Irish leaders wrangling amongst themselves and the Irish people still recovering from the shattering of Parnell's image, a kind of tenuous order was restored. Finally, in October 1891, Salisbury appointed his nephew to be the new leader of the House of Commons in place of W. H. Smith who had died, and Balfour's connection with Ireland was over.

Before leaving Dublin for the last time, he wrote to Goschen, expressing sentiments that echo down the ages with a terrifying truth. 'I feel,' he observed, 'as if I had had a good time which has forever come to an end; and the thought is not agreeable . . . There are other reasons for regret . . . about which I will only say that I have never before so clearly understood how much more important in the eyes of ordinary men are nominal differences than real ones; how indifferent they are to substantial agreement if only the catchwords are not identical.'[1] The post had made him into the most formidable parliamentarian of his party. Within eleven years he would be its leader.

Throughout his time at the Irish Office Arthur Balfour had enjoyed the companionship of George Wyndham. 'Arthur and I,' Wyndham wrote to his wife on January 13th 1888, 'have had an interesting talk about Shakespeare, Shelley, the story of

Hero and Leander, the difference of accent, quantity and num-
bering of syllables in English, Latin and French poetry; politics,
principles, warfare etcetera etcetera.'² There was work to do
as well. One of Wyndham's duties was to reply to letters of protest about the government's Irish policy. This gained him a
degree of notoriety as the answers were usually printed in *The
Times*.

Apart from a brief trip to France in May 1888, there was
little relief from work. The Plan of Campaign and Balfour's
coercion policy were in direct opposition. Wyndham felt
stiffened by the battle. 'All the work here,' he told Sibell on
October 22nd, 'is very interesting, but sad in a way because
you can count on your hand the men who are really trying
for the sake of winning, all the others are merely jibbing and
hedging and tying to hunt with the hounds and run with the
hare. The brave ones are stupid and the clever ones cowards.
Our friends and foes alike are contemptible (there's a little
private grumble). But this will only make it more wonderful
if Arthur wins. I think he will, or at any rate fail gloriously.'³
At times it was exhausting. 'Last night,' he wrote on October
25th, 'I could not sleep for hours and when I slept my head
kept on writing letters and arguing about the Clanricarde
estate till I felt quite mad.' Later Wyndham told Sibell : 'It is
one o'clock . . . I have been steadily reading the "Parnell Commission" since 11.15 – sheets and sheets – Arthur has no time to
read it so I tell him how it is going along.'⁴

1889 began badly for the Wyndham family, with the ful-
filling of a prophecy. At the time of the building of Clouds
an old woman of East Knoyle had told the workmen that within
three years the house would be burnt down. On the night of
January 5th, Clouds was almost entirely destroyed by a fire
which had broken out in an upper floor. Although nobody
was injured and the contents were saved, both children and
parents were distraught. 'Mama and Papa,' his sister Pamela
told George Wyndham, 'are both too wonderfully brave and
patient and it makes one wonder why it should have hap-

pened to them, except that Clouds was too ideal to live, and "who the Gods love die young".[5] Madeline Wyndham sent her son a telegram in Dublin to say that they were safe and he replied: 'I do not know how bad it is, but if you are well all is well. I love you.'[6] It was immediately decided that the house must be reconstructed in exactly the same way. In the meantime the Wyndhams moved into the servants' quarters which, they observed, were extremely comfortable, having been built by the socialist Webb.

In the summer George Wyndham's good fortune returned. The Member for Dover, Major Dickson, died and he was adopted as Conservative candidate for the seat. As he was unopposed (Dover was solidly Tory) the campaign need not have been strenuous. But Wyndham was determined to make a good impression. 'I have called,' he told his wife on July 10th, 'on quite thirty people today and spoken to one hundred in the streets, been twice photographed and expect to be photographed by the remaining three photographers during the intervals of speaking and eating tomorrow. Over-eating, over-speaking, and photography are the three great props of democracy in Dover.'[7] On July 12th he was elected and on the 15th arrived at Westminster to take his seat.

Not everyone was enthusiastic about the new Member. The Star declared: 'Mr Wyndham is Mr Balfour's devil in Ireland. He writes his most insolent letters, concocts his most unreliable statistics, and generally outdoes his chief for the impudence and vulgarity which Mr Balfour mistakes for strength and wisdom.' The Irish Nationalists took a similar view. 'When questions were over,' The Freeman's Journal noted in its parliamentary report on July 16th, 'a new Member of some importance and a good deal of notoriety took his seat. This was Mr George Wyndham, who acts as "devil" to Mr Balfour. He was introduced with much eclat. His sponsors were the Chief Secretary and Mr Akers-Douglas, the Senior Whip of the Tory party. He was greeted, however, with but the very faintest of cheers from his colleagues, while a little ironical laughter only came from the Irish benches . . . Mr Wyndham is a stolid and solemn looking young man – he is only twenty-six – tall and slim of figure à la Balfour. Indeed he looks as if he had been cast in the same mould as the Chief Secretary, but there are differences. Balfour is fair – Wyndham is dark, with his jet-black hair. He is a great grandson, on the maternal side, of Lord Edward Fitzgerald.'

Wyndham waited until February 17th 1890 before making his maiden speech, on Parnell's amendment to the address. He spoke out strongly against the practice of boycotting. He was still assisting Balfour and felt particular enthusiasm for the Chief Secretary's Higher Education project, to establish a Catholic university in Ireland. The measure did not succeed. Rigid Unionists protested, and, although Parnell approved, some Irish Members spoke of 'Mr Balfour's bribing university'. In addition the Catholic Church proved to be incapable of agreeing upon what form the college should take.

In October 1890 Balfour decided that he should see more of his domain for himself. Earlier in the year he had set up the Congested Districts Board and bought up large quantities of potatoes to avert an expected famine. Now he felt he must tour these distressed areas. Wyndham was to accompany him. Also of the party were Sir Joseph Ridgeway (the Permanent Under-Secretary) and the Chief Secretary's niece. They were to drive through the distressed districts of Mayo, Galway and the west. 'We hope,' Wyndham informed his father, 'to see more than Trevelyan who is said to have visited the Congested Districts in a brougham with the blinds down.'[8] He told his wife that they would be dressed 'I am glad to say in shooting jackets and knickerbockers. We shall see and talk to all the nationalist priests. It will be a real experience and I am keenly looking forward to such a new departure in the round of our Irish life.'[9]

The country was at its most beautiful. 'We now had glorious scenery,' Wyndham wrote to Sibell from Belmullet on October 25th. 'The road runs along the heathery edge of the cliff against the base of which the Atlantic thunders and falls back with a loud rock-thwarted roar. We stopped often to go and talk to the men digging potatoes and all were delighted to meet Arthur. At one place we got down to look at an inlet of the sea hollowed out from the land like an arena with precipitous sides. About three hundred yards across, we went to the very verge and Arthur and I, lying on our faces, peered over and down on the gulls, seeming no bigger than sparrows, that skimmed along and paused in their flight between us and the water of a blue deeper than lapis lazuli clouded over with white breakers. A little stream fell over the cliff close at hand but the wind never let it fall but blew it about continually upward like a fountain.'[10]

Wyndham found some of the people exotic and strange. 'We began,' he wrote, 'to meet the folk returning from Belmullet fair. All the women with their white faces and bare legs gleaming out from dark folds of loose indigo. Many of them riding pillion on the cruppers of horses, like princesses in disguise. I cannot make you feel how mysterious and wonderful it is.'[11] But the poverty could intrude on all this. 'For the first time,' he wrote from Costello in County Galway, 'the people looked pinched and yellow and frightened. They all turned out and gave Arthur shrill cheers. A most pathetic sight. You cannot conceive the poverty of this district. Hardly anyone can talk English, the majority have never seen a plough or harrow. There is no mill nearer than twenty miles. They never eat meat and are always on the brink of starvation. I do trust we may be able to help them. The whole country is nothing but yellow marshy grass growing between grey boulders and yet the people are crowded into it like rabbits in a warren . . . Tonight I can only think of the iniquity of the hundreds and thousands of pounds which the Parnellites have screwed out of the people and spent on war, with this kind of desolation standing to be redressed.'[12]

There were no moments of danger, which was fortunate because they had no detectives with them. Indeed the only awkward incidents were when Balfour caught his thumb in the window of one of the inns and when 'Pongo' McNeill the Nationalist MP for Donegal suddenly attacked the Chief Secretary in a hotel in that county for his policy of coercion. Balfour, characteristically, replied: 'What I have done I have done, and if I had to do it again I would do it again in the way that I have done it.' McNeill termed Balfour a 'spiteful tyrant'; yet the people of Donegal, true to Irish tradition, gave him a polite enough welcome. The 'spiteful tyrant', Wyndham wrote to his sister on November 5th, '. . . held a crowded meeting in the school-house, spoke for twenty minutes amid loud and prolonged cheers which fairly blew the roof off when he announced that the Railway was given for nothing.'[13]

After Arthur Balfour's departure from the Irish Office in 1891 Wyndham's connection with Ireland temporarily ceased. Then, with the Conservative defeat of 1892, his party lost office. The election was strenuous, with speeches at Worksop, Birmingham, Battersea, Farnham, Bourne, Ashford and Lichfield, besides his own Dover campaign. 'The silence,' he wrote in July after it was over, 'is profound and delicious, but my head is still haunted with the ghastly cheering and booing and the ceaseless rattling of the train.'[14] Yet even during his Irish duties, he had managed to lead a full life outside the confines of politics. His career in journalism and literature, pursued through the pages of Henley's *National Observer*, began in earnest in 1890; and his many friendships kept his evenings and weekends exceptionally busy. It was in 1889, after a brief period of voluntary exile in Europe, that Wilfrid Scawen Blunt came back into his life. Each was now prepared to forget the past. 'On my return to England in 1889,' Blunt wrote of Wyndham, 'I found him full of affectionate endeavour to make things pleasant for me on my re-emergence into social life. In this he showed himself no idle friend. I had hardly arrived in London when he had arranged occasions of meeting for me at his house in Park Lane with our mutual friends, and eventually one with Arthur Balfour, at which we buried our political hatchet in mutual amiabilities, an attitude we have ever since preserved as often as we have met.'[15]

The meeting had been carefully arranged. Wyndham had written to his master saying: 'I want you to be very forgiving and come and dine with me to meet Wilfrid Blunt.' Balfour answered airily: 'My dear George, I don't know that I am very forgiving but I do know that I am very forgetting, and, not having the least idea to what you refer, I can only say that I shall be delighted to dine with you to meet Wilfrid Blunt.'[16] There was an amusing end to the dinner when Blunt, in view of the coldness of the evening, lent Balfour his overcoat, thus recalling the struggles over a similar garment in Galway jail.

Blunt was grateful to Wyndham. He saw him as a true friend; and in the summer of 1889 invited his cousin to join the privileged assembly of the Crabbet Club.

Chapter 11
At Ease

Crabbet Park, near Three Bridges in Sussex, was Wilfrid Scawen Blunt's house in the country. It had been a small, rather unprepossessing residence; but in the early years of his marriage he had entirely rebuilt it, with the assistance of Lady Anne who, amongst her many other attributes, was an enthusiastic amateur architect. The design was their own, and surprisingly out of spirit with the fashion of the time. The style is, in the words of the historian of *The Victorian Country House*, 'more representative of 1910 than 1870'.[1] The rooms were large, in order to accommodate their many and varied possessions including Lady Anne's vast equestrian portrait of her husband, but not ornately decorated. Indeed, Blunt once spoke, in a conversation at Kelmscott with William Morris, of his preference for 'the old-fashioned square cardboard box style' and his distaste for 'any kind of prettiness'.[2]

Yet if the house itself was not a product of its owner's romanticism, its garden and surroundings were. Here nature was given virtually a free hand, and the impression was one of a partially untamed wilderness, with the lawns and shrubberies deliberately left untended. In 1890 George Wyndham told his friend Charles Gatty of the delights of Crabbet. 'The woods,' he wrote, 'grow up in virginal unconsciousness of the axe to the very door. On one side a wilderness sown with Desert plants and dotted with wind-sown English bushes, on the other a Sussex paddock with Arab brood mares and their foals. Below in the hollow a pond full of trout, on which the swans sleep and swim lazily through the day. The house is overgrown with June roses and the lawns after dark are very silent and conducive to the complete and satisfactory solution of all problems, moral and aesthetic . . .'[3]

With the house had come the estate. This Blunt regarded with love and respect, believing it to be his duty to ensure that, after his own death, his heir would inherit a tradition of good stewardship. In the preface to his privately printed *History of the Crabbet Estate* he wrote that the book 'has been a labour of love with me, for in my view of things the individuality of a landed estate is hardly less real that that of a kingdom, and equally deserves the loyal respect and reverence of those entrusted with its ownership and its faithfully narrating for the sake of those who shall come after'.[4] Even at the height of his political activity Blunt never forgot his duties towards his 'kingdom'. Like most absolute monarchs he often dreamed of expansion. On April 8th 1884 he noted in his diary : 'At Crabbet, dawdling about among the horses and going to see the Vardon property, which is for sale, and which I must buy if I can. This property has for the best part of a century been a thorn in our flesh, running like a wedge into Crabbet. There is an entry in the shooting diary of 1824 in which complaint is made of "old Vardon's poaching". Now is the time to rectify our frontier. An estate is like a kingdom, with its wars and intrigues and ambitions and thirst for new territory, and, though I have no personal wish to increase mine, I consider this purchase a duty of my reign.'[5]

There were those who saw this combination of the revolutionary and the squire as unnatural. Certainly his life there was hardly typical of most radicals' domestic repose. 'He took enormous pride,' his son-in-law Neville Lytton recalls, 'in his position as a country gentleman, and he would pay laborious afternoon calls on his neighbours who were also landed gentlemen, no matter how boring they might be. His faithful and adoring agent, Mr Caffin, always used to call him "Squire" and this title gave him untold pleasure.'[6] Yet, if there was a contradiction here, Blunt never appeared to notice it. His domestic politics were soundly conservative, with the exception of his views on Ireland, and his brief association with the Liberal party that had resulted from his Irish opinions had been an unhappy one. 'I leave today for Egypt,' he was to declare in 1904, 'after having taken all my male servants down to Shipley to vote for Turnour, the Tory candidate.'[7] He always thought of himself as a Conservative Nationalist, being generally in favour of the landowners (unless, as in Ireland, they were cruel or incompetent) and the House of Lords. Socialism had little appeal to him, although its rhetoric could momentarily stir his emotions.

When he was at Crabbet he did not confine himself to following the traditional pursuits of a Sussex squire, watching over his estate and fraternizing with his neighbours. He also entertained his friends and bred Arab horses. Each year the Arabian stud sale was the occasion of a great garden party, attended by horse lovers and innumerable friends and admirers of the Blunts who would come from London to take pleasure in this unusual spectacle. Naturally, the host was very much the principal figure. 'It was,' his diplomatic friend Esmé Howard wrote of the scene, 'really a cheery picnic rather than anything else, and Wilfrid Blunt used to provide his guests with a sumptuous luncheon at which he always harangued them in a little speech. In order to keep up his reputation as a revolutionary, with a profound contempt for all class difference – which he was very far from feeling – he often began by saying: "Ladies and Gentlemen", and then, looking round him he would add, as an afterthought, "and Lords", which was always greeted with laughter and cheers.'[8] Sometimes as many as five hundred would sit down to lunch, and, at Crabbet, this was the most considerable event of the year.

Blunt enjoyed receiving visitors. Friendships were important to him. He needed companionship and also, being a man of some vanity, admiration. He greatly enjoyed conversation and gossip, as his diaries reveal, loving to feel that he was up to date with the latest social and political news. On his release from prison one of his greatest fears was that he might have lost, by his actions, a large number of his friends. For a short time it seemed as if his fear was justified. In his diaries for 1888, he describes the aridity of his first few months of freedom. 'All my relations,' he wrote, 'and nearly all my intimate friends were in the Tory camp and I had no natural footing in any other. With the exception of the Carlisles and the Harcourts, I was at home in none of the great Whig houses, and in my own country of Sussex I stood absolutely alone in my opinions. Nothing can be conceived more dispiriting than the attempts at social entertainment made that Spring in London by the few Liberal peers who had declared for Home Rule, unwilling followers of Gladstone. I went with my wife to one of these, at Spencer House, but we found ourselves among strangers and did not go to another.'[9] At Crabbet he did not fare so badly for he was 'Lord there of my own manor, cock of my own dunghill', but he was shocked to be greeted on his return by a deputation of three Irish Home Rule MPs and the village cobbler who was the only radical in the district. These people, Blunt imagined, were to be his future associates, all others having taken flight because of their disapproval of his conduct.

Thus he left England in the autumn for France, Greece and Egypt, staying away until the next year. On his return in 1889 he found that the dust had settled. George Wyndham, Lytton and his old friends began to return to him. Wyndham, in particular, went out of his way to smooth his cousin's social rehabilitation; and when, in the summer of that year, Wilfrid Blunt embarked upon a reanimation of the Crabbet Club he invited George, as a representative of the younger generation, to play a leading part.

On June 30th 1889, George Wyndham wrote to his wife from Crabbet. 'The party,' he declared, 'is not literary but "lawn-tennisy". It is the "Crabbet Club"; of which Wilfrid spoke to me in '87 . . . The club consists of Wilfrid, who is president – and a number of young and fairly intelligent men, from Oxford, Cambridge, etcetera. Those here this time are two of the Speaker's sons (Peels), Lord Morpeth (George Howard's son), a cousin of mine "Percy" Wyndham, Mark Napier who defended Arabi etcetera; twelve in all. The weather is glorious and the place is a hushed Eden of sleepy summer foliaged trees and rampant roses. The roses are beyond anything I remember. Driving here yesterday every cottage wall was splashed all over with crimson roses, and outside my window pink roses fell in cascades to the lawn. The motto of the Club is "In youth and Crabbed age". I will bring you a copy of the rules, which forbid all seriousness. Any person who becomes an Archbishop or a Cabinet minister ceases *ipso facto* to be a member of the Club. There is a lawn tennis competition for a silver mug, and a poetical competition for the post of Poet Laureate for the year. Besides the President and Laureate there are other offices, among them a public jester and Public Orator. Morpeth, Kingscote and I were admitted members last night and, after our healths were drunk, responded in suitable words. I said that the club was called the "Crabbet Club" on the principle of *lucus a non lucendo* as no one could possibly "Crab it".'[10]

Apparently the President conducted himself in a typically flamboyant manner. 'Wilfrid,' wrote Wyndham, 'presided in the presidential robes, i.e. those of an Arabian Prince, glittering with gold embroidery and crimson, from "silken Samarkand".' To add to the pleasure of its guest, Crabbet, that summer, was at its most exotic. 'I woke at dawn,' Wyndham told Sibell, 'and watched the Arab mares and foals wake and begin to feed under the low sweeping boughs of the beech trees. There are some thirty Arab mares and foals, all perfectly tame as dogs, letting you rub their soft muzzles and ride them bareback.'

The club had originated in 1871, but not at Crabbet. Lord

Pembroke, on his coming of age, had wished to institute some form of annual summer gathering for his friends at Wilton, where they could play cricket, row and partake in various other seasonal diversions. Therefore he had formed the Wilton, or 'Wagger', club. Blunt had been invited to join in 1876 having known the Herberts since their schooldays. Meetings were then instituted at Crabbet, and were thought to have been such a success that the members decided to come there annually as well. In its first incarnation the membership had included Sir Edward Hamilton (Gladstone's private secretary), Mark Napier (lawyer and defender of Arabi), 'Button' Bourke (of *The Times* and Wilfrid's cousin) and Harry Brand (later Speaker of the House of Commons).

Blunt's political activities brought an end to all this. Although the club was supposedly apolitical, a large part of the membership was Tory. After Blunt's Home Rule stand and his efforts on behalf of Egyptian Nationalism few of them would even answer his invitations to its meetings. Pembroke, although, as Blunt said, a most tolerant man, was an Irish landlord with property in Dublin. He was particularly upset by his friend's association with the Land League and the Plan of Campaign. Blunt understood the strong feelings that his activities had aroused. 'All this,' he wrote, 'was natural enough and I could not complain of the defection.'[11] But he was determined not to allow the club to sink into oblivion, and after his release from prison restocked it with members, most of them undergraduates from Oxford and Cambridge, who were more in sympathy with his views.

Then in 1889 the Crabbet Club took on a new lease of life. The undergraduates were joined by a gifted group of young men, most of them, again, Tories, who had now forgotten, or forgiven, their president's political aberrations. It was George Wyndham, urged on by Blunt, who had been the instigator of their joining. 'George Wyndham,' Blunt observed, 'becoming a member, took it in hand, and seeing its intellectual capabilities brought new blood into it by introducing friends of his own, already holding a certain position in the political world, and who have since no few of them climbed to fame.'[12] Among these august recruits were George Curzon, Harry Cust (editor of the *Pall Mall Gazette* and Member of Parliament), Lord Houghton (later, as Lord Crewe, Liberal leader in the House of Lords, ambassador in Paris and Viceroy of Ireland), Eddy Tennant (Liberal MP and husband of George Wyndham's sister Pamela), Esmé Howard (diplomat, later Lord Howard of Penrith), Lord Elcho (George Wyndham's brother-in-law, husband of Mary), Lord Alfred Douglas, Charles Gatty (littérateur and later one of Wyndham's greatest friends) and, on one occasion, Oscar Wilde. Blunt was justly proud of his creation. 'They were,' he wrote, 'really brilliant meetings, with post-prandial oratory of the most amusing kind, and were productive of verse of a quite high order. The number of members was limited to twenty, and there was much competition when a vacancy occurred. The poetry of the Crabbet Club has been preserved in print, and is one of the curiosities of literature, deserving a place, I venture to think, in company with the best verse of a not serious kind.'[13]

Although George Wyndham defined the club's purpose as being 'to play lawn-tennis, the piano, the fool and other instruments of gaiety', its members always took considerable trouble over their poetic contributions. In 1893, Curzon's poem, entitled 'Sin', won the laureateship, ending on a rousing note with two robust verses acclaiming both the club and its subject :

'And so when some historian
Of the period Victorian
Shall crown the greatest exploit of this wonder-working age
His eye shall light on Crabbet,
And, if truth shall be his habit,
The name of everyone of us will shine upon that page.

To us will be the glory
That ne'er shall fade in story,
Of reviving the old axiom that all the world's akin,
That the true link of union
Which holds men in communion
Is frank and systematic and premeditated Sin!'[14]

Indeed Curzon, somewhat surprisingly, flourished at Crabbet, causing Blunt to note after the July 1893 meeting: 'George Curzon was, as usual, the most brilliant, he never flags for an instant either in speech or repartee; after him George Wyndham, Mark Napier and Webber,'[15] (Godfrey Webb). Wyndham's performance could also startle. In July 1892 Blunt remarked: 'George Wyndham performed a wonderful feat, writing a long poem in a most complicated metre, and full of excellent things in hardly more than an hour, between sets of lawn tennis.'[16]

Frivolity, sometimes sought with almost too much determination, was deemed the true purpose of these gatherings. On the Saturday evening the business of the club was transacted, new members elected and speeches made, generally in a satirical vein, proposing and seconding the candidates, or, in Esmé Howard's words, 'regretting absent friends, congratulating the President, Wilfrid Blunt, who sat at the head of the table, dressed in gorgeous silks like an Arab sheik, with an enormous turban. This always caused Mark Napier . . . to refer to Wilfrid as "the flower pot man".'[17] Howard himself, at his first experience of the club, suffered from this desire to tease. Mark Napier proposed him, saying: 'I hardly know this fellow, Esmé Howard, whom I have been told to propose, and it matters little to me whether one fool more or less joins this club, but there is one matter which may be of great importance to you all. It is that I have, in Westminster, a charming little house that I want to let.' Howard was then told to describe his own merits and, overwhelmed by the rumbustious easy self-confidence of the others, termed himself 'a respectable

mediocrity'. Whereupon Curzon bellowed : 'I really must protest against this outrage, with all the vigour of which I am
capable. We have had, hitherto, all sorts of people elected to
the club, of whom the less said, perhaps, the better. But we
have never yet had one who laid claim to the title of a Respectable Mediocrity. A Mediocrity, I might perhaps, *à la rigueur*,
have put up with, but a respectable one would be past endurance.' Despite this the candidate was elected.

Blunt made certain that the rules were obeyed. When
Curzon was appointed Viceroy of India, a post that, because of
its worldly distinction, barred its holder from the club, he
wrote to his president : 'I know well that I have merited expul-
sion from the Crabbet Club, but I hope by a consistent course
of disaster to be unanimously re-elected on my return . . . Of
one thing I am certain – that the surest way in which to do
honour to the bygone traditions of the Club – if they are bygone – will be for me to pursue in India the precepts of its
president. Only you must not come out and compel me to
lock you up which would be subversive to Club discipline.'[18]
Blunt answered : 'I write to condole with you on the appointment which I grieve to think severs your long and meritorious
connection with the Crabbet Club'; and went on to say that he
hoped Curzon would be the 'best, the most frivolous (even
remembering Lytton) and the last of our viceroys'.[19] When
Harry Cust became editor of the *Pall Mall Gazette*, Blunt
declared : 'I feel it incumbent upon me as President of the C.C.
to write to you a few words of warning in regard to the
dangerous form of public life on which you are about to embark . . . We have as examples before us Stead and Morley,
who have made use of *The Pall Mall* as a stepping stone to their
positions of dull respectability . . . You have been put forward
at this critical moment of England's social history to do battle
against the Non-Conformist conscience . . . The Club has its eye
on you.'[20]

The evening sessions at Crabbet often lasted, without a break,
until the dawn of the next day. The members would listen to

poems and to extempore speeches and then, after sunrise, if it was warm, strip off for a swim in the lake. Early one morning one could have seen Harry Cust and Curzon defeating Blunt and Wyndham at lawn-tennis – all four playing stark naked. Blunt looked forward, almost above everything else, to these annual festivities. 'These occasions,' he declared, 'are the salt of the earth';[21] and Wyndham similarly delighted in them. The frivolity provided an admirable complement to the heaviness of his political duties. 'I am here resting,' he wrote to the President from Cliveden on July 21st 1892, 'after the General Election. During a three weeks' campaign throughout the length and breadth of the land I travelled two thousand four hundred and seventy-six miles and delivered sixteen set speeches besides a number of short ones . . . During all those weary hours Crabbet was my "beaconing" star.'[22]

The beauty of the surroundings and the endless congeniality of the company were bound to appeal to Wyndham's aesthetic and social sensibilities. 'This morn,' he wrote to Sibell of the 1893 meeting, 'I woke at eight. The birds singing and all the world steeped in sunshine. Mark [Napier] and I then bathed in the lake. I love running wild more than anything. We jumped in from our boat. I swam and swam in the warm water; lay on my back looking up at the blue sky; climbed out of the water into the boughs of an overhanging tree and finally lay on a mossy bank in the sunshine. I wish there was a lake at Saighton.'[23] It is not difficult to see how the Crabbet Club managed to give such pleasure to its members. The gatherings were in the true English aristocratic tradition of confident masculine exclusiveness (the only women allowed to attend were Lady Anne and Blunt's daughter Judith). In such an atmosphere there must have been an air of complete relaxation, born of shared backgrounds, shared experiences and, at the bottom, despite political differences, shared ideals. None of them would have questioned their right to the position into which they had been born. Wilfrid Blunt might campaign for the break-up of empires but, in the words of his son-in-law Neville Lytton, 'the thought of the ruin of his own family estates was an unthinkable disaster'.[24]

At its best this self-confidence could result in a very real sense of duty, selfless public service and adherence to causes for their intrinsic virtue rather than their ability to advance ambitions or a career. At its worst it might lead to the advent of the hectoring, arrogant bully, insensitive to worlds outside his own and protected from them by the shield of his material advantages. Most members of the Crabbet were too intelligent and sensitive to indulge in such excesses, although when Oscar Wilde attended Curzon's speech was a model of unthinking crudeness. But at times a disdain for everyday constraints, which seemed to the members both trivial and unnecessary, could manifest itself with typical Crabbet flamboyance.

Such was the case one year during a visit to the Derby from Crabbet. It was Blunt's habit to drive his friends to Epsom in a brake drawn by four Arab horses, and there was usually a place reserved for him on the course, at a point inside the ring. This time, however, the party arrived late, to find the entrance blocked by the police as a race was about to be run. Undeterred, Blunt tried to get through, but the crowds were too much for him. So he turned on to the course itself and galloped up it, the centre, in Esmé Howard's words, 'of all attraction, cheers, hoots and cat calls mingling in a strange sympathy'. It must have been a curious sight; the Arab horses straining in front of the brake loaded with the laughing, convivial spirits of the Crabbet Club who were waving at the astonished but admiring onlookers. The police quickly cleared a space for them further up and Blunt, who was a skilful driver, turned into it, having triumphantly made the authorities bow to his will. 'I have,' Esmé Howard wrote, 'never heard that he got into any trouble for this little adventure which was singularly typical of him.'[25]

Although women may not have attended meetings of the Crabbet Club, they were certainly not prohibited in other circles frequented by Blunt and Wyndham. One such group was the Souls, much written about in the memoirs of their

Wilfrid Scawen Blunt in prison in Ireland.
is photograph was taken while he was being transferred from Galway to Kilmainham jail.
It was assiduously circulated in the Mayfair drawing rooms.

above: Clouds, East Knoyle, Wiltshire. A photograph taken in 1908, on the occasion of a meet of the S. and W. Wilts Hounds during the celebrations for the coming of age of George Wyndham's son, Percy.

below: Crabbet Park near Crawley. Home of Wilfrid Scawen Blunt.

time and now celebrated as an example of late-Victorian cultural and social elitism. In his diary for 1891, Wilfrid Blunt records his participation in their pleasures. 'In my disappointment about Egypt,' he wrote, 'I turned with redoubled zest to my social pleasures of the year before, and at this time saw much of that interesting group of clever men and pretty women known as the "Souls", than whom no section of London society was better worth frequenting, including as it did all that there was most intellectually amusing and least conventional. It was a group of men and women bent on pleasure, but pleasure of a superior kind, eschewing the vulgarities of racing and card-playing indulged in by the majority of the rich and noble, and looking for their excitement in romance and sentiment.'[26]

The 'Souls' gained their nickname in 1887, at a dinner party given by Lady Brownlow, when Lord Charles Beresford, the Prince of Wales's great friend, announced that, as they were always talking about their souls, this was what they should, collectively, be called. Many members of the Crabbet Club, including Curzon, Cust, Wyndham, Elcho and Blunt himself, were among their ranks. But the central figure, the pivot around which they gyrated, was Arthur Balfour. In his autobiography he speaks of the nature of the group. 'To me,' he writes, 'the name of "Souls" seemed always meaningless and slightly ludicrous. It seems to imply some kind of organization and purpose, where no organization or purpose was dreamed of. It seems to suggest a process of selection, possibly even of rejection, by a group which, in so far as it had any separate existence, was a spontaneous and natural growth, born of casual friendship and unpremeditated sympathy.'[27] However, despite this almost dismissive tone, he was in little doubt as to his opinion of their importance, telling Margot Asquith that 'no history of our time will be complete unless the influence of the Souls upon society is dispassionately and accurately recorded'.[28]

Too much has been written about the Souls to merit a long

analysis here of their aspirations and activities. Suffice it to say that they were a group of men and women, almost exclusively of aristocratic origin, who preferred conversation and lawn-tennis to shooting, hunting and gambling, which were at that time the customary pursuits of their class. The Souls would meet at weekend parties in country houses. Clouds was a favourite venue, as was the Elchos' home at Stanway in Gloucestershire. Lord Cowper at Panshanger and the Desboroughs at Taplow also entertained them. The ritual was much the same as that of the Clouds house party of 1887 when Blunt and Balfour had their fateful conversation. Lawn-tennis was a favourite form of recreation (it was much enjoyed by Balfour) and after-dinner games kept the party amused well into the small hours of the morning. The conversation was generally wide ranging and well informed, taking in literature, politics and social gossip. Traditional country pursuits, such as hunting and shooting, were practised, but not to excess. The fastidious Soul was rather repelled by the dedication shown by the rest of his class to these bucolic pleasures. A visit to one of their meeting places could be intellectually stimulating and aesthetically enjoyable. In the talk and the games, there was often an air of competition, particularly among the women; and the beauty of the great country houses, set in their carefully landscaped parks, provided a suitable background to the intellectual elegance. John Morley remarked to his friend at the end of one such party : 'My dear Brodrick, these two days have been delightful, but most blighting to one's democracy.'[29]

The Souls were exceptionally closely linked, by ties of blood and affection. George Wyndham's sister Mary was the hostess of Stanway, one of their main meeting places. His other sister Pamela married Eddy Tennant, brother of Margot Asquith, and Wilfrid Blunt was a cousin of the Wyndhams. Brodrick had been at Eton at the same time as Curzon. Because of the rather incestuous nature of the group and their unabashed attempts to be different from their class contemporaries, there were those who believed that the Souls were trying almost too hard and thus did not deserve to be taken altogether seriously. In 1892 certain of them were considering bringing out a newspaper, to give vent to their literary aspirations. This became a topic for discussion when Blunt lunched at 11 Downing Street with Sir William Harcourt on November 8th of that year. 'Great joking,' noted Blunt, 'by Sir William about the "Souls" journal. I suggested as a motto for it, *solus cum sola*, with an armorial coat, bearing two flat fish osculant all proper. "Ah," he said, "it is their bodies that I like, and now they are going to show us their souls all naked in print, I shall not care for them." '[30]

Harcourt need not have worried unduly about the primness of Soul women. At a dinner given by Lord Cowper in 1898 to celebrate Curzon's appointment as Viceroy of India, St John Brodrick asked his neighbour how many people in the room had proposed to her. She answered five, and divided the rest of the company into two categories; those who would have proposed had they not already been married (she claimed six of these, including Brodrick) and those who 'abided in darkness as to her charms'.[31] It was on this occasion that Godfrey Webb remarked ruefully : 'What shall it profit a man if he gain the whole world and lose his own particular soul?' But when love was declared it was usually accompanied by the whole panoply of romantic despair. In the early 1890s, Pamela Wyndham, as yet unmarried to Eddy Tennant, fell in love with Harry Cust who, with his charm, looks and intelligence, had a powerful effect on many women. Some considered Cust to be the most brilliant of all the Souls; but he was forced to marry another whose virtue he was thought to have trifled with, so Pamela had to be sent out to India to recover from him. His letters of this time to Sibell, George Wyndham's wife, whom he treated as a confidante, reveal the intensity with which such matters were conducted.

'I must,' he once declared, writing from Paris, 'I must write my soul out to you or I shall suffocate. There is none other I can turn to who will know and understand and at least for a while the punishment is greater than I can bear. Do not say a word to my darling little Pamela, but help me first for a little while; for I sometimes feel simply mad and murderous and have to cling close to Pamela's darling hand to help and save me as always. Do you understand, do you feel what it is, every dragging miserable minute of the twenty-four hours, with the one pure perfect love of my life, always always with me, filling all my heart and all my mind and all the room of all my love, and turned to whatever happens, whether it be funny or tragic or beautiful or interesting or good or bad or high or low or rich or poor, and then – But first if I ask your help and, for her sake, your love and patience, I must make one thing very clear; which I could not tell to her and yet which I want her in some way to know. Except by English law I am not one bit married save to Pamela only. Not before God and still less before my legal wife: of the ways of married men and women, of merest touch of hand or glance of eye there is not the faintest possible remotest question. As I am spiritually Pamela's I am legally someone else's: the rest of life and all that pure if earthly joy of intimacy and closest friendship is not. It belongs of right to Pamela, and if I may not give it to her none other shall ever have it. Do you understand?'[32]

Certainly Cust, at this time, displayed signs that he was undergoing an emotional upheaval. H. G. Wells, calling at the offices of the *Pall Mall Gazette*, witnessed an example of this. 'I was sent up to the editor's room,' he remembered, 'I remember it as a magnificent drawing-room. There was certainly one grand piano in it and my memory is inclined to put in another. There was a vast editor's desk, marvellously equipped, like a desk out of Hollywood. There were chairs and sofas. But for the moment I saw nobody amidst these splendours. I advanced slowly across a space of noiseless carpet. Then I became aware of a sound of sobbing and realized that someone almost completely hidden from me lay prostrate on a sofa indulging in paroxysms of grief.' This was Harry Cust, who instantly recovered enough to receive Wells with great aplomb, combining 'the agreeable manners of an elder brother with those of a fellow adventurer'. 'Whether he went on with his crisis,' wrote Wells, 'or forgot about it I cannot say, but from my later acquaintance with him, I think he most probably forgot about it.'[33]

If Wyndham's social world was almost entirely populated with the Souls and the reanimated Crabbet Club, Wilfrid Blunt had one old and exceptionally close friend who, by virtue of his long absences abroad, had never been a part of these two groups. This was Robert Lytton. Now, in the 1890s, he was British Ambassador in Paris, and Blunt would frequently visit him at his embassy. Lytton was a success. 'His literary bohemianism and lack of pomposity,' wrote Blunt, 'his devotion to the stage, his ready patronage of artists, actors, and those littérateurs who count for so much in Paris journalism, had been a passport for him to favour with the Press, and through the Press to public opinion. Lytton was by taste a bohemian, and Paris, which is also so largely bohemian, recognized him as a brother artist.'[34]

The success was not to last. In January 1890 he was writing to Blunt: 'For my long silence I have the excuse of long ill-health – I have been feeling really very ill . . . with fever and with congestion of the lungs – the result of a relapse when but half recovered from a first attack of the horrid influenza.'[35] By 1891, the situation was worse and when the Blunts were staying at the embassy in November they were taken to see him on his sick-bed. 'Give my love to Dufferin,' he said to them, 'when you are in Rome – that he always has – and tell him I am a wreck, but do not mean to make a vacancy yet.'[36] Less than a fortnight later a telegram reached them in Italy, giving the news of his death.

'His death,' wrote Blunt, 'was a loss I can hardly estimate, and to many more than me, for by the public in Paris it was looked on as a state calamity.'[37] Lytton had been close to Blunt since they were both in their twenties, and the friendship had flourished, despite their political differences. At the time of Blunt's painful break-up with Skittles Lytton had comforted and sustained him. Together they had been poets and men of vigorous achievement, although one had chosen the path of respectable service while the other had opted for that of rebellion and resistance. For the survivor, the sadness was acute. In an appreciation in *Nineteenth Century* Blunt wrote of his friend: 'His work is imperishable, but, alas! how shall we perpetuate the memory of his personality which has perished from amongst us? This was more wonderful and rare than all his work. We can only weep and hold it dear to our hearts, for in truth he was the brightest, best and most beloved of men.'[38]

Chapter 12
'The Sacred Fire'

In the same way that Lytton had encouraged Wilfrid Blunt in his literary endeavours, so Blunt also was quick to observe, and encourage, talent in his own friends. On July 2nd 1887 he lunched with George Wyndham in London. The conversation turned to literature. 'George,' noted Blunt, 'is full of his poetry, some of which he has showed me. I think he has the sacred fire. He has ear and a certain power of putting what he says effectively. More will come later unless I am mistaken; and I encouraged him to go on.' Yet the older man added a note of qualification to the praise. 'He is,' declared Blunt, 'a charming young man, married to a very charming person, two things not the most productive of poetry. If he could be unhappy, he would write really well.'[1] Later in the year, during the Balfour weekend at Clouds, Blunt was pleased with his cousin's literary progress. 'George and I,' he remarked on September 4th, 'spent the morning and part of the afternoon reading out our respective poetries. Besides several excellent sonnets he read me two longer pieces of very superior merit. He is only twenty-four, the age I was when I first met Lytton at Lisbon, and I certainly had not at that time written anything at all better than these. He has great facility and ought to go far.'[2]

To receive praise from Wilfrid Scawen Blunt, already a poet of some standing, was satisfying to the young Wyndham, particularly as he enthusiastically returned the other's admiration. 'How very good of you,' Wyndham wrote in December 1888 on receiving Blunt's *In Vinculis*, a collection of sonnets written while the author was in prison in Ireland, 'to send me a copy of your book. I am very much obliged for it. I read it last night before going to bed and liked it very much . . .'⁸ Reading his cousin's latest work led to a feeling of disappointment that he, now firmly embarked upon a political career, had been forced, for the moment, to abandon literature. 'I am sorry to say,' Wyndham continued, 'that I have had but little time to write and see no prospect of a more rational life for some time to come. Some day I hope for a pure breath of poetry to clear my lungs of the poisonous dust of political controversy.' Both Wyndham and Blunt were torn between the two worlds of literature and politics. For both of them, and for their readers, the dividing line was often exceedingly obscure; and, in the true romantic style, their lives would constantly impinge upon their writings.

Wilfrid Blunt's first volume of poetry, *The Sonnets and Songs of Proteus*, was published in 1875; and he went on to produce some fourteen volumes of poems, finishing with the two-volume edition of his poetry that was published by Macmillan's in 1914. To read his work is to travel the path of an individual's political and emotional development, for with Blunt it is impossible to separate the man from his art. His poetry is not great poetry, but a vivid record of a varied life and intense enthusiasms, and in this sense can provide a useful clue to the poet's character. Blunt, more than most, believed that, by themselves, 'the tales of poets are but scholars' themes'. Therefore he consciously made his verses reflect the reality of his own life, whether this took the form of love affairs, political campaigns or journeys; and, as he was an active man, opposed to 'the noblest dreaming of mere dreams', it is activity that they primarily celebrate. The activity that has the greatest number of poems dedicated to it is the pursuit, and love, of woman.

It is not the purpose of this book to embark upon a long catalogue of Blunt's love affairs or an examination of his methods of seduction. Contained within his papers in the

Fitzwilliam Museum in Cambridge are packets of love letters from his many and various mistresses, waiting to be sifted by a biographer. Certainly no life of Blunt could be complete without a thorough examination of this side of his character, although a considerable disservice would be done to him if his philanderings were allowed to obscure his other more substantial achievements. Since his affair with Catherine Walters in Paris in the 1860s, women had come to play a large part in his life. The relationship with Skittles had been especially passionate, leading first to intense pleasure and then to despair; but after this there was a more measured tone to these involvements. The self-confidence gained through his association with the famous courtesan, his good looks and charm coupled with his romantic approach, made Blunt an alluring figure. His marriage to Lady Anne did not put a stop to this side of his life. Indeed his grandson has observed that Blunt developed, over the years, a Mohammedan attitude to women which made long-standing attachment impossible.

However, despite the last line in his sonnet sequence *To Manon*, whose heroine is Skittles, Wilfrid Blunt was no callous unthinking womanizer. He might declare, in a moment of fury:

> 'Oh, Manon, there are women yet unborn
> Shall rue thy frailty, else am I foresworn.'

But, in fact his affairs came to be calmly conducted, almost without passion, with the participants eventually parting the best of friends. Yet the lack of emotional upheaval did not preclude outbursts of romanticism, in which these associations were linked with such concepts as delight in nature, the ennobling qualities of physical activity, and even, ultimately, a brief glimpse of immortality. In his sonnet 'St Valentine's Day', perhaps his most famous poem, we see these brought together in ecstatic celebration.

'Today, all day, I rode upon the Down,
With hounds and horsemen, a brave company.
On this side in its glory lay the sea,
On that the Sussex Weald, a sea of brown.
The wind was light, and brightly the sun shone,
And still we galloped on from gorse to gorse,
And once, when checked, a thrush sang, and my horse
Pricked his quick ears as to a sound unknown.
I knew the Spring was come. I knew it even
Better than all this, that through my chase
In bush and stone and hill and sea and heaven
I seemed to see and follow still your face.
Your face my quarry was. For it I rode,
My horse a thing of wings, myself a god.'

Blunt did not exclude the Wyndhams from his romantic
escapades. He found Madeline, as we have seen, a particularly
warm and reassuring companion; and later he was to discover
her oldest daughter Mary Elcho to be similarly captivating.
In this he was not alone. Her most celebrated admirer was
Arthur Balfour, although the extent of his involvement with her
remains doubtful, and others, from a greater distance,
appreciated her charms, not the least of which was a touching, if sometimes bewildering, vagueness. 'She was,' wrote
Margot Asquith, 'always a great joy, but she was physically
and mentally badly equipped for the little things of life.'[4] Yet
beneath the surface chaos there were real qualities. 'Indeed,'
continued Margot, 'she is almost the only woman I can think of
who is without touchiness or smallness of any kind. It might
have been written for her: "She nothing common did or
mean".' H. G. Wells was another admirer, and was grateful
to her for standing by him when conformist opinion, led by St
Loe Strachey of the *Spectator*, attacked the immorality of his
novel *Ann Veronica*.

Mary had married Lord Elcho, son of the Earl of Wemyss,
and they lived at Stanway, a beautiful old manor house in

Gloucestershire. Set amid idyllic surroundings, Stanway became a gathering place for the Souls. George Wyndham has described her domestic contentment. 'You must,' he told Sibell in March 1894, 'come once quietly like this to see darling Mary in her proper frame, this lovely old quiet house, with no luxury, no hot air, few servants, only one cheap horse to ride, but devoted children and a ring of worshipping neighbours. Here she is doing everything for its own sake and nothing for *réclame*. Riding simply but jumping everything with no fuss. Reading her books and educating her babes, making a little speech in the school; having an impossible missionary to lunch and discussing philosophy and aesthetics. A pleasant deep life full of repose and dignity, grace and charm.'[5]

Often, with the arrival of guests, this world would change from the humdrum to the exotic. In August 1894, Wyndham wrote to Sibell from Stanway to say that 'Arthur [Balfour], Wilfrid Blunt and Alfred Douglas (on a driving tour) all dropped in here yesterday afternoon to find a village cricket match . . . in full swing, and a band of young ladies and their admirers playing guitars, mandolines, the flute and castanets in Neapolitan costume. Darling Mary dividing the day between entertaining neighbours and riding a bicycle. The Neapolitans played "The Conquering Hero" as Arthur came up; and Wilfrid turned his two Arabs out to graze in the cricket field. I thought the whole, if put in a French novel as a picture of English life, would be amusing.'[6] In 1895 Mary Elcho accompanied the Blunts to Egypt and, from Sheykh Obeyd, they rode in the desert, pushing their explorations as far as the Red Sea, and following the coastline down between the mountain range of Kalála and the Gulf of Suez. Returning from these journeys they would sit in the oasis's beautiful garden which was full, as Frederick Harrison described, 'of oranges, olives, apricots in blossom and roses in bloom – so that, although it is in the Desert, it is a wilderness of water and greenery'.[7]

Blunt's deep respect for ties of blood was nowhere better shown than in his relationship with the Wyndhams. 'I like,' he wrote to Madeline Wyndham in January 1896, 'to hear of your being happy in a matriarchal way and envy you not a little your many grandchildren. You are right to talk of them as the roots which hold you to the Earth, and I think that now-a-days with our diminishing certainty of a world beyond they are of more value than ever to us as a real physical form of future life. The Chinese have believed this for five or six thousand years. I extend their feeling to a certain extent to all my blood relations.'[8] His poetry reveals this concern with ancestry and family links, and the continuity that common blood can provide. *In Anniversario Mortuis* is written to his dead brother, and contained within it is a description of how the poet regards himself not as the owner of Crabbet after his brother's death, but still a mere tenant in his family's name. Similarly his long pastoral, 'Worth Forest', is dedicated to his son, who died four days after his birth and who was to be his heir.

If the love of women was important to Blunt, his philanderings should not be seen in too garish a light. In effect they provided a background to his other equally intense activities; and, while of importance to him, they rarely turned him aside from these for long. As his amorous adventures spilled over into his verse so did his politics. Initially the poet regarded the political side of his life as being of greater importance than the literary; but later, after a series of disappointments, he came to think differently. Yet he did write four long polemical poems, propagating his political ideas. The earliest, 'The Wind and the Whirlwind', concerns the campaign on behalf of Arabi in Egypt; and begins with a rousing declaration:

'I have a thing to say. But how to say it?
I have a cause to plead. But to what ears?
How shall I move a world by lamentation,
A world which heeded not a Nation's tears?'

In the 'Canon of Aughrim' it is Dr Duggan, the old Bishop of Clonfert, who is the poet's hero and the Irish Nationalist movement his cause. 'Satan Absolved' is a tract, written in 1899, against imperialism and dedicated to Herbert Spencer; and 'Coronation Ode', written in 1911 on the occasion of George V's coronation, speaks out against the exploitation of the weaker nations.

When his contemporaries came to assess Blunt's poetry, his political opinion counted against it. Many regarded him foremost as a poet, who also happened to possess remarkably eccentric ideals, and thus his polemical verse was generally swept aside. 'Undoubtedly,' the critic Percy Addleshaw wrote in the *National Review*, 'his reputation as a poet has suffered from his vehement partisanship as a politician',[9] and went on to observe of *In Vinculis* 'doubtless its composition went far to make the tedium of prison life bearable, but it is full of hysterical screaming, and some of us would forget it gladly'. Byron, both in character and poetry, was a figure to whom Blunt was much compared; but although his verse at times has a Byronic fierceness, it does not have the tempestuous, even satanic, vigour of his wife's forebear's greatest creations. An example of this is *Griselda*, which Blunt termed 'a society novel in rhymed verse' and which is clearly descended from *Don Juan*, although it lacks the brittle economy and cynical humour of its ancestor. Like Canto I of *Don Juan* it concerns the activities of a young woman married to an older man, and is an accomplished performance, more expert than Owen Meredith's *Lucile* to which Blunt acknowledged its indebtedness. He himself disclaims admiration for Byron's work on several occasions, stating that, as a Sussex man, he preferred Shelley. But throughout his diaries, particularly in the early days, there are references to Byron, if only on account of his similar dedication to nationalist causes.

One who believed that Byron's work was a major influence on Blunt was W. E. Henley. In 1898, Henley, arch-imperialist, edited, with George Wyndham, a volume of Blunt's poetry for publication. Naturally the political verse was ignored, but in a brief introduction Henley explained his admiration for the poet. 'These poems,' he declared, 'deal in fresh, clean, living English with life and love, the romance of travel, the delight in woods and fields and skies, the pride of ancestry and race, the joy and sorrow of being, the terror of decay, the pathos and cruelty of death – all the elements of mortal destiny as mortal destiny has been revealed to one forceful, passionate, understanding witness.'[10] To win the enthusiasm of Henley, himself a 'passionate witness', was then a considerable achievement, for he was one of the leading literary figures of the 1890s, and a poet in tune with the spirit of his time. He was also George Wyndham's literary mentor and valued friend.

On May 9th 1893, Blunt wrote in his diary : 'I found George Wyndham with Henley, the hospital poet (a bitter talker but sayer of good things) . . .'[11] But Blunt did not care for this 'bitter talker', however much Henley might profess to admire the other's poetry. 'I confess,' he wrote on the occasion of Henley's death in 1903, 'I do not like Henley, though I have tried to like him for George's sake. But he is both physically and intellectually repugnant to me. He has the bodily horror of the dwarf, with the dwarf's huge bust and head and shrunken nether limbs, and he had also the dwarf's malignity of tongue and defiant attitude towards the world at large. Moreover I am quite out of sympathy with Henley's deification of brute strength and courage, things I wholly despise.'[12]

Henley's bitterness, growing no doubt out of his own infirmities (he had been a cripple since birth), led him to take some strange stances. Born in Edinburgh, a great friend of Robert Louis Stevenson who had used him as a model for Long John Silver, Henley was in 1891 editor of the *National Observer*. He was also a poet whose verse had recently taken on a markedly shrill imperialistic tone, very different from his first productions which had consisted of gentle ballades and grey portraits of life in a general hospital. As a naturalistic poet Henley could be poignant and effective, as is shown by the *In Hospital* series and his sketches of London Types, but, in common with other physically infirm intellectuals, he possessed a fervent admiration for what he was to term 'the dignity of resistance', or blood and thunder. This took the form of a devotion to patriotism and the Empire. Together with Kipling, Henley was one of the foremost literary proponents of late-Victorian imperialism, thus providing, in the 1890s, a formidable counterblast to the aesthetic movement of Wilde, Dowson and Lionel Johnson.

The *National Observer* was an avowedly imperialistic paper, publishing Kipling's *Barrack Room Ballads* for the first time. Soon the editor gathered around him a group of contributors who would meet in Solferino's restaurant near Leicester Square and who were called, by Max Beerbohm, 'The Henley Regatta'. Among these was W. B. Yeats, who termed him 'a man whose power no others can know because it has not found expression in words'. Yeats did not care either for Henley's poetry or his prose; yet he fell completely under the power of the man's personality. 'He alarmed me,' the young Irishman wrote, 'and impressed me exactly as he did those others who were called Henley's young men, and even today [when I meet] someone among them, showing perhaps the first signs of age, we recognize at once the bond.' Yeats gives a hint of the cripple's power when he speaks of 'his unanalysable gift of keeping all men near him at the stretch, of sending all away wearied out with the prolonged giving of their best'. Indeed Oscar Wilde once said to Yeats, after being in Henley's company, 'I had to strain every nerve to equal that man at all,' and yet, as Yeats remembered, 'Wilde himself had said all the brilliant things – Henley had done little more than listen.'[13]

Wyndham was one of Henley's contributors. His knowledge of literature had grown steadily since his departure from Eton. While on guard duty he had read Voltaire and Scott, and even taught himself Italian; but, as with Wilfrid Blunt, he had neither the time nor the inclination to devote himself permanently to its pursuit. In a letter to his wife in 1891 from Clouds he says: 'I wrote all my business letters in bed, have translated a sonnet of Ronsard, made my toilet, read Benvenuto

Cellini and am now writing to you';[14] and of such ferocious activity was most of his life composed. But Henley, after Wyndham began to contribute to the *Scots Observer* in 1890 and became one of the mainstays of the *National Observer* (and its later incarnations, the *Outlook* and the *New Review*), provided valuable encouragement and advice. He persuaded the politician to undertake, amongst other things, the introduction to the Tudor Classics edition of North's Plutarch; and in 1894 Wyndham was enthusiastically writing to his mother: 'Now I must work every day at my Introduction to Plutarch. It entails reading all the lives in old English and old French, and tracing Shakespeare's debt in *Coriolanus, Julius Caesar* and *Anthony*.'[15]

Wyndham, in his turn, helped Henley, promoting him as a candidate for the professorship of English Literature at Edinburgh University (it eventually went to George Saintsbury) and doing much to facilitate the grant to him of a civil list pension in 1897. However he baulked at the suggestion that he should push the writer's candidature for the Poet Laureateship in 1895.

Whether writing or talking about literature, enthusiasm was the hallmark of George Wyndham's approach. Charles Gatty, who shared his literary tastes, often experienced this. 'I felt,' Gatty wrote, 'that he unpacked my brain quite as soon as the footman unpacked my portmanteau. – "Ah, you are working at the vernacular, it's a splendid subject. I'll settle you down in the room below me in the tower, there are lots of books there, and we'll put in a fortnight's talk and work. There's a new book on the origin of the French Language, a perfect mine of stuff for you. And then of course, you'll have to tackle Carmichael's *Carmina Gadelica*. I have a lot of problems for you about the sonnets, astronomical, heraldic and literary, we'll have a glorious time and throw off all the cares of politics and plunge into literature." '[16] Against this, it was natural that vigour and colour were the two literary qualities Wyndham prized above almost any other. 'I have,' he told Wilfrid Blunt, 'never cared much for prose, however excellent, which

The First Earl of Lytton, a sketch for the portrait by G.F. Watts.

George Wyndham towards
the end of his life.

The Poets' Luncheon at
Newbuildings, January 1914.
From left to right:
Victor Plarr, T. Sturge Moore,
W.B. Yeats, Blunt,
Ezra Pound, Richard Aldington,
F.S. Flint.

does not abound naturally in vivid images.'[17]

Wyndham's enthusiasms ranged over Ronsard, du Bellay, the poems of Shakespeare, the Elizabethans, and Sir Walter Scott – in fact over a field of Romance – and these are the subjects celebrated in his *Essays in Romantic Literature*, published after his death with an introduction by Charles Whibley. Whibley points out how, as with Blunt, the life was inseparable from the writing. Indeed, outwardly there was no hint of the cloister about George Wyndham. He was a man 'who', as he wrote of Ronsard, 'argues from the rostrum and pommels from the ring, a conservative with a catholic pleasure in life, delighting in all the treasures garnered into the citadel of the past, and ready [as in Egypt] to die for its defence.'[18] Yet, in a sense, it was this very participation in the spirit of his time and class that did build around him a kind of cloister, as firm and secluded as any hermit's cell. Wyndham's tower room at Saighton, with its wonderful view over the Welsh hills, where he did his writing and would stay up half the night talking and reading; his rushing from the House of Commons to the *National Observer*; his dashing off sonnets in between sets of tennis; his intense literary conversations over the port – all these are evidence of an enthusiasm as serious as it was admirable, but an enthusiasm limited by having to be spread over such a broad and, ultimately, predictable field. While staying at Merton Abbey in Norfolk, Henley noted in 1897: 'A very pleasant experience and the most delightful place conceivable. G. W. [George Wyndham] and I talked Shakespeare (the rest abed and the last whisky on the spot) under a wonderful moon in a landscape liker Watteau than Watteau ever dreamed. I say no more.'[19] There was no need to, for this is as neat a vignette of Wyndham's world as any could provide. Here, with the murmur of voices rising and falling against the firm background of the great country house and the quiet deserted garden, he was at home, resting from politics, at ease in literature.

T. S. Eliot has tellingly remarked of Wyndham as a critic

that 'his literature and his politics and his country life are one and the same thing. They are not in separate compartments, they are one career. Together they make up his world — literature, politics, riding to hounds.' Eliot goes on to observe that 'Wyndham was not a scholar, but his scholarship was incidental; he was a good critic, within the range allowed him by his enthusiasms; but it is neither as Scholar nor as Critic that we can criticize him. We can criticize his writings only as the expression of this peculiar English type, the aristocrat, the Imperialist, the Romantic, riding to hounds across his prose, looking with wonder upon the world as upon a fairyland.'[20]

Some of his contemporaries were very content with 'this peculiar English type'. Walter Raleigh dedicated his Tudor Translations edition of Hoby's The Courtier to 'George Wyndham, soldier, courtier, scholar, in a year of high emotion [this was 1900 and Boer war jingoism was at its height] and the accomplishing of unimaginable destinies, this treatise of amenity in deed, this old-faced but ever lustrous mirror of the complete gentleman'. Henley believed the introduction of North's Plutarch to be a remarkable piece of scholarship and understanding; and the essay on Shakespeare's sonnets, with its allusions to hawking and heraldry, earned similar plaudits. Not only those who shared his political opinions admired his work. Wilfrid Scawen Blunt believed he should have concentrated on his poetry (reading these neo-Keatsian ventures in manuscript today, it is difficult to agree) and eschewed criticism of the works of others. Wyndham himself was ready to take advice from almost anybody, and Henley could suggest whatever changes he wished for the National Observer. But there were certain stylistic principles to which he adhered. Once Charles Boyd challenged him to make his style sparer and less self-indulgent, to which Wyndham replied : 'But, then, old boy, the plainer way of writing wouldn't be me!'[21] Indeed it would not have been. Neither Blunt nor Wyndham were 'plain people'.

Chapter 13
The Height of Empire

In September 1892 Wilfrid Scawen Blunt was staying with his
friend Brinsley Sheridan, 'a typical country gentleman given
to sport', at Frampton. Also of the party was a Miss Fether-
stonhaugh who, misjudging the political complexion of her
fellow guest, showed him some enthusiastic letters she had
recently received from a young man in Uganda. Blunt gave
vent to his wrath in his diary. 'These people,' he wrote, 'believe
they have a mission from God to establish the British flag,
"the dear old Union Jack", throughout the world and to maintain it there with fire and sword. Pizarro, no doubt, wrote in
the same strain from Peru, when he destroyed the beautiful
old world of the Incas. Truly civilization is poison.'[1] With the
arrival of the last decade of the nineteenth century, the
imperial spirit, already well-established, was abroad with a
vengeance; and the zealotry of its promoters had taken on an
almost messianic tone. In 1895 Joseph Chamberlain became
Colonial Secretary. A former radical who had left the Liberals
over Home Rule, he brought to the cause of the Empire new
energy and dedication. Aided by the jingoistic posturings of
the popular Press, imperialism, and belief in the 'civilizing
mission', grew in strength. Commercial and philosophical
justification of its spread had long ago met in the new Colonial
Secretary's rhetoric. 'Experience teaches us,' he observed at the
Devonshire Club in 1887, 'that trade follows the flag' and earlier
in the same year at Toronto he had remarked upon 'the greatness and importance of the destiny which is reserved for the

Anglo-Saxon race – for that proud, persistent, self-asserting and resolute stock, that no change of climate or condition can alter, and which is infallibly destined to be the predominant force in the future history and civilization of the world'.[2]

Blunt, undeterred, remained enthusiastic for the cause of Egyptian Nationalism, and spoke out fiercely against British intervention to quell the rebellion led by the Mahdi's heirs, the Khalifa Abdullah and his lieutenant Osman Digna. He still campaigned in vain for the return of Arabi. However, in January 1890 his efforts were regarded with tolerance by those in authority, as if they were casting a tired but understanding eye on the antics of a wrong-headed schoolboy. Since 1883 he had not seen the English Consul-General Sir Evelyn Baring (later first Earl of Cromer); but now the abetter of rebellion believed that, by making contact with officialdom, he would be able to do more for his cause. An appointment with the Consul-General, who had once banned him from Egypt, was arranged; and Blunt left surprisingly impressed. 'In business matters,' he wrote, 'I found Sir Evelyn a pleasant man to deal with. He was quick to understand a case and straightforward in his replies, willing always to listen to arguments, however opposed to his own opinions, and with nothing of the conventional insincerities of diplomacy.' He now understood the reasons for Baring's success in attracting support for his policies, seeing how 'many English Radical MPs who, arriving at Cairo with the idea of hastening on the evacuation, left it persuaded that the proposal was impossible or at least premature, and that the occupation must be maintained'.[3]

Baring did seem to be, as British representative, firmly ensconced as governor of Egypt. Although the British were supposedly in the country purely as advisers, their supervisory presence was sufficiently obvious to give them the appearance of an occupying force. Against the cry that they were usurping the rights of the Khedive and the Sultan, Baring could answer that the Khedive was still ostensibly the country's ruler and that since the British arrival, the fortunes of Egypt had enjoyed a

considerable upsurge. This, on the face of it, was true. By the
end of 1886 the budget was balanced, after years of disastrous
mismanagement. Improvements in agriculture and irrigation
were also under way.

As befittted a former Indian Civil Servant, Baring's rule was
autocratic but effective. It was in India that he had earned
his nickname 'Over Baring' because of his lofty manner. There
was something of the machine about him. His industry was
prodigious. Frequently he would work at his desk from 6 a.m.
to 8 p.m. But he had the power to attract devotion from his sub-
ordinates, many of whom particularly admired him for refusing to change his approach for anybody, no matter what their
station in life. Once, at the Residency in Cairo, when the Prince
of Wales, later Edward VII, demanded a third helping of prawn
curry, Baring remarked: 'You had much better not. It is rich
enough as it is, and you have already had two ample helpings.'[4]
Later it was said that even Kitchener was frightened of him.
But this ability to inspire awe was accompanied by a tendency
to steam-roller opposition which, in its turn, could lead to
startling displays of insensitivity. As long as the submissive
Tewfik was Khedive, all was well. However, in 1892, Tewfik
died and was succeeded by his son Abbas Hilmy. With considerable alarm Baring telegraphed to Salisbury that he
believed the new Khedive was going to be 'very Egyptian'.

Blunt saw how the Consul-General approached the new ruler
of Egypt. After being taken by Baring to meet the new Khedive
at the Abdin Palace, he observed that 'Baring's manner on this
occasion was very abrupt, like that of a schoolmaster to a
schoolboy, and that on our way back from the palace I
remarked to him that I thought the Khedive would not bear
driving with any but a very light rein, his answer being that
it was necessary to treat Orientals firmly; also I warned him
that he might have trouble'.[5] In 1893 Blunt, typically, tried to
instigate this trouble. He went to Constantinople in an attempt
to get the Sultan to be sympathetic to the cause of Egyptian
Nationalism. Here, for the first time since the umbrella incident,

he encountered his old Moslem teacher and friend, Jemal-ed-Din, now in favour with Sultan Abdul-Hamid. Their disagreement was forgotten, and they fell into each other's arms. But an audience was not forthcoming, and eventually Blunt said in desperation to one of the courtiers: 'I am not a fakir . . . to sit at the palace door waiting. I am not the Sultan's servant, nor will I dance attendance on any king in the world. If the Sultan wants to see me he must send and say so and I will come, but tonight I go home.'[6] He left with only the vague promise of a future audience and an arrangement whereby Jemal-ed-Din would show the Sultan letters from Blunt concerning political affairs in England. There never was such a meeting and his letters seem to have had little effect on the policies of the Ottoman Empire.

During the 1890s Blunt's views were still at odds with those of the majority of his fellow countrymen. Now his position was made even worse by the growing tide of imperialist sentiment. For the moment it appeared as if his day were over. This saddened him, but he felt no undue loss of hope. Indeed, as he grew older, his temperament became less prone to depression, partly because he had discovered reliable refuges into which he could retire with satisfaction. For example, at Sheykh Obeyd, he always managed to attain a state of benign contentment that allowed him to regard setbacks with comfortable stoicism. 'The longer I live,' he wrote from Egypt to Lady Currie, the wife of his cousin Philip, 'the more attached I become to the life of these old fashioned countries where age still meets with respect and lethargy is indulged without reproach. I love to sit all day long pretending to write but really doing nothing but listen to the drone of the waterwheels and the cooing of doves.'[7]

At times like these he came to believe that the only sensible aim in life was the attainment of an almost mystical serenity from whose heights the rest of the world could be observed and gently pitied. In 1897 Blunt wrote to George Wyndham from Sheykh Obeyd, in this philosophical vein. 'The real thing in life,' he observed, 'is to be happy. The older I get the more convinced I am that no ambition is worth pursuing except that of being rather happier than other men. Fame of any kind is only of use in so far as it leads to this, even the fame of being a poet which is perhaps more satisfactory and lasting than the rest. I would not give a brass button to be the greatest general that ever won a battle or even I think the greatest statesman that ever bamboozled the world. But I should like to be quite happy to the last day of my life, and to be able to inspire affection at the age of eighty, as I believe Goethe is said to have done.'[8]

In 1897 Blunt compared his idea of heaven with that of the other guests of Alfred Austin, the Poet Laureate, with whom he was staying. Austin's idea was to sit in a garden receiving constant telegrams announcing alternately a British victory by sea and a British victory by land; whereas Blunt was content merely to be laid out to sleep, also in a garden, for a hundred years, then to be woken by a bird singing and to call out to the person whom he loved best : 'Are you there?' and, after she had answered 'Yes, are you?' to turn round and sleep for another hundred thousand years. Yet this was only half the story. It belies the intense enjoyment he obtained, well into old age, from an active life of travel and adventure. The true pleasure of rest came for him only after activity, as one might lie down with relief at the end of a long day. While activity was physically possible there could be no enduring solace in repose; after a few weeks, the urge to be on one's way again would lead to a regeneration of the once battered self.

So the last decade of the nineteenth century saw Blunt still as active as many who were half his age. In 1894 he travelled with his young cousin Terence Bourke to Kerouan in Tunis, and in 1895 journeyed up the Nile to Wadi Halfa. In 1897 he experienced what was perhaps the most alarming of all his journeys – into the Tripolitan desert. Here he was taken prisoner by hostile Arabs at Siwah, and was only released because at length he managed to make them understand that he was an Englishman. Blunt, after reading Doughty, followed his fellow Arabist's advice as to presenting a passive front to the attack, and was convinced that this also contributed to his survival. The journey back to Sheykh Obeyd was similarly unpleasant. The guides were virtually useless, the water position frequently desperate, and Blunt uncertain as to the right route. His entry in his diary for March 24th records the enormity of his relief at returning at last to domestic peace. 'I returned,' he wrote, 'from my Siwah journey on the 17th at a quarter past eleven, meeting Anne accidentally on her way through the palm grove from the station. I could hardly speak for tears of joy. I had been away for forty days, during which she was to expect no news of me, and this was the forty-first, and during the whole of that time I had not spoken a word of any language but Arabic, till I had come even to think in Arabic, and I was weak and worn out, and famished in mind and body. Our last run from Siwah, four hundred and thirteen miles, had been accomplished in fourteen days and a half.'[9] It is hardly surprising that he should go on to observe: 'From this point my more violent activities in life may be said to have ended.'

Another result of his experiences in the Tripolitan desert was disillusion with Mohammedanism. Shocked by the brutality of his captors and their frenzied, almost manic, celebrations of the ending of Ramadan, Blunt wondered if so fanatical a religion could ever be susceptible to the liberalizing influences which he had once found so appealing. Eventually he decided that he had been duped, and recorded in 1897: 'My experience of the Senussia at Siwah has convinced me that there is no hope anywhere to be found in Islam. I had made myself a romance about these reformers, but I now see that it has no substantial basis, and I shall never go farther than I am now in the Mohammedan direction. The less religion in the world perhaps, the better.'[10]

Throughout all this his friendships remained unimpaired. They too were a source of comfort as he passed through the middle years of his life, and he tended them as carefully as his Egyptian garden. From Sussex he would drive his Arab team out across the country, perhaps to visit the Elchos at Stanway or the Morrises at Kelmscott. William Morris he liked and admired. The poet and designer made a tapestry of Botticelli's *Spring* for Blunt, which still hangs in Newbuildings, the house he moved to from Crabbet in 1895. Newbuildings, a Charles II manor house at Southwater in Sussex, became his home now for the rest of his life. Smaller, and therefore easier to manage, than Crabbet, it possessed, and still possesses, an intimate domestic atmosphere that is especially conducive to ease. New-buildings represented Blunt in old age – 'a fire', as T. E. Lawrence observed, 'yet flickering over the ashes of old fury . . . a careless work of art in well-worn Arab robes, his chiselled face framed in silver curling hair'[11] – when peace had partially come to him but when, as with a dormant volcano, there was the constant threat of further eruption.

Blunt would travel long distances to see those whose company he enjoyed. In France he visited Prince and Princess Wagram at Gros Bois, where the old feudal ways of the estate delighted him, and in 1895 saw his cousin Philip Currie, by now ambassador to the Porte, in Turkey before going on to Poland to Count Joseph Potocki and his Arab horses. From the Count he went further east, to the Ukraine and the residence of Countess Branicka. In English society his rehabilitation was now complete, and in the diaries there are some deliciously acute descriptions of London drawing-room life in the 1890s. On July 17th Blunt was present at a lunch given by the Asquiths. Among the other guests was Oscar Wilde. 'Of all those present,' the diarist wrote afterwards, 'and they were most of them brilliant talkers, he was without comparison the most brilliant, and in a perverse mood he chose to cross swords with one after the other of them, overpowering each in turn with his wit, and making special fun of Asquith his host that day, who only a few months later, as Home Secretary, was prosecuting him on the notorious criminal charge which sent him to hard labour in prison.'[12] To give added poignancy to the story, Asquith was apparently so overwhelmed by the flood of epigrams from his guest that he had been almost entirely silent for the duration of the meal. Blunt and Wilde were the last to leave. When the former proposed that they should walk together as far as Grosvenor Square, the great aesthete remarked: 'I never walk,' and summoned a passing hansom.

In such society, and in family circles, Blunt and George Wyndham were often together. Their friendship flourished as memories of the Irish imbroglio faded into history. In September 1892 Wyndham took his cousin, who was staying at Saighton, to visit Gladstone at Hawarden, and Blunt described the old statesman as being 'very cordial with George, but not as I think with me'. Gladstone was by now well settled into a loquacious old age. 'He talked,' said Blunt, 'about his books in the absorbed way he has, going on, without paying the least attention to the person he is speaking to, especially if it is his wife and she ventures to interpose a remark.' Gladstone decried the revised version of the Bible and Mrs Gladstone used this in an attempt to demonstrate her husband's essential conservatism. 'But,' observed Blunt, 'the old man paid no attention and went prattling on, talking of all things in the same absorbed way, apparently without sense of their proportion and for talking's sake, heedless of our remarks, until at last he settled down into a *Quarterly Review* article and said no more. That, I fancy is his common domestic life.'[13] Blunt was pleased, however, to find in the Hawarden library *In Vinculis*, with the leaves cut, although *Sonnets to Proteus*, which he had presented to Gladstone in 1884, was not there.

Another jaunt with Wyndham was a visit to Stratford in 1896. In the company of Sibell and George's mother the cousins stayed at the Shakespeare Hotel and in the evening read *Venus and Adonis* and *Lucrece*. They then explored the town itself, later driving out to Charlecote, where Shakespeare is said to have shot a deer in the park, and on to Anne Hathaway's cottage, at that stage still lived in by a descendant of the Hathaway family. 'George,' wrote Blunt, 'is a capital companion for a visit of this kind, he enjoys sightseeing, and besides knows all about Shakespeare, and has his theories about everything.'[14] The two were now very close, revelling in each other's successes. Wyndham was entering politics and literature with an enthusiasm which Blunt, however much he may have disapproved of the younger man's political conformity, clearly found irresistible. In 1895, after Pamela Wyndham's marriage to Eddy Tennant, George and Sibell gave a dance, at which the host regaled his cousin with epicureanism. 'What we want in modern life,' he said, 'is to have more feasting, song and flowers, and noise, and to sit long and late with beautiful ladies, ourselves crowned with wreaths.' Blunt remarked : 'Certainly his own entertainment, the first he has ever given, was perfection . . . His is a happy nature.'[15] In June 1896 there was a similarly euphoric encounter, of which Blunt noted : 'Breakfasted with George, who was in the highest of his high spirits, having been up at a ball till five at Grosvenor House, and then out at nine to try a new bicycle on Hampstead Heath, which is to run forty miles an hour. His triumphs are my triumphs, and I delight in his happiness.'[16]

Occasionally the political gulf between the two became too much for the older man. A typical evening was spent 'arguing with some heat the eternal question of the right of savage nations to existence'. 'George,' Blunt noted with alarm, 'who represents the general sense of modern imperial England, denies them any such right at all.'[17] Another time they had a furious dispute about Fashoda, with Wyndham declaring : 'We don't care whether the Nile is called English or Egyptian or what it is called, but we mean to have it and we don't mean the French to have it . . . It is not worthwhile drawing distinctions of right and wrong in the matter, it is a matter entirely of interest.' Blunt furiously declared in his diary : 'George represents all that is most extreme, most outrageous, in modern

English politics, and it marks the decline of the higher traditions to find one like him proclaiming and defending it.'[18]

In the 1890s, in South Africa, there was one voice which had been remarkably successful in its resistance to Joseph Chamberlain's 'predominant force', and that was the voice of the Boer. Chamberlain did not seek the supreme manifestation of imperial feeling that resulted from the Boer war and the British public's reaction to it. Indeed, as a prudent businessman, he wished to avoid the untidiness and risk of a military clash with Kruger. But, if the Empire were threatened then there must be war. 'England without an empire!' he exclaimed a few years later. 'Can you conceive it? England in that case would not be the England we love . . .'

Those who could conceive Britain without her empire were moved to an equally passionate expression of their beliefs. On August 12th 1899, Blunt noted in his diary: 'Chamberlain has made another violent speech, and it is clear now, as, indeed, it has been all through, that he is forcing a war with the Boers . . . The Liberal Party has swallowed so many violences and so many diplomatic frauds in the last twenty years that it may as well make up its mind to swallow this too. I, as an enemy of Empire, shall not say a word.'[19] With two races of colonizers at each other's throats Blunt might well have simply sat back and revelled in the spectacle. But he had to applaud the resistance of the Boers to British bullying. 'I read in the papers,' he wrote, 'the Boers' refusal of Chamberlain's ultimatum. A very dignified document it is, and one very difficult for our people to answer.'[20] He condemned the Liberals for lining up with Salisbury's government. Manifestations of jingoism disgusted him, and he was particularly alarmed to hear from George Wyndham that Shakespeare's *King John*, which they went to see together on October 12th at Her Majesty's Theatre, had been especially put on by Beerbohm Tree because it was 'full of jingo tags and no popery talk'.

The cousins' views on the war differed vastly. Wyndham thought that Kruger was bluffing and, after a token fight, would surrender to Buller, the British general, and make terms. Blunt, on the other hand, dreaded a rapid conclusion to hostilities. 'My chief fear,' he declared, 'had been lest the Boers should be jockeyed out of their independence without fighting. Besides, I look upon the war as perhaps the first nail driven into the coffin of the British Empire. I believe that if the Boers can hold out for six months Europe will intervene.'[21]

George Wyndham was merely conforming to the romantic Conservative imperialism of his generation. At this time he admired Chamberlain, Rhodes and Dr Jameson. He spoke in the House of Commons so fiercely for the interests of colonials that he became known, briefly, as the 'Member for South Africa'. In 1896 he visited that country, and went on to sit on the committee of enquiry into the Jameson raid, at which he defended Rhodes and Dr Jameson. He was also instrumental in the formation of the South African Association. South Africa fascinated Wyndham but he was impatient with its condition. On September 19th 1896 he wrote to Arthur Balfour from Cape Town : 'Here is a country with the greatest industrial possibilities in the world and yet with five separate states in it taxing and impeding each other; a war with barbarism; rinderpest annihilating all transport and Foreign intrigue fostering the suicidal vanity of the Transvaal.'[22]

South Africa was in ferment. The independent Boer republic of the Transvaal, under Paul Kruger, had become its richest state. People flocked to Johannesburg, to the great Witwatersrand gold-field, thus creating a large population of *Uitlanders*, or foreigners, whom the Boer government proceeded to tax at a high rate without allowing them any representation or official recognition. Kruger, although the 1884 London convention had insisted upon British control over the Transvaal's foreign relations, began to seek German support. He felt hemmed in by the British presence in Bechuanaland to the west, and Rhodesia to the north. Matters were further complicated by

Cecil Rhodes who, as managing director of the Charter Company and Prime Minister of Cape Town, had long objected to Kruger's efforts to frustrate trade with areas that could only be reached by crossing the Transvaal. Only an ultimatum issued by Chamberlain in 1895 put a stop to these obstructions.

The situation of the *Uitlanders* was a challenge to British national pride as well as to commerce. In August 1895 they presented a petition with over 35,000 signatures to the Transvaal government, demanding redress of their grievances. But the *Uitlanders* were far from united. Many of them were not British and thus would have been ill at ease in a coup inspired by Rhodes and other British influences. Thus, on December 29th, when Dr Jameson, with four hundred and seventy men, eight machine guns and three pieces of artillery, rode towards Johannesburg to take on the Transvaal Republic, those whom he was supposedly rescuing were still undecided as to whether they should hoist the Union Jack or the flag of the Transvaal.

Chamberlain, not hearing of the raid until the day of its occurrence, instantly condemned it. Rhodes, its true instigator, resigned his premiership of the Cape, and the Kaiser sent his celebrated telegram to Kruger congratulating the Transvaal president on his country's escape. The raiders themselves, having been apprehended with ease, were handed over to the British government, and the leaders of the abortive *Uitlander* rebellion were sentenced to death in Johannesburg. Only Chamberlain's intervention saved their lives. Dr Jameson and his associates stood trial at Bow Street. Here, although they were convicted and sentenced, jingoistic sentiment took their side. To some foreign observers, indeed, it seemed as if the British public was entirely unrepentant.

It was against such a background that George Wyndham began to take an interest in South Africa. On October 12th he wrote to Wilfrid Scawen Blunt from the base of the Matoppo Hills, where Rhodes was attempting to pacify a Matabele rebellion: 'You probably dislike Rhodes, but he has acted here as you would have done. He found the soldiers pounding away twice a week into these hills, losing and killing men, so he went into the Hills and invited the natives to talk it over with him. They now call him "the man who came between two bulls fighting" and "the cow who is given when the calf's mother is dead".'[23] Wyndham's role in the select committee of the House of Commons set up to investigate the circumstances of the raid was to be strongly on the side of Rhodes. He refused to sign the report, believing it to be too critical of the former Prime Minister of Cape Province, and in the Commons debate defended the 'colossus'. Rhodes, who had previously dismissed Wyndham as a 'spring poet', was so delighted that, when his champion came to visit him one morning, he appeared, covered in shaving soap, to say : 'Wyndham, I won't embrace you but you know what I mean.'[24]

Towards Dr Jameson Wyndham was equally trusting and enthusiastic. 'First,' he told Sibell on March 1st 1896, after dining with the Doctor in London, 'let me say that Jameson is a most impressive and charming personality. Not, as I feared, from some of the pictures and from his action as one pieced it together, a fanatic or exalted enthusiast, but a kind, strong, frank, clever man, with wide-open clear eyes, nostrils of a race horse. His voice is always pleasant and controlled and, to put it shortly, I should say from what I see him to be and from what I know of all the facts, that he has the best right and the fullest power to go to sleep every night with a clear conscience, of every single person who has touched the business in England and Africa.'[25] Blunt found his cousin delighted with his own efforts after the committee of enquiry. Even though Rhodes had been condemned in the report, Chamberlain had later, in the House of Commons, gone out of his way to soften the blow. 'With regard to Chamberlain,' Blunt wrote, 'George admires him as the grandest specimen of the courageous, unscrupulous schemer our politics have ever seen. He says that Chamberlain was not an accomplice of the actual armed raid made by Jameson – though he certainly was in the political intrigue – and he [Chamberlain] would not deny it – against the independence of the Transvaal.'[26]

If Wyndham believed the raid to be 'dead and buried' he was mistaken. Its effects, both in England and South Africa, had been considerable. The jingoes had taken the Doctor and his associates to their hearts, as is exemplified by Alfred Austin's fearsome poem 'Jameson's Ride'. They wanted revenge, and noisily sought it. From afar, it seemed to Kruger and the Transvaal as if England was riddled with the spirit of the raiders. Accordingly, the Boers began to rearm, their confidence having received an immeasurable boost from the chaotic last attack on their borders. The situation was further changed by the arrival of a new British High Commissioner, the determined and formidable Sir Alfred Milner. Milner was an aggressive imperialist who had served under Cromer in Egypt. He regarded war as the only solution to the problem of the Transvaal, particularly after the February 1898 presidential election had led to Kruger's overwhelming victory, and looked upon imperial sentiment as an asset rather than an embarrassment.

In October 1898, George Wyndham received a letter marked 'private'. The writer estimated the year to be 1896; but the news was good enough. 'My dear Mr Wyndham,' it began. 'You will perhaps have observed in the newspapers that St John Broderick [misspelt: it should have been Brodrick] has accepted Curzon's place in the Foreign Office. After consultation with Lord Lansdowne and Arthur Balfour, I have little doubt that you would be the person whom the opinions of competent persons in the House, and of our side generally, would indicate as the fittest to succeed him, if you are disposed to accept the office. I have no doubt that you will fill it in a manner equally advantageous to the War Office and to the Unionist Party . . . Will you allow me to submit your name to the Queen? No re-election will be necessary.' It was signed 'Salisbury'.[27]

Thus, after nine years in Parliament, political office came to Wyndham. Sibell received a letter a few days later from St John Brodrick, the man whose place her husband was to take.

'I have no time,' he said, 'to write to George, dear Lady Grosvenor, and I think he knows all I feel. But in reply to your dear kind letter I must tell you what a joy it is – both from personal feeling, for I know my old post will be in the best hands – and from the public standpoint for he is far the ablest of those in or out of the government who could take it . . . I think it's a great compliment. He is the youngest man who has ever represented the W.O. in the House of Commons since Lord Hartington in 1865.'[28]

If activity was what the new under-secretary was after, his appointment could not have come at a better date. Initially, on account of the Fashoda incident in which the British regarded as 'an unfriendly act' the French penetration into the Nile Valley, war with a European power appeared even more likely than war in South Africa. In fact, diplomacy settled the matter and the French climbed down. But in October 1898, Blunt had recorded the militancy of the War Office's latest recruit. 'George,' he wrote, 'is in high spirits . . . Things look more and more war-like, as Russia seems to be backing France, and I suspect most of the Continental powers are against us . . . George says that the British fleet has its programme ready, and the French fleet would be shut up in their ports in a few days. He and the ultra-Jingo section of the party are all for war. He gets £1500 a year by his appointment.'[29]

Chapter 14
At the War Office

At this time, with Wyndham on the brink of his brief tenure of office, it might be asked what sort of politician, or what sort of man, this young Conservative romantic had become after passing through the several stages of a late-Victorian youth. Leaving the domestic calm and affections of a united family, he had stepped, almost immediately, into a happy marriage and the beginnings of a political career. In his twenties, George Wyndham was almost absurdly promising. But to be a young man of promise is not difficult, particularly if circumstances work as hard in one's favour as they appeared to be working here. His advantages came not only from his social prominence, but also from certain undeniably attractive personal attributes. Later these, so beguiling at an early age, began to take on an element of the grotesque as their possessor evolved from the charming, occasionally artless, youth into the tired garrulous middle-aged man, but in the 1890s they were still fresh enough to be effective.

Fluency and confidence, tempered with sufficient sensitivity to prevent a lapse into brashness, are undeniable assets to one who aspires to a career in public life. When accompanied by good looks their effect is further heightened. Charles Boyd wrote, after Wyndham's death in 1913: 'Twenty years ago George Wyndham's good looks were of a kind to take one's breath away. As he sat on his horse at a meet, or passed through a public place, people's eyes followed him . . .'[1] Sarah Bernhardt once said that he was the handsomest man she had ever seen. To the demanding eye of the young, his oratorical powers could be similarly impressive. In 1891, Lord Willoughby de Broke, then an Oxford undergraduate, was present at a dinner held jointly by the university's Chatham and Canning Clubs. He described himself as being dazzled by hearing George Wyndham for the first time'. At this dinner were some of the leading lights of the Conservative party in the House of Commons, such as Sir Stafford Northcote, Sir Michael Hicks Beach, and Arthur Smith-Barry. 'But,' Willoughby de Broke remembered, 'the things that stand out through all these years are the person and eloquence of George Wyndham. It is doubtful if he ever made a bad speech in his life; and when he was in his best manner he was very good indeed. He was then twenty-eight years of age, richly endowed with good looks, talent and charm . . . He illuminated the Tory cause with that graceful manner and happy phrase which made him one of the most attractive speakers in England.'[2]

Wyndham at twenty-eight was already a polished performer. His oratory, backed up by his literary sensibility, flowed with an ease that was rare, even in a veteran parliamentarian. Yet this ease did not give the impression of spontaneity, but rather of fluency, and this fluency could lead to a disturbing obfuscation. Often there seemed to be too much art and activity at the back of it. He was apt to qualify his statements to excess, smothering his message with a blanket of words, and taking too long to say too little. Sometimes the latter could lend to his speeches a gravity that, for his age, was both misplaced and even a little ridiculous. In conversation his gifts were displayed to a greater advantage, although here again he demonstrated a facility that could occasionally overawe less articulate listeners. In 1893, while staying at Petworth, he especially impressed his cousin Mary Wyndham who wrote in her diary: 'George . . . has been holding forth at great length tonight, both at and after dinner, as I believe he always loves to do. He is very clever and amusing, and it is interesting to hear his daring criticisms demolishing writers, magazines and other opinions right and left. Perhaps a little too sweeping for Papa. His language is wonderfully well chosen and eloquent, even in ordinary conversation.'[3]

There were those in politics who believed that, if allowed to go unchecked, this fluency must eventually count against him. On a platform outside the House of Commons it might be impressive, but within the more intimate confines of the chamber a laboured style, reeking of midnight oil, appeared artificial and rigid. Arthur Balfour, on being asked for advice after hearing one of his early speeches, said: 'My dear George, dilute, dilute, dilute.'[4] Wyndham was aware of his tendency to overcrowd his ideas into an aggressively ornate framework. 'Mark Napier,' he wrote to Sibbel on May 4th 1894, 'was very kind to me yesterday before my speech telling me (as they all do) that I must take lessons from an actor in elocution and adopt a more conversational and easy style. But it is not the want of knowledge and intention, only my nervousness and want of skill. I mean, however, to learn. Yesterday I was really better, but perhaps, a little over fluent and alliterative. *The Daily Graphic* and *Westminster* are accordingly down on me. "Fatal gift of fluency", "hear him but do not understand", "carefully balanced sentences", "pounded laboriously away".'[5] In 1893, however, Chamberlain, sitting next to Wyndham at lunch with the Londonderrys, offered other advice. 'He strongly recommended,' Sibell was told, 'preparation, and said that when he began he was ill for a month before speaking, could not eat or sleep or talk to his family but brooded alone and toiled over his speech point for point after making elaborate notes two or three times. Fired by this I have walked straight back, am at the desk and shall not leave it till I dine.'[6]

Chamberlain's advice did not conflict with Napier's. Preparation can shorten a speech as well as lengthen it, and it can also simplify the images and alliterations of an aggressively literary style. Lord Salisbury, when speaking of Wyndham, once remarked: 'I don't like poets';[7] and traditional Tories tended to be either stunned into vaguely uncomprehending admiration, like Willoughby de Broke, or moved to a typically English distrust of such oratorical ostentation. 'Damn that fellow,' one said to Lord Lee in the early 1900s while listening to Wyndham, 'he pirouettes like a dancing master.'[8] The trouble was that pirouetting, which was permissible, even attractive, in a youth of promise appeared exceedingly ungainly in a middle-aged Cabinet Minister.

With his fluent style, his urbane confidence (probably not as great as it seemed), his looks and his ease of manner, the young Wyndham must have appeared almost too good to be true. To be termed the best-dressed man in the House of Commons was not perhaps to receive the ultimate sartorial accolade, but to some this sobriquet epitomized Wyndham's manner and approach. His close connection with Arthur Balfour, another seemingly effete figure with an unnaturally intellectual outlook, earned him the nickname 'Miss Arthur'. The Press, quick as ever to jump upon the caricature rather than the man, would portray him as a handsome young guards officer with a rather distant expression on his face, and constantly referred to his society habits, friends and pleasures. This, naturally, rankled. In 1900 he wrote to Charles Boyd, after the newspapers had attacked the War Office and its ministers: 'The high society tack won't really wash. I never go into society. I fought in the Sudan. I have been a railway director for ten years. I plugged away at the Irish Office through all the scrimmage. I am plugging away now. You know that.'[9]

For Wyndham to say that he did not go into society was patently ridiculous. He enjoyed its conversation and delights as much as anybody. However he did not allow it to sap his industry, and the results of leading life at such a pace soon became evident. Whether attending parties, pursuing literature or the fox or politics all his energies were devoted to the enthusiasm of the moment. The result was occasional exhaustion and illness. In February 1893, at Petworth, Mary Wyndham saw evidence of this. 'He was frightfully tired,' she wrote to her cousin, 'and looks so careworn and old, more like fifty than twenty-nine.'[10] After all this, the reward of an under-secretaryship was especially gratifying, particularly as Wyndham had been disappointed at being passed over in 1895, when both Curzon and St John Brodrick were given office for the first time.

Yet the lack of success in 1895 was not only due to Wyndham's inexperience and Salisbury's dislike of poets. In 1893 he had had the courage to go against the dictates of his party to support a friend. Charles Gatty, an ex-curator of the Liverpool Museum and expert on early sacred music, stood as Home Rule candidate for West Dorset in 1892. The Home Rulers lost what had become a rather nasty campaign. Gatty, who had met Wyndham in literary circles and certain grand houses (for which he had a weakness) was accused by his Tory opponent of having been sacked from Charterhouse for homosexuality and promptly, after encouragement from Wyndham, brought an action of libel. Wyndham appeared as a witness in Gatty's favour and damages of £2500 were awarded. However the matter was complicated by the publication, shortly after the trial, in *Pulman's Weekly News* of flattering letters to Gatty's opponent from Lord Salisbury and Balfour. In September 1893 Wyndham told his wife that he believed that Balfour and all the senior Conservatives thought he had done the wrong thing in defending a Liberal; and in her diary for 1898 Marie Mallet, one of Queen Victoria's Maids of Honour, noted that because of the Gatty affair, 'I do not fancy from what Lord George Hamilton says, that the government are best pleased at having to place George Wyndham. It appears that he is the best hated man in the House of Commons . . .'[11] This was clearly an exaggeration, born of gossip; but his loyalty to a friend had cost Wyndham his place in certain Tory affections. Thus it was not an entirely unscarred politician who walked into the War Office in 1898. The surface gloss concealed, all too effectively, a nervous, intensely eager person of sensitivity, desperately anxious to improve himself, conscious of his own shortcomings and a victim of remorse.

Wilfrid Blunt believed that he had the measure of Milner, Britain's aggressive new High Commissioner in South Africa. 'Milner,' he wrote, 'was sent to Egypt ten years ago to convert English Liberal opinion to the plan of remaining on there instead of withdrawing the garrison, and having succeeded in that mission he has been sent to the Cape to convert English Liberal opinion to the idea of annexing the Transvaal.' Blunt believed that hostilities were imminent. 'Now,' he declared, 'there will certainly be war in South Africa. They have tried every kind of fraud to get their way, but old Kruger has been too astute for them, so they will try force.' The Colonial Secretary was depicted as the major villain. 'Chamberlain,' Blunt said, 'will not rest until he has Kruger's head on a charger . . . It will also be a beautiful exposure of our English sham philanthropy, if at the very moment the Peace Congress is sitting at the Hague, we flout its mediation and launch into an aggressive war. Anything better than the general handshaking of the great white thieves and their amicable division of the spoils.' He welcomed the move towards war which he thought would 'alleviate the condition of the only people there whose interests I really care for in the quarrel, namely the blacks'.[12] His view of the South African colonists coincided with that expressed by Milner in 1897 when he remarked that they were mostly 'slave-owners at heart, thinking that Natives are chattels with no rights, to be used, abused, taken on and made away with at pleasure'.[13]

The difference between them was that the new High Commissioner saw the only choice in South Africa as being between two rival sets of 'slave-owners', and acted accordingly. Towards the end of 1898 an English workman called Tom Edgar was shot and killed in Johannesburg by a Boer policeman. The

Uitlander population regarded the shooting as being entirely without justification, and demanded that the policeman be tried for murder. He was arrested, but on a charge of manslaughter, brought before a jury of Boers and acquitted. To make matters worse, at the end of the trial the judge saw fit to commend him for his actions. Foreign residents of the Transvaal were outraged, demonstrations followed – which the Boers put down with a savage ferocity – and a petition of over twenty-seven thousand signatures was got up by British subjects in the Transvaal and sent to Queen Victoria.

Milner strongly supported the *Uitlanders'* complaints, and in May 1899 the British government decided to take up the petition. Later in the month Milner met Kruger at Bloemfontein. The High Commissioner made little effort to come to any sort of compromise with the old Dutchman, and after five days the talks were called off, a telegram from Chamberlain urging their continuance and suggesting new negotiating ploys reaching Milner too late. Chamberlain continued to offer the olive branch, and the Cape Dutch also attempted to open up some kind of understanding with their Transvaal counterparts; but further attempts to secure peace foundered upon the obduracy of Kruger. Milner's superciliousness at Bloemfontein had done much to encourage this obduracy. On June 29th Wilfrid Blunt breakfasted with George Wyndham and Sibell, and letters from Sibell's eldest son Bendor (later Duke of Westminster) who was then serving on Milner's staff, were displayed. 'The letters,' Blunt wrote, 'were actually written during the conference, and contained sketches of old Krugers whom he described as very old and infirm, and also very sly. He talked of Kruger as "bluffing". He writes with a boy's enthusiasm for his chief, and seems to be enjoying himself greatly.'[14]

Kruger was not bluffing. The Boers saw a fight as the one way to escape from the clutches of a British South Africa. On September 27th the Orange Free State allied itself with the Transvaal and war was declared in October. Since the breakdown at Bloemfontein such a declaration had been virtually inevitable. In Britain the reaction was a strange mixture of ecstasy and relief. It is difficult in these days to imagine how, before the terrible slaughter of 1914-18, war could so easily be represented as a glorious crusade whose possible ending – the sacrifice of one's own life or of the lives of those whom one loved – was, in effect, its most ennobling feature. The outburst of national sentiment mirrored this, from the displays of bunting in Trafalgar Square to the ranting poetry of Kipling, Henley and Austin. On October 17th Blunt noted : 'Swinburne has published a ridiculous sonnet in favour of the war, and Kipling has also been in *The Times*.'[15] When Sir Redvers Buller left Southampton with the British troops he was given a rousing send off; and even the news of the first casualties did not dim the euphoria. After all the dead gave added lustre to the cause, by demonstrating that it was greater than their lives. 'So let us pray,' George Wyndham wrote to his mother on October 23rd, 'and be quietly cheerful in the thought that all these Englishmen are heroes.'[16]

Wyndham had believed to the last moment that there would be no war. On September 24th he was writing to his mother : 'I still think the chances are against war . . . Every day on which the Boers do not cross the border confirms my view. For now is their time and opportunity.'[17] But by October 6th he was resigned to the prospect. 'Well, darling,' he told her, 'we are giving our best for this Empire; and that is quite right and what we wish to do . . . Between you and me and the gatepost we mobilize on Monday. I trust all will go well. I know we have worked hard here for success. And I believe the Army is more efficient than at any time since Waterloo.'[18] On October 11th the Under-Secretary was equally optimistic. 'Well,' he declared, 'it has come and we are in "a state of war". Don't pay the slightest attention to alarmist rumours. We are all well enough ahead with our work.'[19]

In the light of history it appears rather ridiculous that the Under-Secretary at the War Office could be so woefully ill-informed as to misjudge entirely the timing of the outbreak of war and then, equally absurdly, to remark that an army upon which a series of humiliating defeats was about to be inflicted, was 'more efficient than at any time since Waterloo'. But Wyndham's attitude is understandable if one takes into account the condition of the military at the time. The intelligence department at the War Office was understaffed and inexpert; there was no general staff; and the contingency planning for a war in South Africa was non-existent. It was not realized that, until Buller's forces of 47,000 men arrived from England, the Boers outnumbered the British by nearly two to one. They knew the terrain; they would have help from the country people of Cape Province and the Natal border, who were almost all of Dutch extraction; and their Krupp artillery was far superior to the British guns. In fact, had the Boers made for Cape Town without delay in October instead of engaging in the time-consuming seiges of Kimberley, Ladysmith and Mafeking, they might well have forced the British to make terms with them as the new masters of South Africa.

George Wyndham's brother Guy was Brigade Major to three cavalry regiments in Natal, and by the end of October was locked up in Ladysmith with Sir George White and 14,000 men. On November 3rd his older brother wrote: 'How I wish I could be in Ladysmith with something to do! We all go on here preparing to hit as hard and as fast as we can until we establish an overwhelming superiority. But you are a long way off and it takes time to get the blows planted.'[20] On November 10th he offered further encouragement, saying: 'We are only thinking of relieving you and hope to do it in three weeks. What a horrid time you must be having under the bombardment. But no matter. You have saved Natal, and the nation will be for ever your debtor. All well here.'[21] The suggestion of relief in three weeks turned out to be wildly inaccurate, and provides another example of misplaced War Office optimism. Presumably it was imagined that Buller's arrival would entirely change the situation, whereas the Commander-in-Chief merely added to the humiliation. Fatally splitting his army corps of three divisions, he advanced, with one division under General Clery, towards Ladysmith and, on December 15th was defeated by Louis Botha at Colenso, completing a series of engagements known as Black Week in which his other two generals, Methuen and Gatacre, had been beaten at Magersfontein and Stormberg. On December 16th Wyndham wrote to his mother in a less euphoric tone, saying: 'We must acknowledge that Buller's failure is a disappointment. And we must all pull ourselves together and pull together. Our grandfathers had a much worse time of it. They must have felt bitterly disappointed when the Walcheren expedition failed.'[22]

The defeats were a terrible blow. The Cabinet acted quickly. Buller was relieved of his command and replaced by Lord Roberts, whose only son had been killed at Colenso, with Kitchener as the new commander's chief of staff. National pride was considerably deflated. The music-hall songs, previously so swaggering and self-confident, now jarred against the grim reality. Wilfrid Blunt noted one, written on December 7th 1899, called 'Kruger's Dinner Party' whose exhortations after Black Week, possessed more pathos than encouragement. It ended:

'Pretoria's a place we've often wanted for to see,
We'll be there!
The air with us, there is no doubt, will splendidly agree,
We'll be there!
Perhaps I may just mention, we are coming up in style,
And with the firm intention of remaining for a while;
Still, Uncle, don't you worry, for mother's paid the fare
We'll be there!

CHORUS:
So please you, Uncle Paul, see that there's enough for all.
There's fifty thousand Tommies on the way,
And somewhere in a bag they have got a little flag
To stick in the pudding on Christmas Day!'[23]

Indeed, as Blunt observed, several regiments did dine with
Kruger on Christmas Day, but as prisoners of war.

However, resolution soon took over from gloom. Queen
Victoria told Balfour, when he made a reference to the disas-
ters: 'Please understand that there is no one depressed in
this house; we are not interested in the possibilities of defeat;
they do not exist.'[24] Even in Egypt, where he was staying at
Sheykh Obeyd, Blunt was confronted with similar sentiments
from his own family. He was now prepared to sympathize
almost entirely with the Boers, believing that the war had
been forced upon them by a bellicose Chamberlain. He did not
appear to take into account Kruger's dream of a United South
Africa under the Dutch, and had little or no sympathy for the
Uitlanders whom he saw as a collection of crude profiteering
businessmen. Of a guest, who accepted the British case, he
remarked, 'To me it is incredible how any reasonable creature
should believe such trash.' Yet even Lady Anne doubted the
wisdom of her husband's approach. 'Today,' he recorded, 'when
I say, "Now we ought to make peace with the Boers" they are
all against me. Even Anne thinks that the rights of the blood
feud forbid that. Yet what nonsense!'[25]

As a counterblast to the jingoistic verses of Kipling and
Austin Blunt had produced a poetic diatribe against imperialism
entitled 'Satan Absolved'. The idea for this had come from
Herbert Spencer, who had originally suggested that a poem
should demonstrate that Satan's original rebellion 'has been
less flagitious than that of man', having not, like men, 'professed to worship the Christian God while perpetually worshipping the pagan gods', sacrificing 'with zeal to Thor and Odin
while nominally sacrificing to Jehova'. Blunt did not entirely

abide by Spencer's original conception. He made the basis of
Satan's case for his own absolution the behaviour of the
colonizing races towards those whom they colonized. Spencer
was disappointed that the poet had not stuck to his ideas,
yet admitted that the work had power. But the public reaction,
with jingoistic fervour at its height, was not favourable, and,
as the war began to go against the British forces, the critics
became more forceful. When Satan spoke, in ringing tones,
of:

'The ignoble shouting crowds, the prophets of their Press,
Pouring their daily flood of bald self-righteousness,
Their poets who write big of the "White Burden" – Trash!
The White Man's Burden, Lord, is the burden of his cash.'

he was striking home at what Blunt believed to be the ludicrously hysterical imperialism of the time.

At the War Office the search for more reinforcements, in
the form of yeomanry, militia and volunteers – got under
way in earnest. George Wyndham played his part with typical
gusto. 'The "Imperial Yeomanry",' he told his father on
December 20th, 'is my child. I invented it after lunch on
Sunday and it is already in fine bantling. May it live and
prosper.'[26] Naturally the work was hard, but with this extra
labour came a new sense of contentment. 'I am wonderfully
well,' Wyndham told his mother in December 27th, 'less tired
every day. Things come easy to me that used to be difficult.
I sleep like a top eight hours a night and take on committees
and long memoranda without any previous nervousness . . .'[27]
He had no doubt of the value and importance of his work.
'Buller,' he told Guy on December 30th, 'has asked for eight
thousand Mounted Infantry. Phew! But we mean to do it.
We are working through the Yeomanry, using the Colonels
and depots as recruiting and drill centres. The men are coming
in . . .'[28]

On January 6th the Boers tried to storm Ladysmith and were

beaten off, losing a large number of men; but on January 24th Buller and General Warren, once more attempting to relieve the town, had a serious reverse at Spion Kop, losing over a thousand men. They were forced to retreat, and George Wyndham wrote to Guy : 'It is disappointing . . . Take great care of yourself whatever happens.'[29] Blunt, on the other hand, was pleased. General Warren he particularly disliked as he remembered him from the days of Tel-el-Kebir. He sent £50 to the 'Stop the War Committee', although reluctantly, as he believed that 'if the war goes on another six months it may really smash up the British Empire'.[30]

In the middle of these uncertainties George Wyndham went down to Osborne to speak to Queen Victoria about the situation in South Africa. The Queen was resolute but upset. She would often break down and cry over the long lists of casualties. Possessing no knowledge of the local conditions, she could not understand why the British Army was proving incapable of supplying the one great victory which she believed was all that was necessary to win the war. Wyndham's visit was a success. 'I was afraid,' Sir Frederick Ponsonby, the Queen's assistant private secretary, wrote, 'that his literary studies might have made him priggish, and that now he was Under-Secretary for War he would be too great a man to speak to; but I was most agreeably surprised to find that he was a delightful human being and full of humour.'[31] The Queen too, despite her dissatisfaction, 'was much pleased with him and thought him charming'. A hint of how immersed Wyndham had become in his new activities is given by Ponsonby's description of their conversation later that night in Wyndham's bedroom, during which the Under-Secretary apparently 'listened attentively to all the questions I asked'. However he seemed to have developed already the politician's tendency to lecture rather than converse, for Ponsonby records how 'he then addressed me as if a question had been asked in the House of Commons, and having all his facts and figures at his fingers' ends, he more than answered the questions'. Yet both found themselves so intrigued that it was not until 1.30 that they parted.

After such a string of defeats there was a good deal of criticism of the government's handling of the campaign. On January 6th Wyndham wrote to his brother: 'The *Daily Mail* is attacking the Government in a violent and ignorant manner and the Opposition will go for us when the House meets. That, I regret to say will probably be on February 1st. I think I have a pretty good case. Anyway, I am keeping low like a Boer and shall not fire until they come into the open.'[32] On January 26th he grimly observed: 'The House meets on Thursday. I shall have hard work.'[33] Lord Lansdowne, the Minister, was in the Lords, so Wyndham was the senior representative of his department in the House of Commons. The Liberals, divided by the war into the Liberal Imperialists, among whom were Rosebery and Asquith, who supported it and the pro-Boers, like Morley and Lloyd George, who did not, had produced an amendment to the Address deploring 'the want of knowledge, foresight and judgment of Her Majesty's Ministers in preparation for the war now proceeding'. It was Wyndham's unenviable duty to speak in defence of his party.

He rose to the occasion and made the greatest speech of his political life. Having acquired, through the past months of hard work, an extraordinarily comprehensive knowledge of the country's state of military preparedness he dazzled his opponents with his mastery of the subject. If, he said, mistakes had been made they were now the mistakes of the past. Within two or three weeks there would be 180,000 men in South Africa, equipped on a level with any force in the world. Before disposing of the technical minutiae, he raised the whole debate on to a different plane by making a fervent appeal to patriotic sentiment, regardless of party disagreements. 'I never for one moment,' he said, 'believed that such an attack would be delivered from such a quarter at such a time. What is the time? We are in the midst of the most anxious stage of a war which is filling the breasts of our countrymen with poignant emotion, and which is taxing even their splendid qualities of stoical endurance. That is the time. What is the quarter? This attack is delivered by the Right Hon Gentlemen on the Front Opposition Bench, who, next to the Government of the day, are under the most onerous obligations to the whole country to avoid any course which may embarrass our army – any course which may add to the anxiety only too naturally felt by those who watch the efforts of our brave soldiers upon the field.'[34]

The speech did much to promote Wyndham's career. Its fame reached out far beyond the boundaries of Parliament. At Sheykh Obeyd Blunt noted: 'George Wyndham has made a very able speech in defence of the War Office and his political fortune is made. I am glad of this, though his principles in politics have been up to now abominable.' While disapproving of his cause, Blunt could not help admiring his cousin's tactics. 'He was wise enough,' the diarist wrote, 'to confine his speech strictly to the War Office, and did not attempt to explain the policy of the war: being a subordinate of very short standing in the Government he will not be held responsible, and people will only see in him what they most appreciate, a very clever parliamentarian defending a bad party cause in the best possible way.'[35]

Wyndham's success was not the only heartening news for the government. Lord Roberts appeared to have transformed the face of the war. Kimberley and Ladysmith were relieved in February, and on March 13th he entered Bloemfontein. Despite setbacks he was in Johannesburg by May 31st, Mafeking having been relieved on May 17th after two hundred and seventeen days' siege. On June 5th Roberts was in Pretoria, liberating three thousand British prisoners of war. The end was thought to be only a matter of months away. Parliament was dissolved on September 25th and a General Election followed at once. On August 30th George Wyndham wrote to his mother: 'I still think that the war will be practically over by

September 26th.'[36] In fact the Boers' guerilla campaign had hardly begun.

Wyndham was exhausted. In the House of Commons he was constantly on his feet, and the administrative work was proving to be equally hard. 'The daily strain,' he wrote in May, '. . . has given me such a seven months at the gallop as I trust never to endure again.'[37] The 'Khaki' election was, at Chamberlain's instigation, a blatant attempt to make use of the popular emotion generated by the recent run of South African successes. In fact it changed the position of the two parties very little, recovering only three seats for the Tories. A government reshuffle followed. Lord Salisbury, now almost seventy-two, left the Foreign Office, which he had held jointly with the premiership, and appointed Lord Lansdowne as his successor. This left the War Office vacant; and its Under-Secretary wondered if he might not become its minister. He was to be disappointed. The job was given to St John Brodrick, and Wyndham was promoted to be Chief Secretary for Ireland, without a seat in the Cabinet. Thus in November he returned to the forbidding challenges of Dublin Castle. Blunt wrote of the appointment : 'I am glad of it as a step in his ambition, but it is a thankless task, if he thinks to reconcile Ireland to English rule.'[38]

Chapter 15
The Chief Secretary

The nineteenth century closed unhappily for Wilfrid Blunt. He saw Chamberlain and the new aggressive imperialism as the negation of all that he had stood for. He also felt the encroachment of old age, and wondered if he should despair of there ever being any change for the better in the world. His health, never entirely reliable since one of his lungs had collapsed in 1873, was becoming an almost constant source of pain and worry. On November 25th, he wrote gloomily in his diary : 'I am closing my accounts of all kinds for the year, and shut up this journal in no sanguine mood of having anything happier to relate in the diaries of another year. The only thing I love is my cat, and I am obliged, alas! to leave it behind.'[1]

This melancholy was further increased by the loss of friends and valued acquaintances. Lytton's death had been a sad blow; and in 1896 William Morris, whom Blunt had come to regard as 'the most wonderful man I have known', had also died. Blunt and Morris had not been particularly close. 'He never,' Blunt noted, 'I am sure, returned the affection I gave him,' and the diarist felt that Morris would not, if he thought the other had not seen him, 'have crossed the street to speak to me'.[2] Yet despite this Blunt had come to admire immensely Morris's dedication to his work and his lack of worldly ambition.

On December 10th 1900 he recorded the death of Oscar Wilde, again not a great friend but an admired acquaintance.

Both Morris and Wilde, in their different ways, had possessed the power to dazzle Blunt, the one with his integrity and dedication, the other with his conversational powers. Wilde, he believed, was 'without exception the most brilliant talker I have ever come across, the most ready, the most witty, the most audacious. Nobody could pretend to outshine him, or even to shine at all in his company.'[3] Morris and Wilde were two of the few figures of whom the persistent rebel was in awe, and their deaths affected him for this reason.

The passing of friends was not the only hardship of these years. In 1900, while in Egypt, Blunt decided, in the company of his new secretary Sydney Cockerell, his nurse Miss Lawrence and two Arabs, to sail to Tor on the Khedival steamer *Chibine*, in order to visit Mount Sinai. On March 8th they joined the ship at Suez, to find themselves closeted with three hundred and fifty Moslem pilgrims who were bound for Mecca. Disaster came quickly. On the first night the *Chibine* struck a coral reef; and could not move. After a day the situation became desperate, with the wind rising and waves crashing over the deck. One man was drowned while attempting to leave in a lifeboat, thus bringing their total of these craft down to three. In his cabin, to the sound of the pilgrims praying, Blunt read Tolstoy's *Resurrection*, hardly a cheering book, and pondered grimly upon the likelihood of death. He felt unafraid of whatever might come after this life, but fearful of the physical agonies that must accompany drowning or being dashed to pieces on the reef.

Two ships were sighted, but they took no notice of the *Chibine*'s signals. As the pilgrims turned to the Koran, so Blunt sought solace in the gospels, returning, in this moment of desperation, to the old comforts of his childhood faith. Eventually, during the fourth day on the reef, the naval gunboat, H. M. S. *Hebe*, was sighted, steaming to their rescue. It was just in time, for water had almost run out and practically the only liquid available was soda-water which the stewards were selling to the richer passengers at exorbitant prices.

Blunt's party had made themselves popular by giving out oranges which they had providentially brought with them, and he himself had taken morphia to assuage his thirst and hunger.

Chastened by this experience, Blunt made it his business to see that the chaotic manner in which pilgrims were transported from Egypt was investigated. He wrote an account of the wreck for *The Times* and urged Cromer to take action. New regulations were issued with regard to pilgrim traffic in the Red Sea, and they made provisions for greater security and safety.

On December 31st 1899 he found, despite his personal melancholy, the political situation moderately pleasing. 'The last year,' he noted, 'of the 1800s ends disastrously for England, or rather for the British Empire. For England can only gain by the break up of that imposture. I think now there really is some chance of a consummation, for we are sending the whole of our armed force into South Africa, where it is likely to become engulfed, and we have got the whole sentiment of the world, civilized and uncivilized, against us.'[4] Certainly, at this time, Britain was paying a price for Lord Salisbury's policy of 'splendid isolation'. The war in South Africa found international opinion arraigned against her.

On December 31st 1900, with the Boers supposedly near to surrender, Blunt was less sangine. In Egypt, however, he was, as always, philosophical and moderately content. 'I bid goodbye,' he wrote, 'to the old century [the Moslem century ended a year after the Western], may it rest in peace as it has lived in war. Of the new century I prophesy nothing except that it will see the decline of the British Empire. Other worse Empires will rise perhaps in its place, but I shall not live to see the day. It all seems to matter very little here in Egypt, with the Pyramids watching us as they watched Joseph, when, as a young man four thousand years ago, perhaps in this very garden, he walked and gazed at the sunset behind them, wondering about the future just as I did this evening. And so, poor wicked nineteenth century, farewell!'[5]

At the end of 1900 George Wyndham could consider himself to be, with his acceptance of the Irish Secretaryship, one of the brightest Conservative stars of his generation. 'I see,' the young Winston Churchill wrote to him in November 1900, 'it is decided that you go to Ireland. I am sorry on public grounds, for you could have carried some real measure of reform at the War Office, and I fear such will not be carried now. For your sake it is perhaps the best thing. You will be in the front line again and with regard to the War Office, remember the lines:

> "Who lay the world's false idols low
> Oft perish in the overthrow."

. . . I am going to stake my energy in writing a great book – something historical – will you suggest me a subject or character? Please advise me on any matter you think fitting whether of taste or tactics.'[6]

But in a sense Churchill was wrong about Wyndham's new job taking him 'into the front line again'. The Irish Office could make a man's reputation, as it made Arthur Balfour's, but it had also broken many of Wyndham's predecessors. This was not only because of the rough ways of Irish agitation. While he was in Dublin, where he was bound to spend half the year, the Chief Secretary was out of touch with day-to-day manoeuvrings and developments at Westminster. During the Boer war Wyndham might write to his brother: 'Arthur Balfour, Lansdowne and self lunch and dine together most days and keep at it';[7] but such intimate contact with his political colleagues was less easily attained when he was cut off in Dublin. Even the connection with Balfour weakened. 'Up to the time,' J. S. Saunders, Balfour's private secretary, wrote, 'of his appointment as Chief Secretary there was no one who was so intimate in political confidence with the First Lord – no one upon whom Balfour relied more. But, when Wyndham received the Irish appointment, these close relations necessarily ceased, and he played no part of importance in the Inner Cabinet.'[8] This was even more true under Salisbury, when the Lord-Lieutenant, Lord Cadogan, spoke on Irish affairs in the Cabinet – an arrangement with which Wyndham was to become far from satisfied. However it ended in 1901, with Salisbury's departure, when Balfour installed Lord Dudley as the Viceroy and brought his Chief Secretary into the Cabinet in place of Cadogan.

Wyndham appeared to have no illusions as to the difficulty of his task. 'I am,' he wrote to his sister Madeline from the Chief Secretary's Lodge on November 25th 1900, 'very happy here. Not that I hope to succeed personally. A man who expected personal success in Ireland would be ripe for Hanwell.'[9] But, conscious of his Irish ancestry, he became enthralled in his new position. With this came a typical eruption of romanticism. 'I feel,' he told Madeline, 'that I was destined to come here. My solitary trump is Mama. Dear old things remember dancing with her. And everyone in the country says "at any rate his mother was born in Ireland". It is a land of sorcery; false, but so fair that the adventurer willingly dives beneath the waters to reach the enchanted palace of the Princess Arianrhod. This means that I swim in "Celtic twilight", but through the green and golden witchery comes the piercing appeal of grinding and hopeless poverty. I walk like the mermaid in Andersen on pointed knives.'[10]

His allusion to his path of 'pointed knives' was, in 1900, an apt one. During the 1890s it had seemed as if Ireland was settling down at last. Parnell's fall had disastrously divided the Nationalists and the Conservative policy of killing Home Rule by kindness appeared to be working. Agricultural prices recovered from their low level of the late 1880s. In 1896 the

Chief Secretary, Gerald Balfour, (Arthur's brother) had introduced another land Act which abolished the less attractive provisions of his brother's measure of 1891. This was meant to encourage further purchase, but it soon became obvious that the old idea of payment in government stock was not proving sufficiently attractive. Although the terms, since 1885, had been favourable to the tenant, he was still frightened by their complexity, and the landlord, particularly if unencumbered by a mortgage and not battered by an agricultural depression, clearly needed additional inducement to sell.

Gerald Balfour's Irish Local Government Act of 1898 was more effective. Irish local government was reconstructed on the British model, with elected County Councils. This, at a stroke, caused a shift in power away from the landlords and Protestant ascendancy class to the Roman Catholics and Nationalists who, because of their greater numbers, came to dominate the new apparatus. Both sides seemed satisfied. Indeed at this time there was a new spirit of unity abroad in Ireland, bringing moderates of both Nationalist and Unionist persuasions together over such non-controversial matters as agricultural improvement. Yet, as was so often the case in Irish affairs, the picture was far from clear. The coming-together of certain moderates and their resulting proposals appeared encouraging to the Irish Office, as did Parnell's legacy of a divided parliamentary party; but, in 1898, with William O'Brien's formation of the United Irish League, agrarian disorder came again to the countryside.

At first the League merely called for the redistribution of land. Then it came to demand that landlords should be entirely bought out by means of compulsory purchase. The League grew fast. In June 1899 there were 33,000 members; in June 1900, 63,000; and in August 1901, 100,000. Its tactics were not so rough as those that had been employed by the Land League or the Plan of Campaign, although boycotting and intimidation were used. The British government, and George Wyndham, met it with coercion. By 1902 half Ireland was proclaimed and from 1901 to 1902, eleven sitting Irish Members of Parliament were imprisoned. One of the consequences of this was that the Irish parliamentary party united under the leadership of John Redmond. Another was the dealing of a hard blow to the new moderation. When the moderate Sir Horace Plunkett, who had lost his seat in Dublin to another Unionist in 1900, pressed ahead with his plans for agricultural co-operation he was met with a resurgence of defiance. An inhabitant of Rathkeale exemplified this when, apprised of the possibility of a co-operative creamery starting in his town, he remarked: 'Rathkeale is a Nationalist town – Nationalist to the backbone – and every pound of butter made in this creamery must be made upon Nationalist principles or it shan't be made at all.'[11]

Wyndham was a most reluctant coercionist. 'He is,' wrote Blunt after speaking to his cousin in January 1902, 'far more in sympathy with the Nationalists than with the Castle party which he despises for its sycophancy or the Ulster Protestants whom he dislikes for their sour bigotry. His own people, however, are constantly worrying him to coerce, and he has been obliged to make a show of doing something in that way though most unwillingly. He told me he had quite come to agree with me that there was no possibility of doing anything of real good in Ireland under present conditions and the less done by a Chief Secretary, the less the harm.'[12] Some of the Nationalists, however, had already become suspicious of the Chief Secretary. In June Blunt went to see John Dillon and noted: 'He is rather sceptical of George Wyndham's Nationalist sympathies, and says that he is putting the Coercion Act in force more vigorously in some ways than Arthur Balfour did formerly.'[13]

In the House of Commons Wyndham encountered, particularly within his own party, a new attitude towards Ireland – one of fatigue and disdain. Wyndham himself had been angered by the Irish Nationalist party's opposition to the

South African war, but now that he was at the Irish Office he wished to see proper attention given to Irish problems. 'Nobody,' he told Sibell, 'thinks of Ireland; yet the problem, the old problem, is here in a new shape. The three old forces in Ireland – Agrarian, Priestly and Physical Force – are all revived and in full swing but luckily disunited; each playing for its own hand. And the new parliamentary party is angling for funds from each of them. It is a complicated and most interesting conundrum.'[14]

In a speech at Bradford on October 24th 1901 Wyndham stated publicly the aims of his Irish policy; and the spirit of Arthur Balfour clearly loomed behind them. 'The policy,' he declared, 'of the Government, and especially of Lord Cadogan and myself in Ireland, is in absolute consonance and harmony with the policy of the Unionist administration in which Mr Arthur Balfour was Chief Secretary. The Government now, as then, are bent upon two objects . . . The first of these objects is the suppression of agrarian crime, of intimidation, and the protection of liberty. That is a matter of immediate, of urgent, of constant obligation. The second object – the enlarging of opportunities for the Irish people – is a goal to be approached whenever and wherever advance can be made without prejudice to the successful accomplishment of the first object.'[15]

His ancestry made him doubly keen to succeed. He believed that it gave him a unique insight into the character of those whom he had been appointed to govern. 'In this country,' he told his sister Madeline, 'you must never be tired and never in a hurry. You must listen and laugh with everyone and master the land acts and agricultural returns in stolen moments.'[16] He tackled the administration in the same spirit of optimism. The hours of work were often long, although no longer than they had been at the War Office. In July 1901 he wrote to Sibell from the Irish Office in London: 'I am forging ahead now, through arrears of work: worked with Hanson from 11 a.m. to 1 a.m. this morning, dining together at the House. As a result I woke at five today. But feel very fresh all the same and am determined to drive things through . . .'[17]

Philip Hanson, Wyndham's private secretary, has left a genial impression of how the Chief Secretary could occasionally find his routine work a little wearing. 'In every office,' Hanson remarks, 'there is this miscellaneous mass of work, consisting of numerous questions, some important and all requiring settlement in one way or other, but uninteresting because they come up as detached fragments of subjects with which there is no opportunity and perhaps no need to deal as wholes. The Chief's attitude towards this sort of thing was amusing; he did the work, when it was put before him, with an air of half-humorous melancholy, as one making concessions to the unreasonable prejudices of a friend . . . The Chief was accustomed to work with me at the special things in which he was interested – Land Purchase, the Congested Districts, Harbours, etcetera. One day at the Castle we had been at these things for some hours, and the Chief said it was time to go home. I said : "Dowdall has got a lot of papers here which he has been going through, and I think he could get a good many of them settled with you in a short time; will you take them before you go?" "Certainly," said the Chief, with an air of magnanimity; 'I think it's only fair." '[18]

One grave disadvantage of Wyndham's administrative style was his old fault – that of verbosity. What frightened some was not so much the amount of time that he took to make a point, but rather the difficulty of discovering, amongst the thicket of words, exactly what the point might be. 'He used,' Sir Henry Robinson said, 'to frighten me sometimes, when I went to see him about very ordinary matters of Local Government policy by speaking so incomprehensibly that I thought I had got a migraine, to which I have always been rather subject, as I had been quite unable to take in what he said.'[19] Robinson gives another example, told to him by a priest, of his master's tendency to obfuscate the issue. Wyndham went to Belmullet and, while there, agreed to speak about the railway to a deputation who were demanding that it should be brought to them. As he stood up in his carriage, the crowd were apparently immensely impressed with his appearance. 'Oh,' the priest told Sir Henry, 'a grand, lovely man he was, with black hair swep' off his forehead an' his tall figure an' his broad shoulders, with the little slim waist on him an' the glory of the face he had, an' all the girls were claspin' their hands and cryin' out for the love of him so they were.' Wyndham drove off to cheers; but afterwards the good humour ceased. 'Some of us,' the priest related, 'said he'd given us the railway, an' more of us said he had not.' Eventually the issue led to a fight between the two different schools of thought, and the police had to be called to calm them down. Later the same priest, while visiting a cousin in Glasgow, chanced to hear the Chief Secretary, as Rector of the University, lecturing the students on 'The Development of the State', and claimed that the lecture was exactly the same as the oration that had been delivered at Belmullet.[20]

It was not surprising that he felt some strain. The South African war, thought only a few months before to be virtually over, was not going well. The Boers' guerilla operations were proving remarkably successful; and these successes were an embarrassment to the government of which he was a member. Other departments appeared to have little time for his Irish policy and his ambition to produce a comprehensive land bill. 'I am,' he told his mother in November, 'having a hard time with the Treasury and the Cabinet. I want a holiday badly.'[21] He felt hampered by the fact that to reach the Cabinet he had to go through Lord Cadogan. Cadogan was thought by some to owe his position to his wealth rather than his ability. Wyndham appeared to echo this opinion. 'My spirits sink,' he told Balfour on September 20th, 'in the face of eight sheets received today from Cadogan. I would gladly devote days to talking to him if I ever supposed he understood what I am saying. But I know that he does not, and I have reason to fear that, with the best will in the world, he misrepresents my views to others.'[22]

On July 11th Wyndham wrote to Sibell: 'Absolutely secret. Lord S. [Salisbury] resigned yesterday. Arthur is engaged on forming a government. Not a word!'[23] He must have known that this augured well for him. Salisbury had never found Wyndham a particularly alluring figure, being unappreciative of his rather flamboyant charm, whereas Balfour was his old friend and mentor. Wyndham admired the new Prime Minister without reservation, reporting to Sibell on July 14th: 'Arthur spoke at the Party meeting with wonderful simplicity and perfect taste. He has won more affection than any party leader.'[24] The reward was forthcoming. Joseph Chamberlain, on urging Balfour to put fresh blood into the somewhat tired administration, was told: 'The first question I ask myself is: What men are there who, if introduced into the Cabinet, would add to its distinction and efficiency? There really are only two – Austen and George Wyndham, both of them in their respective ways quite first rate . . .'[25]

Austen Chamberlain came into the Cabinet as Postmaster-General and Lord Cadogan resigned the Irish Lord-Lieutenancy – being replaced by Lord Dudley – and gave up his Cabinet post to George Wyndham. Lord Lansdowne, Arthur Balfour's Foreign Secretary, was particularly interested in Ireland. In 1880, at the time of the first wave of land agitation, his estates were, after those of the Conynghams, the largest in that country, consisting of 121,349 acres valued at £34,342 a year. He was one of the Nationalists' chief targets although, in fact, his land was among the best administered in Ireland. Lansdowne was an exceptionally conscientious man who had entered politics in the patrician spirit of service rather than to pursue personal ambitions. With so great a stake in Ireland, he felt it was his duty to seek, as best he could, some practical method of calming the Irish uproar. As a landlord he recognized the landlords' claim for what they regarded as a fair deal over land purchase; but he had sufficient prescience to be able to understand the emotive force of Nationalism. Therefore when George Wyndham sought his advice as to who might be the most suitable candidate to succeed his departing permanent under-secretary, Sir David Harrel, Lansdowne went to great pains to draw on his experience as a holder of four great offices of state (the Governor-Generalship of Canada, the Vice-royalty of India, the War Office and the Foreign Office) in order to assist his former Under-Secretary.

One of Wyndham's candidates was Sir Antony MacDonnell, 'the Bengal Tiger', a brilliant Indian administrator who, as Lieutenant-Governor of the North West Provinces and Oudh and, latterly, a member of the Council of the Secretary of State for India, had risen to the top of the formidable Indian Civil Service. He was an Irishman, born in County Mayo, the son of a Roman Catholic landowner, in 1844 and educated at the Roman Catholic College, Summerhill, Athlone and Queen's College, Galway. A dominant figure, of medium height and with a heavy moustache, he had, over the years, become something of a martinet. William O'Brien, on meeting him, observed that he 'suggested a resemblance to an Indian curry such as they serve in all the pride of its four courses at the Gollfaas Hotel in Colombo to wayfarers from the mail-boats – a dish of startling richness and variety, but of a distinctly peppery flavour . . . Even in two or three not too lengthy interviews it was easy to see traces of the imperious temper of one who had ruled over more settled millions than the dynasty of the Moguls . . .'[26] But of Sir Antony's ability there could not be any doubt.

In Ireland, however, ability was not enough. When Wyndham mentioned MacDonnell's name to Arthur Balfour in August, the Prime Minister said that he did not question Sir Antony's administrative qualifications, but had heard, with alarm, that he was sympathetic towards Home Rule. Balfour advised his Chief Secretary to consult Lansdowne. Lansdowne himself saw MacDonnell in September and reported the result to Wyndham. 'He refused,' wrote the Foreign Secretary, 'to join the H[ome] R[ule] party, altho' they offered him a seat. He considers an Irish Parliament out of the question, and objects to the tactics which have led to the obstruction of useful measures in the hope that such obstruction would eventually bring about H. Rule . . . But he thinks something of the nature of a "convention" for the transaction of purely local business might in time be permitted . . .'[27] Wyndham saw MacDonnell's idea of a 'convention' as insufficient basis for his disqualification for the post.

On September 22nd MacDonnell wrote to Wyndham, after meeting him in Dublin, putting on record that he was an Irishman, a Liberal, a Roman Catholic and opposed to coercion. Nevertheless he saw the possibility of his accepting the Under-Secretaryship under certain conditions which, in effect, allowed him considerably greater latitude than was usually granted to a civil servant. 'I should be willing,' he told the Chief Secretary, 'to take office under you, on this condition – that I am given adequate opportunities of influencing the action and policy of Irish Government, and (subject of course to your control) am allowed freedom of action within the law. My chief aims would be the maintenance of order; assisting you in the solution of the land question on the basis of voluntary sale, and where sale fails to operate on the basis of paying rents on a self-acting principle, excluding local enquiries; the co-ordination, direction and control of Boards and other administrative agencies; the settlement of the Education question in the general spirit of Mr Balfour's views; and administrative conciliation. My best friends tell me that I delude myself. Still I am willing to try, under the colours and conditions I have described. It is for you to decide whether the trial is worth making.'[28]

Wyndham decided with customary speed. He accepted MacDonnell's offer in a letter of September 25th. Balfour's original misgivings had been overcome by Wyndham's enthusiasm and his respect for Lansdowne. He was afterwards to regret his decision.

Chapter 16
The Land Act

On January 23rd 1901, a few months after George Wyndham had gone to the Irish Office, Wilfrid Blunt, watching the foxes play in the garden at Sheykh Obeyd, received the news of Queen Victoria's death. Blunt had never seen himself as a great Victorian. Unlike Wyndham, who had written of his delight at being appointed to the War Office, in 1898 'because I have set my heart on being a minister of Victoria',[1] he felt no emotional link with that seemingly ineluctable sovereign. Indeed, he was proud of being unaffected by monarchy, and the mystique that surrounded it, whereas the more conventional Wyndham venerated the idea of the Crown and its supporting hierarchy, seeing behind these an aspect of history whose tradition he found irresistible. 'You,' he wrote to Sibell in 1889, after a service for the Cheshire Yeomanry, which the Duke of Westminster commanded and of which Wyndham was a member, in Chester Cathedral, 'would have enjoyed the service. It was really affecting. The whole scene belonged completely to the older England that is passing away. A feudal force, serving by tenure under the Duke, wearing his star and listening in a shadowy Cathedral to a sermon breathing the doctrine of "Divine Right" in all temporal and ecclesiastical offices, made a strange and romantic scene.'[2]

Blunt clearly felt there was no 'Divine Right' attached to the dead Victoria. 'As to Her Majesty personally,' he wrote, 'one does not like to say all one thinks even in one's journal. By all I have ever heard of her she was in her old age a dignified but rather commonplace good soul, like many of our dowagers, narrow-minded in her view of things, without taste in art or literature, fond of money, having a certain industry and business capacity in politics, but easily flattered and expecting to be flattered, quite convinced of her own providential position in the world and always ready to do anything to extend and augment it.'[3] On Edward VII he was equally candid, declaring that : 'he has certain good qualities of amiability and a Philistine tolerance of other people's sins which endear him to rich and poor, from archbishops down to turf bookmakers, and the man in the street. He will make an excellent King for twentieth-century England.'[4]

The rebel was soon involved in conflict with the new King's government. In July, while still in England, Blunt had received news that some English officers from the Cairo garrison had broken into the garden at Sheykh Obeyd with their hounds and chased the partially tamed foxes that afforded its owner so much pleasure. The servants had resisted them and in consequence had been arrested. Instantly Blunt telegraphed that he was responsible and went up to the Foreign Office in London to lodge a complaint. From Egypt Cecil Spring-Rice, in a letter to his brother Stephen, gives the official side of the story, also showing how the British authorities in Egypt regarded their old opponent. 'We have,' he wrote, 'a great difficulty with that hero of freedom, Wilfrid Blunt. He appears to have very autocratic views about the right of property and has been in the habit of falling on trespassers and incarcerating and beating them. His Arab servants follow his example. It appears that a few British officers were out hunting the fox and trespassed on to Blunt's property. They were fallen on by W.B.'s servants and severely handled. The servants were prosecuted and punished with considerable imprisonment. W. Blunt telegraphs that he is responsible, which is true. In defence the servants urged that they had seen their master "beat trespassers till the blood ran down their backs"! Isn't this rather a queer aspect of the bird of freedom? I wonder what exactly he will say for himself.'[5]

Blunt had plenty to say for himself. He wrote to Lord Lansdowne, the Foreign Secretary, and to several newspapers. He arranged for questions to be asked in Parliament, and on reaching Egypt in the winter spent a considerable amount of time in Cairo unravelling the case. What particularly annoyed him was that the servants, on being released from prison, bore marks of physical maltreatment, and that his demand for a court martial for the officers had been refused. Lansdowne would not put the results of Blunt's investigations before Parliament, so the evidence was put to use as a 'bomb' against Cromer and his Egyptian policies. This exploded in May 1902, and pleased its manufacturer. Most newspapers gave it good coverage, with the exception of *The Times* and the *Telegraph*, and he believed 'it could hardly have made a bigger noise'. The Foreign Office refused to publish his correspondence with Lansdowne, and Edward VII's illness captured the public's attention. 'The case,' Blunt remarked, 'was of importance, not so much in itself as from the demonstration it gave of the unscrupulous methods resorted to by our diplomacy at Cairo to hide its tampering with the Law Courts and whitewash the misdeeds of the Army of occupation.'[6]

The winter of 1902-3 was spent in Egypt. Then on March 28th 1903 Blunt returned to London, to find an almost universal topic of conversation amongst his friends. He had received a foretaste of this from an English newspaper which had contained a report of the introduction in Parliament of a pioneering Irish land bill. 'I had,' he observed, 'hoped to be in time for it, for it is the biggest piece of legislation that has been attempted for Ireland since Catholic Emancipation.' Wyndham, despite Cabinet vacillation, had had his way. On March 29th Blunt called on Percy and Madeline in Belgrave Square where there were 'new raptures about George and his bill – how could it be otherwise?' Then on March 30th Lady Windsor, a close friend of Wyndham, came to call on Blunt. 'She has,' he noted, 'seen George since yesterday, and brings me a message from him to the effect that I could help him with the Irish members about the bill. Of course I shall be delighted to do this, and it is all the easier because Redmond wrote some weeks ago asking me to let him know as soon as I returned to England. I must see George however first.'[7] Thus the jailer and the jailed were now working hand in hand. If Blunt saw the incongruity of this, he made no mention of it.

The initiative for Wyndham's land Act had come from an unlikely source: the landlords. In September 1902, after the annual landlords' convention, Captain Shawe-Taylor, the younger son of a Galway squire and nephew of Lady Gregory, wrote a letter which appeared in several Irish newspapers proposing a conference of representatives of landlords and tenants to discuss the land issue. Wyndham attempted to encourage this approach; but the more rigid landlords would have nothing to do with it. However Redmond and William O'Brien agreed to represent the tenants; and, on October 7th, George Wyndham wrote to Mary Drew: 'Dunraven has weighed in with a fine letter on land. The pace here is becoming delirious, so that London even with a Cabinet will seem a stagnant place.'[8]

It was the Earl of Dunraven who refused to allow Shawe-Taylor's idea to founder for lack of landlord support. Dunraven was one of the few members of the Protestant ascendancy who could claim Celtic Irish ancestry. His experience of life was varied. As a young man he had dabbled in spiritualism, been as a journalist to Abyssinia and the Franco-Prussian war, made two attempts (as an accomplished amateur yachtsman) on the America Cup, and hunted in the American west with Buffalo Bill Cody as his guide. Since childhood he had loved his country with the fervour of the most ardent Nationalist. He had briefly held office in the Salisbury government; but it was in Ireland that his real interest lay. The famine, with its degradation and suffering, had disturbed him deeply, and over the years he had turned his estates at Adare in County Limerick into a model of their kind. Politically, Dunraven was a moderate Unionist. He had raised men in Ireland to fight in the Boer war, going out to South Africa himself as an officer; and it was after returning from the veld that he resolved to devote 'the very precious years since middle age in endeavouring to do what I could for my country'.[9]

In a letter to Captain Shawe-Taylor, published in the Irish newspapers, Dunraven pledged his support for the conference, providing moderation was to be its keynote. Despite the continued opposition of the landowners' convention the first meeting took place at the Mansion House in Dublin on December 20th 1902. Dunraven was elected chairman, and O'Brien and Redmond were there for the tenants. John Dillon and Michael Davitt, two members of the Irish party who would be certain to object to such an assembly, had recently set sail from New York at the end of an American trip. Both Redmond and Dunraven saw that the conference must be in session before their arrival, or else they would do their utmost to prevent its inception.

The result, published on January 4th 1903, was rightly called by Dunraven 'a great triumph for the forces of peace and conciliation'.[10] It was also a remarkable tribute to his placatory chairmanship. Several improvements were called for, including a reform of the Congested Districts Board, the providing of better housing for agricultural labourers and fairer treatment for evicted tenants. But the most important passage was that which advocated peasant proprietorship of the land in place of the existing system of dual ownership. If this were adopted, a massive scheme of land purchase, financed by the government, would have to be put into operation; and here was contained the essence of George Wyndham's revolutionary land Act of 1903.

The reception given to the conference report was good. Even the landowners' convention gave it a cautious welcome. Lord

Dudley and Sir Antony MacDonnell were publicly enthusiastic, and Wyndham wrote to Dunraven to say that he felt 'fairly confident – nay sanguine – that 1903 will mark an epoch in Irish history'.[11] But opposition came from an unexpected quarter. Michael Davitt had always favoured compulsory purchase of land, and detested individual ownership. On platforms and in *The Freeman's Journal* he and his supporters attacked the report, seeing it as another manifestation of the policy of killing Home Rule by kindness. John Dillon was wary. He wanted a Liberal government who would, he believed, be more sympathetic to Irish national aspirations. The idea of propping up Balfour's administration with Irish support was repugnant to him. In February, when Redmond persuaded the Irish party's convention in Dublin to support the conference report, he was away in Egypt; and it was not until the summer of 1903, after the land bill had become law, that he began to decry its spirit of conciliation.

In the House of Commons on February 25th, with resolutions from his party conference and the directory of the United Irish League to support him, Redmond moved an amendment to the address drawing attention to the results of the land conference. Wyndham moved as quickly as he could. Throughout the spring he had been working on a land bill, elated by this outburst of apparent unity. By March his scheme was ready and on March 24th, the day before he was to introduce it to the House of Commons, he noted: 'The future of Ireland, and my future for what it is worth, turns on what happens tomorrow.'[12]

Cabinet approval had not been easily obtained. 'He told me,' Blunt wrote on March 31st, 'what a desperate fight he had had to get it adopted by the Cabinet and how nearly it had more than once been wrecked. Even within forty-eight hours of his bringing it forward in the House all had seemed lost, and it was only the splendid support given him by Arthur Balfour that had carried the day . . .'[13] Ritchie, the Chancellor of the Exchequer, had also been enthusiastic and therefore the necessary funds had been forthcoming. 'Brodrick [the War Minister],' the Chancellor had remarked, 'asks for millions, but he can't explain what he wants them for. But Wyndham explained everything and convinced one . . .'[14] The difficulty had been the Liberal Unionists, who, having left their own party over the cause of Home Rule, did not look lightly upon any measure that they believed would contribute to its advancement. Devonshire, Londonderry and Lansdowne, all large Irish land-owners, had been doubtful. But the most sceptical voice was that of Joseph Chamberlain, recently returned from South Africa in an obdurate and impatient mood.

Wyndham's bill had grown out of the Conference Report of the Dunraven convention. Its proposals were far-reaching, although they stopped short of compulsory land purchase. Briefly, they entailed the transfer of land, by voluntary action, from the landlord to the tenant, made possible by government loans to the tenant to assist the purchase. It was ensured that tenants' repayments stayed below their original rents. Landlords received an additional inducement to sell, in the form of a cash bonus paid over and above the price of the holding. Payments were made in cash, not stock. Entire estates were to be sold if three-quarters of the tenants on the estate agreed. The purchase price was to be supervised by an Irish Land Commission Court; and landlords were given the right to sell their own demesnes to the Estates Commissioners and then buy them back under the same terms that were available to their tenants. To operate the whole scheme Ritchie and the Treasury had made available £150 million.

These proposals were both complex and masterly. They showed that Wyndham, when anchored to the facts and figures of a particular problem, could transform his impulsive and erratic mind into a most formidable instrument. 'I asked him,' Blunt noted, 'who had suggested the finance of his scheme, and he assured me he had done the whole thing entirely himself, which is also what his mother told me on Sunday when she described to me how he had always had a mathematical head at school and how at an examination he had drawn without a mistake the whole of the figures of the second *Book of Euclid* from memory.'[15]

Joseph Chamberlain was not impressed. He believed that the debts would be impossible to collect and might provide, in a hard year, yet another cause for complaint against the British government. The Colonial Secretary went further. He spoke in Cabinet against the Irish Land Bill, on the morning of the very day that George Wyndham was going to introduce it in the House of Commons. This can have done little to encourage Wyndham, whose admiration for Chamberlain was anyway beginning to wane. In June 1902 he had told Blunt that 'his [Chamberlain's] character was completely misunderstood by the public, who, judging by his face, thought him a cool, unimpassioned calculator. He was just the reverse, being rash and impulsive in his decisions, to a great extent a political gambler, anything but a safe man to be at the head of affairs.' Blunt observed: 'George is beginning to learn things now he is in office.'[16] But Wyndham's wariness was returned. After Chamberlain's Birmingham speech, Sir Almeric Fitzroy, considering possible reasons for it, noted: 'It is notorious that Mr Chamberlain has no love for the Irish Land Bill, and people do not, therefore, hesitate to ascribe to him the intention if possible to wreck it, even going so far as to attribute to him an ungovernable jealousy of George Wyndham's rising reputation . . .'[17]

Balfour supported his Chief Secretary because he knew the force behind many of the reasons for bringing in the bill without delay. For the first time in years a reasonable measure of agreement had been achieved between the two sides over the land question, and it was vital to act on this before the extremists tilted the balance in favour of a renewal of resistance. There was a growing demand for compulsory sale of estates, and in 1902 a candidate standing on this plank had won the safe Tory seat of South Down. Wyndham's bill would go some way to satisfying this. Finally there were the party political considerations. Two by-elections, in Woolwich and Rye, had gone against the Conservatives, and Balfour felt the need of an obvious legislative success.

When Wyndham stood up in the House of Commons to introduce his bill on March 25th he was acutely nervous. 'I felt,' he told Blunt, 'that I . . . was fighting for my life; and, as often happens in such circumstances, I was able to do my very best.'[18] He claimed to have been able to make contact in turn with each section of interest that was represented in the House, so much so that when he reached the financial part of his argument he suddenly exclaimed : 'Am I right ?' whereupon Edgar Vincent, a financier, answered : 'Quite right.' As with his speech of 1900, in which he had defended the War Office, he had enough information and facts at his disposal to tie him down to earth; and, in consequence, was eminently lucid and comprehensible. He was received with acclamation. Redmond was cordial, expressing enthusiasm but saying that the final decision must rest with his party's convention which was due to meet in April in Dublin. This, after all, was only the first reading; but the Chief Secretary had a right to be pleased. 'So far,' he wrote the next day, 'the miracles go on.'[19]

It was under these circumstances that Wyndham, on March 31st, enrolled Wilfrid Blunt as an intermediary. Over breakfast in Park Lane the Chief Secretary explained himself. Apparently representative members of the old and more extreme Tories had been to Arthur Balfour and declared that, although much of the bill was hard to swallow, they would support it if the Irish members accepted it as the final solution to the land question. Such a deputation exemplified the narrowness of the middle path that Wyndham was attempting to walk and he therefore asked his cousin to emphasize to his Irish friends how easily obstinacy on their part might ruin the bill's chances. Blunt agreed to help.

Thus for the next two months Blunt attempted to build an even firmer bridge between the government and the Nationalists. He knew that if the land bill failed Wyndham would resign, the Conservatives would return to coercion and an infinitely less sympathetic Chief Secretary would be installed in Dublin Castle. Redmond soon made him aware of the difficulties on the other side, when they lunched together on April 1st. The Irish leader, a more conciliatory figure than Parnell, was, in essence, a stolid country squire from County Wicklow. Previously Blunt had termed him 'a thoroughly straightforward good fellow, strong and practical and self-reliant but not self-assertive'.[20] The Irishman had always recognized that Wyndham's sympathies were essentially in the right place. 'I am obliged,' he had told Blunt, 'to be fierce with him in public, but I know he is with us in his heart and we all know it.'[21] At lunch he spoke of his concern for the land bill, declaring that there was a strong party in Ireland who were against it and this would inevitably lead to a stormy convention. For it to pass the bill would have to be amended; but would the Chief Secretary accept this? That evening Redmond left for Dublin, to attend his party's convention on April 16th. The next day Wyndham told Blunt that he would certainly accept the amendments in principle, but he would like to meet Redmond at Blunt's house after the Easter recess.

The Nationalist convention in Dublin went off well. Although there was opposition to the bill it was accepted (subject to certain amendments) and the Irish parliamentary party given the necessary powers to decide what their attitude to the measure should be as it passed through its subsequent stages. Redmond told Blunt, however, that if Dillon, who was abroad, decided to join them the struggle would become more difficult. Blunt, Redmond said, must see Dillon when he returned and attempt to influence him. 'Dillon,' he declared, 'has great confidence in your opinion.'[22] But when the Irish leader saw Blunt again on April 30th, he brought bad news. Dillon was back from Egypt, and very much opposed to the bill. He wanted no conciliation with the landlords, or anything less than that they should be driven out of Ireland.

Blunt's efforts were kindled by his own enthusiasm for his

cousin's bill, which grew almost daily. 'I look,' he wrote on May 3rd to Redmond, 'upon the new Land Bill, if as I hope it passes the second reading, as the first piece of quite honest legislation for Ireland which will have been carried through Parliament in my recollection, and the certain prelude, however little the Government may have it in their minds, some day of Home Rule.'[23] John Dillon, out of loyalty to his party, was supporting the bill, albeit in a lukewarm manner; and the Liberal Opposition were also adopting a helpful attitude. But the accord between landlords and tenants was being subjected to strain. The Conference landlords had appointed a committee, under the chairmanship of Dunraven, to watch over the passage of the bill, and this committee had worked closely with the Nationalists. Then towards the end of May, a crisis loomed.

'The crux,' Redmond wrote to Blunt on May 15th, 'is still the question of the maximum reduction, and I have very great apprehensions on this matter.'[24] Blunt too was worried. It seemed as if the moderate Dunraven and Mayo were being pushed by their more extreme colleagues. 'It was,' he told Wyndham on May 20th, 'largely the fault of Dunraven and Mayo, who till the other day had agreed with him [Redmond] to a withdrawal of the limit, and then for some unexpected reason had suddenly turned round . . . Within the last fortnight I have talked with others of the Irish members, and I fear there is no doubt of there being a growing section among them indifferent, if not hostile to the Bill. It seems to be the general opinion that unless the tenants specifically affected are given easier terms than the Bill provides there will be new combinations against purchase.'[25]

Blunt was being less than fair to Dunraven. In fact he managed to swing the landlords away from their old obduracy, and his compromise was represented by the introduction of an amendment in the House of Commons by Henry Duke. To reach this position had not been easy; in fact on June 19th the outlook was bleak enough for Redmond to send a message to Wyndham in which he foresaw that, unless a more conciliatory attitude prevailed, the bill would be wrecked. On June 20th the Landowners Convention met and both Dunraven and the previously obstinate Duke of Abercorn spoke against the landlord opposition to Duke's amendment. The Convention then voted for this compromise and thus, for the moment, appeared to end what Blunt termed 'the vacillation of the landlords who are most of them too stupid to understand the bill . . .'[26]

It remained only to placate the Nationalists. On June 23rd, when Wyndham finally met Redmond at Blunt's house in Chapel Street, he was concerned mainly about the terrible split that seemed to be developing in the Cabinet. On May 15th Joseph Chamberlain had made his Birmingham speech. Wyndham had tried to stay out of the discussion that followed, at least until his bill had been passed. He felt that now Chamberlain had 'blown his steam off' he would forget about Ireland; yet the Chief Secretary still knew that he was performing a most difficult balancing act between opposition within his own party, the landlords and the Nationalists. With Redmond, however, he felt at ease. 'I was much struck,' Blunt noted, 'with the lawyer-like ability both showed in seizing points as they rose, and developing them. The discussion was carried on in all possible good humour, and much personal sympathy.' He observed the contrast between the lively gesticulating Wyndham and the solid, genial Redmond 'nursing his great double chin . . .'; and remarked how both were intensely anxious to come to an understanding and carry the bill.[27]

At length they did come to an agreement. Wyndham said that he would adopt Duke's amendment as his own, and Redmond should express his support for it, thus avoiding any more dispute on this score. Accord was also reached on the subject of evicted tenants and political prisoners, Wyndham releasing one and Redmond complimenting the Chief Secretary for saving another's life by locking him up, thereby halting his ferocious drinking. After three-quarters of an hour the two

parted, having shaken hands. 'This,' Blunt remarked, 'I felt
was an historic event, as I saw George into his hansom at the
door with his red box – a great day for Chapel Street! We consider the bill safe.'[28] That evening he dined with Wyndham and
his mother at Belgrave Square, where the former, fresh from a
successful day's tussling with the Cabinet and the landlords,
was 'in tearing spirits'. As the dinner proceeded he became
more and more eloquent, his fancy leading him to the wildest
optimism about his future. To the others, listening, it was both
delightful and impressive. 'George,' wrote Blunt, 'has in him
the fire of genius, and whether as leader of the Conservative
party, or of Irish Home Rule he will be equally conspicuous,
and as superior to any party leader as Disraeli was in his day.'[29]
Then on July 20th, still triumphant, Wyndham went to Dublin
to receive the King on the occasion of his state visit to Ireland,
leaving Arthur Balfour to steer the land bill, now assured of
victory, through its third reading.

The Chief Secretary crossed the Irish Sea with the King in the
royal yacht. At breakfast the next morning the talk was of
the Pope's death, and Edward was the very picture of benignity.
'The Pope's dead, of course we had expected it,' he remarked to
Wyndham. 'A boiled egg? . . . Did you sleep well? . . . Some
more bacon?' On the drive into Dublin the crowds were
immense, standing on roofs, leaning out of windows to
cheer both the King and the land bill. In the evening came the
Viceroy's official dinner, and Wyndham was next to Princess
Victoria who was 'good, gentle and sensible and absolutely
unselfish'; but the high point came afterwards when 'the
Queen talked to me . . . and is delicious'. Everywhere the royal
party went the reception was delirious. 'We went on,' wrote
Wyndham of one drive in Dublin, 'through the poorest parts
by the North Circular road, and ever and always, there was
the same intense emotion. It brought tears to the Queen's
eyes, and a lump in my throat. No one who did not drive in
their carriage will ever know how mesmeric it was. It made
me understand the Mussulman conquests and the Crusades. For

here was a whole population in hysteria.' Once, as they rode
through Phoenix Park, the cheering was so loud that the horses
took fright and almost bolted. At the Chief Secretary's Lodge
'with their supernatural kindness the King and Queen came
. . . here and loitered and talked and thanked and overpraised
and made me love them – just as if they had done nothing
and had nothing to do except to please Sibell and myself'. The
state visit had received one of the most spectacular of all
Irish welcomes. 'And these,' remarked Wyndham, 'are the
people whom some call disloyal.'[30]

In England, the land bill received the royal assent on August
14th. In five years it enabled 228,938 tenants to take possession
of their holding. Seventy-seven million pounds' worth of property changed hands, and from 1906 to 1908 alone 100,000
tenants took advantage of the terms it offered. In 1870 three
per cent of Irish land holdings were occupied; by 1908 the
figure stood at forty-six per cent. At last the inducements to
both sides to participate were large enough. John Redmond
called the measure: 'The most substantial victory gained for
centuries by the Irish race for the reconquest of the soil of
Ireland by the people.'[31]

Chapter 17
Catastrophe

'Here,' Wilfrid Blunt wrote in his diary on October 31st 1903, 'I close this year's journal as far as my life in England is concerned. The part I was able to play in Irish affairs this summer has given me confidence my life has been not quite wasted. I await the future calmly, feeling that I have almost completed my life's work.'[1] That summer had seen him still active after his Irish intervention; yet conscious that this activity must soon be curtailed by his years. In November he was back in Egypt, having stayed on the way at Gros Bois where, in the course of the summer, his old friend Princess Wagram had died. Here he found 'no visitors and none of the bright talk I had so long enjoyed there'. At Sheykh Obeyd however one link with the past still survived, in the form of Sheykh Mohammed Abdu – an old disciple of Jemal-ed-Din. That summer Mohammed Abdu had been in England, and Blunt had taken him to Brighton to visit Herbert Spencer, whom the Moslem greatly admired, having translated his volume on education into Arabic. The old man, suffering from the after effects of a stroke, was in bed, but had received them kindly, prophesying, amongst other things, that there was coming 'a reign of force in the world, and there will be again a general war for mastery, when every kind of brutality will be practised'.[2] At Sheykh Obeyd Mohammed Abdu's company was a great comfort for, after his campaign against Cromer and the fox hunters, Blunt found himself ostracized by the European society of Cairo.

This seclusion brought a wistful contemplation of the past.

Madeline Wyndham was at Hyères with her relations, where Blunt had once spent part of a summer in her company some twenty years ago. 'I don't know,' he wrote to her on March 8th, 'when anything has given me so much pleasure as getting your letter from Hyères. It is like a child's letter, handwriting, smudges, pictures and all, and it has delighted me that you should remember times that I never forget and things and sayings in the past which I fancied everybody but me had forgotten. The days that were are all like a map to me and I could put a date on every circumstance and make a plan of every house in which I have ever been happy, and I like to find you treasuring the past in the same way . . . The flowers of Hyères, as you say, are not like other flowers and the hills are not like other hills, and you too are not like any other woman that ever was and your letters are not at all like anybody else's letters. It is a victory over time to be able to enjoy them all still. My eyes, like yours, are almost as good as they ever were, and my power of enjoyment with them as strong, and I fancy that to the last we shall both find happiness in the sunlight, especially the early morning light when one breakfasts out of doors.'[3] Then in September he was in England, driving his Arabs across the autumn countryside, to pay another visit to Clouds.

In 1904 Blunt was able to perform one more service for Ireland. This was the age of the Irish literary renaissance, and he, through his friendship with Lady Gregory, was on its periphery. In May, Yeats, whom Blunt described as being 'brilliant in conversation and full of affectations', asked him if he would approach George Wyndham to grant them a patent for their new theatre, the Abbey; and this, the next day, Blunt was delighted to do. 'George,' he noted, 'promised at once to befriend the Abbey theatre as I was sure he would,' and, in consequence, it rapidly flourished, eventually, in 1907, staging one of Blunt's own dramas, *Fand of the Fair Cheek*. Back in Egypt in 1905, Blunt was able to escape from British domestic politics. Before leaving England he had settled Crabbet on his daughter Judith, retaining Newbuildings and Worth Forest, where he was later to build a small house for himself. In December, at Sheykh Obeyd, he fell a victim to a fever which, by reaching his lungs and kidneys, caused acute discomfort. 'I have,' he told Madeline in January, 'had a rough shaking and feel as if I should never be quite the same again. I go out now every day, being lifted on to a mare and taken outside on to the sand where I have a tent and lie all day enjoying the desert air.'[4]

His recovery proved only temporary. At the beginning of February he was ill again, with an even fiercer fever, and decided to return to England as soon as possible. Eventually on March 17th he left Sheykh Obeyd 'as it seems to me forever'. Mohammed Abdu came to see him off at Cairo station, and they stayed talking until the last minute as each believed that it would be the last time they would meet. There then followed a terrible journey, first to Venice and afterwards to London. At such moments friends, and the comfort they could provide, were badly needed. 'I hear,' Cockerell wrote to Madeline after his arrival, 'that he was much comforted by a telegram you sent from Egypt. Please also write to him. Where is G.W.? I saw that he had gone abroad. If by any chance he is in Italy he could come here. The weather is perfect just now, and his presence would be a great help. I hope that he is better in health than he was reported to be, and that you and he are not taking the recent political incidents too much to heart. His turn will come later and for still greater usefulness than before.'[5] George Wyndham could not come to Venice; but he did write to the invalid, saying: 'I am much distressed to hear that you are laid up at Venice. Your last letter was full of new life and anticipation of London before Easter. It reached me just before I started abroad to rest and recover from the wearying consequences of work and excitement following too closely on influenza . . . Fate has emptied a quiver at me and mine and one shaft has struck you.'[6]

In March Wyndham had resigned from the Irish Office, with

his nerves in a state of temporary wreckage. 'I feel,' Blunt told Madeline, 'happy about him and am sure that his release from office is the best thing that could have happened to him';[7] but Wyndham was still simmering with disappointment. 'I will,' he promised his cousin, 'expound to you the Irish situation. I have not spoken of it to anyone else and am enigmatic merely because I have many things better worth doing than railing at Orangemen. The whole gang of *Times* newspaper and whips-room politicians and new journalists have got to hang themselves before I condescend to move a finger.'[8]

Since the triumph of the land Act, the Irish situation had been steadily sliding against the Chief Secretary. At first, in August 1903, it seemed as if Wyndham had brought about a remarkable transformation; and the King's visit, with its tremendous welcome, was held to signify the dawning of a new age of conciliation. On October 14th 1903 Wyndham wrote to Mary Drew of 'the undoubted and growing desire of many interests in Ireland to draw together and treat each other in a more kindly and reasonable spirit'.[9] He was now turning his attention to the old problem of Catholic higher education, but was operating against a far less secure background than that of the land bill. First there was the ministerial crisis brought about by Chamberlain's cry for tariff reform. In September Ritchie, Lord Balfour of Burleigh, Lord George Hamilton and the Duke of Devonshire resigned from the Cabinet. All were free-traders. Devonshire, who had come, for many, to symbolize rocklike dependability, was persuaded to stay on, but on October 6th he resigned again, this time permanently. Meanwhile the Colonial Secretary had departed on September 16th, to pursue his campaign with a greater vehemence.

In October, at Glasgow, Chamberlain thundered against free trade, employing rhetoric that struck a chord with the Chief Secretary. 'I have,' he declared, 'taken up new burdens and come before you as a missionary of the Empire, to urge upon you again, as I did in the old times when I protested against the disruption of the United Kingdom, once again to warn you, to urge you, to implore you to do nothing that will tend towards the disintegration of the Empire, and not to refuse to sacrifice a futile superstition, an inept prejudice, and thereby to lose the results of centuries of noble effort and patriotic endeavour.'[10] On October 7th, after this speech, Wyndham wrote to his old colleague: 'I must break my resolution now to add to your correspondence only to say that I have never felt such exultation in the joy of battle since the anti-Home Rule meeting at Her Majesty's theatre which swept me into politics in 1886.'[11]

But Wyndham's position on protection was ambivalent. He told Blunt that he believed Chamberlain had vastly exaggerated the importance of the colonies, in particular Australia. He felt bound, by ties of loyalty and affection, to stick by Balfour in his effort to find some sort of middle ground on which the protectionist and free-trade wings of the Unionist party could meet. 'I am just forty,' he declared to Blunt in September, 'and find myself with the balance of power in my own hands. I mean of power in the Cabinet . . . In fifteen years' time I shall leave politics for good, the more one sees of them, the more futile they appear, and I shall have had enough of them by the time I am fifty-five. Of course I must be Prime Minister first, I am sure of that. I am constantly approached already to lead the Party, and I can do so when I please. I don't see who is to be my rival in it, George Curzon will be in the House of Lords, and I am younger than all the rest. It is surprising how little ability there is, but I don't mean to go on forever with it. I have other things to do.'[12] But by April Blunt was noting: 'George is getting sick of office, and longs to be away writing poetry.'[13]

This change of attitude did not only have its origins in Wyndham's mercurial temperament. In the Cabinet reshuffle which followed the resignations he could have moved on to higher office; but was restrained – first by his own feeling that he must see the land Act through its early stages of operation, and second by the King's request that he should remain in Dublin to capitalize on the goodwill he had won by his success. As the enthusiasms cooled and the pace slackened, Wyndham came to regret this decision. 'I am still,' he told Sibell on April 16th, 'wrestling with Irish Education: not that I have to make a big speech, rather the reverse. The truth is I do not see my way to a better system without losing some of the good things in the present one. In any case, nothing but rows with everybody.'[14] The difficulties were mounting. In August a split had occurred in the Irish parliamentary party, with John Dillon moving away from his grudging support of the land Act towards outright opposition to any further offering of the olive branch, and William O'Brien remaining in his position of moderation. Dillon spoke out fiercely, wishing to see the Conservatives out of office and determined to prevent a Liberal drift towards Rosebery's position of opposition to Home Rule.

He was strong enough to carry most of his party with him, and O'Brien retired from Parliament. 'I am grieved,' Wyndham wrote to Lord Dunraven, 'by W. O'Brien's resignation and its cause. You know how much I have admired his courage – I might say chivalry – ever since the Land Conference. It is tragic that the jealous journalistic and village wiseacres should defeat his attempt to make Ireland a nation by burying ancient feuds.'[15] Now the 'jealous journalistic and village wiseacres' appeared to be making the running. Many of the Irish MPs began to wonder, after the event, if the landlords had not been given terms that were too generous.

Slowly the recently forged links between the Irish Office and the Nationalists began to break; and Redmond drifted back to his old position of opposing the government. Disagreement between Unionists and Nationalists effectively prevented any further Irish legislation, such as the plan for a Catholic University and an Irish Labourers bill, from reaching the Statute Book. Fatigue was beginning to set in. On July 13th Blunt noted: 'Lunched with George. He is dying to be out of office, and live an irresponsible life away from politics, which he declares to be an abomination. He says that I am the only person who has learnt the secret of how to live. We are to spend the next Saturday to Monday together in Worth Forest, where I have seen deer lately.' The forest was a welcome rest. The two of them slept in a tent 'talking always of past days and the glories of the Crabbet Club, and devising schemes of an ideal life in the woods, with a pleasant society of men and women on Boccaccian lines, which we are to call the Fellowship of the Holy Ghost'.[16]

Wyndham tried to make the best of his burden. 'I have,' he had written to Sibell on June 29th, 'recovered from my slight chill, mainly because there has been too much work, and rather exciting work, to leave time for illness. I told you that I had Cabinet yesterday till 1.45; lunched with Arthur, still on problems; many questions. With Austen Chamberlain from 3 to 4.15, then Arthur and Arnold Forster from 6 to 7.30: Army debate 9 to 12 with (me) on Bench with Arthur etcetera etcetera. We got well out of it, but I have not had a moment for heavy Irish work, and many questions – tiresome ones – So I worked till 1.30. Woke very well and bright at 6.45 and worked in pyjamas and dressing gown in my study from 7.00 to 9.30. Rode: dejeuned with Will (Beauchamp): Another Cabinet conference from 4 to nearly 6 and Cabinet again tomorrow . . . I feel very well for I delight in a hurricane. My spirits have bounded up to meet the battle and the breeze . . . Arthur has been too dear to me. I catch little looks of appreciation, sometimes, when I have helped to steer round a corner. But the pace is very hot just now.'[17]

Eventually, at the end of July, there was a note of despair. 'I cannot force myself to work,' he told Sibell from Hatfield, '. . . The pettiness and malice and ignorance are wearing. But I know that much good remains and will bear fruit some day. For the moment I cannot help being melancholy and irritable . . . I should be all right and quite a joyous companion to you if I could do some real work. But I must rest. Yet – really – I do not want to be selfish and will do whatever you like. I do not want to please myself and have lost the power of pleasing myself. So there is no merit in saying that I will do whatever you like. Only I want you to be happy when the wayward mood is on me. There is a restless spirit in me that breaks out at times and longs for silence and solitude. It will pass soon and then you will be pleased with me again.'[18]

By the time the parliamentary session ended in the middle of August Wyndham was exhausted. Efforts to overcome his fatigue by resorting to drink and bracing exercise had merely exacerbated his condition. In October 1903 Mark Sykes, the aristocratic young traveller and Orientalist, had called on the Chief Secretary in Dublin with a view to serving as his assistant, in the same way as Wyndham had once served Balfour, and had found him in a loquacious, almost unbalanced state. 'The whole sub-melody,' Sykes informed his wife of his prospective master's conversation, 'which runs through everything is Melancholy, Humour, false Hilarity, elemental passions, elemental thought, nobility of soul, etcetera, etcetera, etcetera, blending into a wailing dirge.'[19] By August doctors had been called in. Clearly a complete rest was needed, and a break from artificial stimulants. 'I feared,' his private secretary remembered afterwards, 'that he would have a nervous breakdown before the end of the session, but he managed to hold out somehow. He had not the energy to make plans for the autumn. All he wanted was to get away somewhere, and have a complete rest. He told Sir Antony, and he told me, not to forward any papers which could await his return; and then went off, for the first rest he had had for several years, first to friends and then to Germany with Percy.'[20]

When George Wyndham left for his holiday he was leaving behind an Under-Secretary whose power had recently been significantly increased. MacDonnell now had the machinery of Irish government more closely under his control than before. Through this was created the possibility, particularly if Wyndham was either away or in poor health, of his taking action largely on his own initiative. Certainly in August and

September Wyndham appeared to be in no fit state to involve himself deeply in anything; and when Lord Dunraven approached the government for assistance and advice it was with Sir Antony MacDonnell that he primarily found himself dealing.

Dunraven had been disappointed by recent developments in the Irish parliamentary party, particularly O'Brien's resignation and the vehement campaigning of Dillon, Davitt and Sexton. This had led him to form, as an opposing force to extremism, the Irish Reform Association, which was, in effect, a reconstitution of the old Land Committee. It was set up in August 1904, and on August 31st it produced its first report, in which the idea of decentralization, or devolution, of government for Ireland was proposed. 'While firmly maintaining,' one clause ran, 'that the Parliamentary Union between Great Britain and Ireland is essential to the political stability of the Empire, and to the prosperity of the two islands, we believe that such union is compatible with the devolution to Ireland of a larger measure of local government than she now possesses.'[21] The proposals were given a cautious welcome by the Unionist *Irish Times* and the general reaction seemed to be favourable. 'Our platform,' Dunraven later wrote, 'was a modest one, but the planks were sound,' and it was with considerable confidence that he sought an appointment with Sir Antony.

At first Sir Antony was wary. He knew that the Unionists were suspicious of him on account of his supposed Home Rule sympathies and his enthusiasm for a Catholic University; and thus he refused to have discussions with Dunraven at the Under-Secretary's residence. But in September, when Wyndham was away, he visited Dunraven, who was anchored off the Kerry coast in his yacht *Cariad*, and on September 10th, wrote to Wyndham in Germany to acquaint the Chief Secretary with his actions. 'In the Irish Reform Association Manifesto,' he said, 'I fancy you have recognized the trace of conversations we have had. I have helped and am helping Dunraven in the business, which for many a day seemed to me to offer the best hope of an unravelling of the tangled skein of English and Irish relations.'[22] Receiving no answer, Sir Antony pressed ahead with his deliberations.

There had been, as was so often the case in Irish political manoeuvrings, misunderstanding from the very start. 'During August,' Dunraven remembered, 'I had several conversations with the Chief Secretary and Sir Antony MacDonnell . . . My general impression was that Dudley [the Lord-Lieutenant] and George Wyndham . . . approved of the draft of the scheme agreed upon by Antony MacDonnell . . . and myself. It really looked as though at last a settlement satisfactory to all parties, though, of course, capable of development – as all such instruments must be – would be arrived at.'[23] On September 26th this scheme, in reality more the product of the professional Sir Antony than the amateur Lord Dunraven, was published in the form of the Irish Reform Association's second report.

The report contained four proposals. First the creation of a financial council for Ireland which would control matters of Irish finance, although the power of raising revenue was to stay with Westminster. Secondly, that this council would consist of the Lord-Lieutenant, and twelve elected and twelve nominated members. One of the nominated members was to be the Chief Secretary. Decisions were to be reached by means of a majority vote, which could only be reversed in the House of Commons by not less than a majority of three-quarters. Thirdly the council was to have the power to prepare for Parliament the Irish estimates. Fourthly there was to be an additional delegation of business and authority to a body consisting of Irish representative peers, Irish Members of Parliament and both sitting and retired members of the financial council. This body should be able to draft Irish bills for discussion at Westminster, and a Royal Commission should be set up to look into the best form its composition should take.

Unionist opposition to this was inevitable. On September 26th the tempest broke. *The Times*, on September 27th, thundered in an editorial that 'this insidious project' had originated in 'an influential clique in Dublin Castle of which Sir Antony MacDonnell is regarded by numbers of Irish Unionists as the head'; and on the same day the Irish Alliance passed a firmly worded resolution in which it was roundly condemned. The more extreme Nationalists were equally dismissive of the proposals, with Davitt terming them 'a wooden horse stratagem', although John Redmond cabled from America : 'The announcement is of the utmost importance. It is simply a declaration for Home Rule and is quite a wonderful thing. With these men with us Home Rule may come at any moment.'

Wyndham, just back from Germany, saw the manifesto in the Press and was horrified. Having no recollection of MacDonnell's letter of September 10th he was entirely unprepared for it, and quickly wrote to *The Times* to protest his ignorance and opposition. 'No report,' he declared in a letter published on September 27th, 'of the earlier proceedings of the Irish Reform Association has reached me, and no correspondent has invited my opinion on the aims and proposed methods of that body, in so far as I might have been able to glean them from the press . . . I have to say, without reserve or qualification, that the Unionist Government is opposed to the multiplication of legislative bodies within the United Kingdom, whether in pursuance of the policy generally known as "Home Rule for Ireland" or in pursuance of the policy generally known as "Home Rule all round" . . . I do not for a moment question the sincerity of the Irish Reform Association's intentions to avoid any course which might impair the Parliamentary Union of Great Britain and Ireland. I am convinced of their devotion to the Imperial ideal. I welcome their desire to stimulate energy and foster collaboration among their countrymen for the promotion of education, commerce and industry. These aspirations are unimpeachable. But the chances of their realization are prejudiced, and not enhanced, when they are confused with any plan, however tentative, for the multiplication of legislative Assemblies within the limits of the United Kingdom. To any such plan, however contracted in scope and vague in feature, the Unionist party is opposed.' Heeding his master's words, Sir Antony at once withdrew from any contact with the Irish Reform Association.

The Times praised the Chief Secretary for his prompt response. On September 28th, when Blunt dined with the Wyndhams in Belgrave Square, George seemed confident that he had avoided trouble. 'He has,' Blunt noted, 'just published a letter in *The Times* repudiating a programme put out in his absence by Dunraven of a kind of Home Rule for Ireland. I know this kind of Home Rule to be in accordance with his views, but he gets out of the difficulty by declaring that it is absolutely contrary to those of the Unionist Party, a distinction which has so far escaped the criticism of his opponents.'[24] It was not to do so for long. The Irish Unionists were, numerically, a hard-pressed bunch. Of the one hundred and three Irish MPs they constituted only twenty, and held only two seats outside Ulster, both of which were in Dublin University. They therefore felt obliged to fight and fight hard, whenever their position appeared to be threatened. On September 27th an ominous letter was published in the *Belfast News-Letter*, from William Moore and Charles Curtis Craig, two prominent Ulster Unionists, in which they demonstrated their concern by a call to arms.

'Unfortunately,' it ran, 'there would appear to be good grounds for assuming the closest connection between the new scheme and the Irish administration . . . We think that the present would be an opportune moment to revive on a war footing for active work the various Ulster defence associations. Lord Dunraven and his associates can be ignored, but the administration which, though masquerading as Unionist, plots behind them, cannot.' The chief accusation was that Sir Antony had taken charge; and they felt themselves to be faced with their greatest challenge since the Home Rule bill of 1893. Wyndham never found these men easy, remarking in August: 'My contact with Ulster members is like catching the "itch" from Park Pests. It is very unpleasant; not your fault; but still degrading.'[25] Now, with their traditional dourness, they set their faces against this new alliance which seemed determined to bring in Home Rule by stealth.

Within the government Carson and Lord Londonderry were known to be outraged by the scheme. Eventually, out of the Cabinet's deliberations, there came a 'measured censure' passed on Sir Antony MacDonnell, in which his actions were condemned but he was informed that it was the ministers' opinion that he 'acted without disloyalty' to his official superiors. The positions of the leading figures grew more difficult with each succeeding day. Sir Antony, confident that he had done no wrong, was determined to see himself exonerated, and would not accept the official censure. Neither would he ease the situation by moving to the India Council without seeing his name cleared first. Wyndham was plunged back into the neurotic turmoil from which he had briefly emerged during and after his trip to Germany. He was desperately attempting to get to the bottom of a dispute with his Under-Secretary. MacDonnell claimed that he had given his superiors adequate information about his actions, most particularly in Wyndham's case, through the letters written previous to and on September 10th. He also stated that he had kept well within his unusually flexible terms of employment. What most distressed the Chief Secretary was that he had no recollection of the passages in Sir Antony's letters that had referred to devolution; and he began to doubt both his memory and the opinion that his colleagues might have of his honour.

By the middle of January his mental condition was serious enough to merit Prime Ministerial intervention. 'I am,' Arthur Balfour sat down to write to Sibell at 1 a.m. on the morning of January 23rd, 'seriously alarmed about George's state. His nerves seem to me – nay are – (for the moment) utterly ruined. He is really hardly sane, and has worked himself into such a state of mind that he actually believes that his colleagues doubt his honour! There is not one of them who would not go to the stake for it. But he cannot be made to see this – and has delusions only possible to an unbalanced mind. I do beg of you to call in at once a competent physician for I am sure the case is serious.'[26]

This was the condition in which he was to face Parliament in mid-February. *The Times*, on January 28th, added to his discomfort with a particularly vicious leading article. 'Since,' the paper declared, 'Mr Wyndham's repudiation in the autumn of the policy of veiled Home Rule propounded under the name of devolution, by the wiseacres of the "Irish Reform Association", the Chief Secretary – owing, it is understood, to enfeebled health, the result of influenza – has seen little or nothing of the country for the administration of which he remains responsible. His utterances on Irish affairs have been so rare and scanty that they abide in no man's memory.' Ulster Unionists, *The Times* complained, had been treated neither sympathetically nor even fairly. 'His nominal subordinate,' it claimed, 'treats their remonstrances with indifference or contempt, while the appeals or protests of Nationalist politicians or the Roman Catholic clergy are received with deferential compliance.'

Two days before the debate, in a state of exhaustion, Wyndham conceded to MacDonnell the three points upon which they had been in correspondence since the Cabinet's 'measured censure'. These were: first, that Sir Antony had been justified in helping Lord Dunraven; second, that he had not concealed the fact that he was helping Lord Dunraven from his superiors; and third, that he had not given evidence of any disloyalty. On February 17th Dunraven spoke in the Lords to say that the devolution proposals had had their origins with him and not with Sir Antony MacDonnell. Lansdowne then declared, in a further effort to defend Sir Antony, that 'when Sir Antony took up this appointment it was understood by both himself and by the Chief Secretary that he was to have greater opportunities for initiative than he would have expected had he been a candidate in the ordinary course'.[27] He also stated that

MacDonnell had acted throughout with the full knowledge and approval of his Lord-Lieutenant.

It was not surprising that, after Lansdowne's speech, Lord Ashbourne should have whispered to him: 'My boy, I have never heard so much fat put into the fire in a few minutes.'[28] For Lansdowne had given to the Ulstermen and the more unbending Unionists even firmer reason to suspect that there had been a government plot to bring in some measure of Home Rule without either their knowledge or consent. In the House of Commons Balfour contradicted him by saying that Mac-Donnell's appointment had not been made under exceptional terms; but the damage had been done. On February 20th, when Redmond moved his customary motion of disapproval of the Irish government, he did it with considerable Unionist support. The government's majority was down to fifty; and only six Irish Unionists were with them. The imbroglio was not disentangled by the reading out of the Wyndham-MacDonnell correspondence of 1902, which showed that Sir Antony had, in fact, stayed well within his terms of employment. Redmond and the Nationalists, delighted to have a chance to disconcert the government, pressed their attack with no thought for the frail unity of two years ago; and Asquith had little difficulty in demonstrating the contradictions between the statements of Balfour and Lansdowne.

Wyndham, his nerves in pieces, was at his circumlocutory worst. J. S. Sandars wrote of his explanations in the Commons as being 'involved, unconvincing and prolonged . . . He wholly failed in the steadiness of plain sense which is the essence of political defence.'[29] 'Cannot,' one opponent cried out, with justification, during one stage of the debate, 'the Right Hon. Gentleman give a plain answer to a plain question?'; and every utterance was 'fretted with nice distinctions'. Within a few days the government's position had drastically declined. On March 1st Mrs Joseph Chamberlain wrote to her mother of 'the general impression of incredible muddle';[30] and on March 6th Sir Almeric Fitzroy described how 'old fashioned Tories, who, in the whole course of their parliamentary lives, had never entertained the thought of voting against their party, now left the House swearing that nothing would induce them to stay and vote. They swept past the Whips at the doors, ignoring their presence and rudely repelling their efforts to detain them, till the Whips themselves deserted their posts in despair, and defeat was only averted by putting up stalwarts to talk against time.'[31] Finally, on March 6th, Arthur Balfour rose in the House of Commons to make the inevitable announcement. 'It is,' he declared, 'with the deepest regret that I have to inform the House that I have not found myself any longer able to resist the appeals made to me by my right honourable friend the member for Dover that he might be permitted to resign his office.'

'The ground,' Balfour continued, 'of his resignation is not ill-health, though I frankly admit that I do not believe that he would be at present able to support all the labours and all the anxieties of a great administrative office. His principal reason is that he is of the opinion that the controversy which has recently taken place both within and outside these walls has greatly impaired, if not wholly destroyed, the value of the work which he could do in the office which he has so long held.'[32]

A few days later George Wyndham went abroad, with Sibell, to recover the balance and ease of mind that had eluded him throughout these last months of stress.

Chapter 18
Reaction

'I felt,' George Wyndham wrote to Wilfrid Scawen Blunt on March 31st 1905, from Bordighera, 'that my life was going to change and it has changed . . . I have spread my wings and am rejoicing in the sunlight and clean air of liberty . . . I have been taking long walks in the hills . . . up through the olive-yards to tangles of Rosemary and juniper and myrtle, and up to the crags and pines. I feel years younger. I am delighted at being out of the Government. And now I wish to foregather with you . . . My only fear is that they may want me back for the War Office or some other expiring effort of this immortal Government. I mean to resist any such appeals. Let us enjoy this summer, simply and fully.'[1]

After such an upheaval, it was natural that he should feel frustration and bitterness. 'The Unionist Party,' he declared, 'has got to learn a good deal from facts before it can learn anything from my words. I shall help them again later on; if they deserve it. Meanwhile there is an English summer and Poetry and these I will share with you . . . Shall we start a new magazine? Or write in *Blackwood*? Let us do something wholesome and primeval . . . If we start a magazine shall we call it *The Detached Review*? Let us denounce "Innovation", the viper that, according to Daniel – is born through its mother's entrails. Let us resist Education and enlarge Liberty.'

But Wyndham's behaviour to his colleagues at the end of the devolution crisis had been both chivalric and humble. 'A section of our party,' he had written to Arthur Balfour from Clouds on

March 2nd, 'will not obey the Whips or give you the support you deserve until there has been a change in the Irish Government; having defended MacDonnell in December and since, and having opposed Dudley's resignation, I should have to insist on resigning if both or either were asked to resign later on.' On March 3rd, when formally tendering his resignation, he wrote: 'Do not think of me. I shall be glad if mis-constructions of my policy and above all of my actions can some day be removed. But I am quite ready to wait for that.'[2] On Sunday March 5th, before Balfour was to announce the resignation in the House of Commons, Wyndham, in a more personal letter, told him: 'I beg you not to praise me tomorrow. It will do you harm. Perhaps that argument will not weigh with you. So let me add, it will do me harm.'

Arthur Balfour had always possessed an almost mesmeric power over George Wyndham. As his earliest political mentor and an old and respected friend, the Prime Minister would anyway have had considerable claims on his affections. In addition there was the matter of personality. Where Wyndham was hot-headed and romantic, Balfour was cool and dispassionate; and the older man's remorseless logical approach must often have fallen like a douche of cold water on the younger's flights of glorious fancy. Now the ultimate awakening had come. 'Put not your trust,' Wyndham was later to observe ruefully, 'in Princes in whom there is no help . . .'; but the Prime Minister could not have saved his Chief Secretary. Wyndham's physical and mental condition made him, at this stage, entirely unsuitable for office. Balfour had been reluctant to part with Wyndham. 'Those,' Winston Churchill wrote in 1937, 'nearest and dearest to George Wyndham declared that the Prime Minister backed him with the whole of his strength, that he refused time after time to allow him to resign, and that it was only when, in the end, Wyndham's health and nerves completely broke down . . . that Balfour finally accepted resignation.'[3] Once this had happened it was important that the transition should be affected smoothly, without any recriminatory statements or attempts at self-justification.

The Prime Minister received none of this from his old colleague, and would never have been likely to, for with the respect and loyalty that Wyndham felt for Balfour there came a measure of fear. The early years in Ireland had revealed to him the steel that lay beneath the other's geniality. 'George,' Blunt wrote on May 13th '. . . . seems to have been captured by Arthur Balfour at Clouds and brought over to a position of mere party obedience.'[4] On May 9th, after his return from Italy, Wyndham made his postponed resignation statement and Jack Seely, the Liberal, remembered later that when he 'came to the passage in his speech exonerating Balfour from any part in the imbroglio, Balfour turned round and seemed to hypnotize him. It was like Svengali and the maid.'[5]

The epilogue was suitably bizarre. On May 2nd Wyndham found one of MacDonnell's letters, that of August 14th, at Clouds. It contained an allusion, of which Wyndham had no previous recollection, to the possibility of Lord Dunraven producing a scheme of decentralized finance and to MacDonnell's readiness to help with this. It was not until 1912 that the second, more detailed, letter, that of September 10th was discovered by Murray Hornibrook between the pages of a Congested Districts Board Report which Wyndham had taken on holiday with him. In his troubled state of mind he had either not read the whole of it or been incapable of taking in its message. The omission had cost him his political career.

Driven back into contemplation by his disaster, George Wyndham began to sharpen his views on life and politics. In 1904 he had delivered, as his Rectorial address at Glasgow, a lecture on the 'Origins of the State'. In this he had warned against 'cosmopolitanism'; and, in April 1905, he seemed, when writing to Wilfrid Blunt, to be narrowing his view of society and government even further. 'My sympathies,' he wrote, 'are more and more with the real Tories; less and less with

255

Americanism and Teutonism, or rather, with their awkward adaptations to our life in these islands . . . My brief sojourn abroad has made me feel that the "gentry", whether of territorial birth or literary distinction, throughout Europe represents something that is valid more truly than the domestic politics of "nation-states" and the world politics of would-be Empires . . . The "Gentry" – so defined – are one people the old world over. The members of it have the same manners and thoughts. They understand each other in spite of imperfect communication in divers tongues . . . What is more they have always been one people, and the same people, in every age for the last three thousand, perhaps in view of Knossos, the last six thousand years.'[6]

Wyndham's departure from the Cabinet had brought the cousins into even closer communication. 'I have been thinking of you,' Wyndham wrote to Blunt on September 3rd, 'constantly during long stretches, day after day. Your presence is strangely insistent. The last two nights I have spent in reading your poetry. Your poetry touched me first when I was very young and turned me into what I am. But, reading it again, I received two vivid impressions; that you are a Poet, without any shadow of doubt, destined to great praise in years still long distant and, again, that the stuff of your poetry is linked very closely with my life.'[7]

Later in October Wyndham went to Newbuildings for a shoot. Wilfrid Blunt was recovering from his illness, which had been diagnosed as Malta fever, but was still an invalid. Soon after his return to England he had heard of the death of his old friend and teacher Mohammed Abdu and this appeared to symbolize a final break with the desert and Eastern travel. Although he was to maintain a close interest in Egypt and her future Blunt was never to leave England again. 'Wilfrid,' Wyndham told Sibell on October 27th, 'is much better; quite himself. He now has, really, only rheumatism in his arms, like a cottager . . . We talked painting, poetry, politics.' He too was still tired, even after the weeks of rest. 'Politics,' he wrote, 'are becoming wearisome. Mr Joseph Chamberlain wrote me a letter which I am answering that may lead to our estrangement.' From the tone of his letters complete rest seemed still to elude him. 'The sun is shining now gloriously,' he declared to Sibell from Newbuildings, ' – I am writing in the Jubilee room with Wilfrid lying on a couch. I am happy here : went to bed at ten last night! But did not sleep for a long time. I got up and wrote some letters and then read old French poetry.'[8]

Wyndham was still a politician, however wearying he might find politics. Chamberlain's letter had sympathized with 'the worry and anxiety which you must have endured in connection with the most difficult of all political offices', and attempted to persuade him to speak for Tariff Reform. Wyndham, although sympathetic, rebuffed Chamberlain. He felt that he must stand by Balfour in his attempts to find some middle way between the two wings of the Tory party. He spoke at Dover in November, the night after the Prime Minister. 'All the people here,' he wrote to Sibell, 'who count think that they are strongly for Joe. They told me they did not understand Arthur, etcetera, etcetera. This is – as I know – simply because they read in the papers that Joe is definite and courageous; Arthur timid and ambiguous . . . I received two telegrams from a Tariff Reformer MP; the second, put into my hands at the Town Hall, before I spoke, begged me to throw over Arthur, offered me – so kind of them! – the Premiership in seven years time, etcetera, etcetera, concluding with the words "Now is your opportunity, the iron is hot. Strike it!" So I got up very quietly and supported Arthur up to the hilt.'[9]

Later that month, after dinner with the Salisburys, Wyndham had a long talk with Balfour who, by his friendliness and lack of reproach, greatly heartened his old admirer. 'I talked too much, no doubt,' Wyndham told Sibell on November 28th, 'but all was for the best. I am happier than I have been for many a long day. The stone of anxiety has rolled from my heart, and, once more, I live and move and have my being. Arthur laughed at me a little and said "You are Sir William

Wyndham" . . . But it is all right. My ideals reign. My traditions are not shattered.'[10]

Balfour, more hard-pressed than ever by Chamberlain, who openly denounced the Prime Minister's attempts to compromise and gained more power for his cause from the support of the National Union of Conservatives, resigned on December 4th. The Liberals under Sir Henry Campbell-Bannerman took office, and a General Election was fixed for January 6th. On December 30th Balfour, writing to Wyndham, showed how difficult it had become to maintain Tory unity. He hoped, he said, that 'Joe' would 'play the game' and fight under the all-embracing slogan of 'Fiscal Reform and no Home Rule'. Then, the Conservative leader declared, 'we shall be able to fight the Election under circumstances more favourable than anybody could have anticipated a month ago'.[11]

The hopes were to be in vain. In the General Election of 1906, the Conservative party suffered one of the greatest defeats of British political history. 'Arthur Balfour's defeat at Manchester has amused me greatly,' Blunt noted in his diary on January 17th, 'and Gerald's [Balfour] at Leeds, and Alfred Lyttelton's at Warwick. With these three front bench men gone, George Wyndham will remain leader of the Tory opposition, for even Hugh Cecil has been submerged in the general deluge. What a debacle!'[12] The electorate had turned on the already battered government. Using the issue of the importation of Chinese labour into the Transvaal as an example of Tory heartlessness, Campbell-Bannerman had swept the country. Nonconformists, rallied by the memory of the offence given to them by the Conservative Education Act, had deserted the Liberal Unionists in droves; and the defeat of St John Brodrick, the War Minister, symbolized an expiation of the military blunders in South Africa.

'I am,' Wyndham wrote to Sibell on January 19th, 'terribly sorry for St John. It was a shock . . . Our people are beginning to lose heart. But Arthur is splendid. It is grand to think of him speaking right up at Inverness. I only wish I could do more . . .'[13] At Dover Wyndham was safe, with a majority of 1564, but by January 29th Blunt was writing: 'The elections are over, giving the Liberals a clear majority over all other sections of some 89. This is immense.' Blunt, who generally voted Conservative (except when he was standing as a Liberal candidate) was almost alarmed by the vastness of the turn-about, however pleased he may have been by individual upsets. The final results were: Liberal 377, Labour 53, Irish 83, and Conservative and Liberal Unionists 157. The true sensation of the moment was the 53 Labour members, representatives of a new era in British politics.

Wyndham, staying with the Windsors at Hewell Grange, wrote of his reaction in terms that evinced a nostalgia for the past and a distinctly pugnacious attitude towards the future. With Windsor he discussed 'the Conservatism of England and the mission of the great families and the new duties to great towns and the Empire. I cited Benny's [the Duke of Westminster] work and, of course, recognized Windsor's work at Barry Docks and elsewhere . . . We felt that life was worth living and our cause and traditions never more glorious than now. I would rather sweep a gutter than be Winston Churchill . . . I am an incorrigible Tory! Never more so than now. I am glad to go on fighting. I do not believe that we are going to forget the Past and foreswear the Future. The Church and the Realm are great spirits urging me on . . . I am glad we are so soundly beaten. We have shed our Financiers and Brewers. We stand, by our names and our breeding, for a tradition of one thousand years. We know how to fight and we know how to love and we KNOW. We are the tried steel of our race. I never felt more confident in my ideals than now. I love the crowd and the aristocracy of my land. I detest cosmopolitans. I will suffer for my church. I will fight for the Empire of English thought that is to be. It is good to feel this.'[14]

Despite his loyalty to Balfour, Wyndham continued his drift towards whole-hearted Tariff Reform. The party was still split. Of the Conservatives elected in 1906, it was estimated that two-thirds were Chamberlainites, the rest being uneasily divided between those who accepted the Balfourian compromise, the Free Fooders and those who were still undecided. Chamberlain was in a powerful position. He had held his seven Birmingham seats, and felt that his programme had been vindicated. Eventually Balfour acceded to most of Chamberlain's proposals. On February 15th a party meeting was held at Lansdowne House where the truce was ratified. With Arthur Balfour still not back in Parliament (he was to be elected eventually for the City of London) Joseph Chamberlain appeared to be triumphant. In the House of Commons in March Wyndham made a strong Tariff Reform speech.

But the triumph was to be short-lived. On February 19th Wyndham told Blunt that 'Chamberlain, though the public does not know it, is becoming senile and talks inordinately'.[15] On Sunday July 8th Birmingham celebrated his seventieth birthday with a massive display of civic enthusiasm. On the Wednesday of the following week he suffered an incapacitating and dangerous stroke. Henceforth, although he lived on until July 1914, his active political career was ended. However, his sons Austen and Neville lived on; and messages from Highbury, his Birmingham home, continued to be received by the faithful like pronouncements from some distant divinity.

1906 was a milestone in the lives of both Wilfrid Scawen Blunt and George Wyndham. For Blunt it was the first year since his early manhood that he was unable, because of his health, to leave England. It was also the year in which Lady Anne left him. Throughout their marriage she had been subjected to indignities and humiliations, mostly the result of his philanderings, and now she felt unable to accept her position any longer. Her stoicism had been formidable, and she still cared deeply for him. 'I cannot help,' she had written in June 1905, in an effort to retrieve the situation, 'writing about tomorrow. Its date recalls the day we began life together and all the joy as well as the sorrow of those thirty-six years rushes to mind. Above all else, I think of happy days alone with you in desert places, would that we had never come back from them. What I found best in life came with or through you and though also suffering, this I should count as nothing, if only we could now make the best of what may be left to us of life.'[16]

This appeal was not successful. Blunt believed that their estrangement had become inevitable when his wife, after a vision in the Persian desert, had become a Roman Catholic in 1890. 'Very likely,' he wrote, 'you thought that it would bring us nearer together – in fact it was quite the contrary and I look upon it as the point where our roads – our spiritual roads – first diverged. I felt then for the first time that you had come under an influence not mine, which was leading you into regions of the future where I knew I had no part.'[17]

Blunt's attitude to women was, as has been noted, influenced by his contacts with Mohammedanism, and, in the Moslem fashion, he expected their attitude towards him to display a suitable degree of submission. Not even God was tolerated as a competitor. 'Though,' he told her, 'I have many times tried to return to a belief in life after death, I have always since I was twenty-one at the bottom of my mind remained incredulous, and your acceptance of it in so very definite a form as the Catholic one I knew so well as making our human affections in this life subordinate to feelings more glorious perhaps but quite different to take their place in another life, destroyed the sense I had up to that time of security and permanence in the devotion you gave me. I have felt ever since that you were, so to say, serving another master, acknowledging another King, worshipping another god.'[18]

The final separation was precipitated by his illness. Cockerell had telegraphed to Lady Anne in Egypt at the beginning of 1905, and she had travelled to London to be with her husband. In Chapel Street they quarrelled, Blunt eventually telling her that, in his present condition, his nurse was of more importance to him than she was. Next year at Newbuildings there was a similar scene when, as she later told her grandson, Lady Anne felt insulted by Miss Lawrence being placed at the head of the table to pour out the tea. 'You will have to put an end,' she wrote to Wilfrid in July 1906, 'to the position you have placed me in. This you can do by putting your nurses on their proper footing – they should have their meals separately and not come into contact with me or with guests, except in the ordinary course of their professional duties – it is necessary that I should be head in household matters in fact as well as in name – but I have no wish and I never have had any wish that you should part with one that suited you. On the contrary I have borne with the most intolerable state of things for your sake – I have never asserted myself and I should not do so now if you had left any other course open to me.'[19]

Lady Anne left, to divide her time between Sheykh Obeyd and a *pied-à-terre* at Crabbet with her daughter and son-in-law. From here she was able to supervise her portion of the Crabbet stud which husband and wife now divided between them. As time passed their relations became less acrimonious, and on the occasion of her death in December 1917 Wilfrid Blunt was genuinely sad. Irritable and difficult with her he may have been but he could never forget her essential goodness.

After her departure, another person was added to the ménage at Newbuildings. Dorothy Carleton, George Wyndham's cousin, was adopted by Blunt as his niece and henceforth also acted as his companion and private secretary. In his *Quatrains of Life* he writes of her :

> 'How came I by this jewel, this sweet friend,
> This best companion of my lone life's end ?
> So young she was, so fair, of soul so gay,
> And I with only wisdom to commend.'

Dorothy Carleton's presence became another barrier against Lady Anne's return. She was a warm-hearted, rather unimaginative woman, fine-looking and utterly devoted to Blunt. At Newbuildings she and Miss Lawrence enjoyed an uneasy relationship, each adoring their master and both jealous of his praise and attention. His daughter Judith came to resent Dorothy Carleton's position intensely; but it is a measure of Dorothy's qualities that Judith's children remember her with affection. Blunt made George Wyndham a trustee of the money that he was settling on her, and Wyndham wrote, on November 5th 1906, 'I will gladly undertake the duties of Trustee for dear Dorothy. She is like a sister to me and I shall enjoy doing anything for her.'[20]

Although his movements may have been restricted by his health, Wilfrid Blunt maintained an acute interest in life, people and politics. Cromer's rule in Egypt still excited his opposition. In 1906 the Consul-General published a report of his administration's achievements, which was promptly answered by Blunt in the *Manchester Guardian* in May. Scott, the *Guardian*'s editor, added a sympathetic editorial urging self-government for Egypt. In June the *Manchester Guardian* carried another piece by Blunt, this time protesting against the proposed execution of some Egyptian peasants for the 'murder' of an English officer.

This was the notorious Denshawai affair. The villagers of Denshawai had protested vigorously after their tame pigeons had been shot for sport by seven English army officers. A quarrel ensued, a gun went off and a woman was wounded. The officers were belaboured with sticks and a villager was clubbed to death. One of the officers attempted to run for help and was found dead four miles from the village. The charge was that the villagers had killed him, but afterwards it was confirmed that he had died of heat-stroke.

On June 28th Blunt heard of the sentences. They had been passed by a special tribunal of three British officials and two Egyptians. Four of the villagers were condemned to death; four to penal servitude for life; three to fifteen years imprisonment; six to seven years imprisonment; three to one year imprisonment with fifty lashes; five to fifty lashes. Thirty-one were acquitted. 'This,' Blunt wrote, 'is a monstrous sentence and ought, I think, to do more to break up the legend of Cromer's paternal rule in Egypt than anything we have seen since its commencement.'[21] There was worse to come. 'What a state of things!' Blunt exploded on July 3rd. 'Here we have a judicial crime of the largest dimensions committed by our representative in Egypt, the thing hardly denied, quite undeniable and defaming the fair face of English justice throughout the world, yet on the very day the hangings take place our Representative is honoured with the supreme award of the Order of Merit!'[22]

Painstakingly he compiled a pamphlet entitled 'the Atrocities of Justice under English Rule in Egypt'. In September it appeared and caused a considerable stir, being praised in the *Manchester Guardian* and denounced in *The Times*. The latter denunciation, by Moberly Bell, led to a correspondence, and Blunt noted that in Egypt 'my pamphlet has had more effect than I expected, and still more my *Times* letters'. However it was not until April 1907 that the good news came. He was in bed, resting before dinner, when a telegram arrived announcing Cromer's resignation. 'I was at once,' Blunt noted in his diary, 'full awake and laughing so that the bed shook under me, nor could I stop for several minutes. I sent back in return the single word, whoo-whoop! I am off to ... Clouds tomorrow, feeling like a huntsman at the end of his day's sport with Cromer's brush in my pocket, and the mask of that ancient red fox dangling from my saddle. Whoo Whoop!'[23]

Cromer was succeeded by Eldon Gorst, who had served under him for sixteen years. Wilfrid Blunt was, at first, full of hope. 'Sir Eldon Gorst,' he later wrote, 'is not without a certain sympathy with oriental ideas, he speaks Arabic; he is amiable and without the British arrogance which was so characteristic of his predecessor; he has the talent of being able to put himself into good relations with the native world.' But Blunt was to be disappointed. Gorst was more willing to compromise than Cromer; but his attitude to the Nationalists was, in reality, no more accommodating. In 1910 Blunt still felt strongly

enough to finance the publication of *Egypt's Ruin*, a diatribe
against the British presence in that country written by Theodore Rothstein; and contributed frequently to the magazine
Egypt, a monthly review published by the 'Egyptian Committee' who called for 'a return to the better tradition of sympathy
with freedom in the East'.

Cromer returned from Egypt to a hero's welcome. Blunt
claimed that he had talked George Wyndham round to his view
of Egyptian matters; but when Redmond and the Irish, largely
at Blunt's instigation, voted against the government's vote of
thanks to Cromer Wyndham did not join them. His feelings
for the Empire ran too high. His views on foreign policy still
earned Blunt's whole-hearted disapproval, causing the older
man to write in March 1906: 'George was with me again
yesterday full of his parliamentary plans. He is taking the
lead in Opposition now, which he does well, though I hate most
of his public politics.'[24]

For Wyndham 1906 was the end of his party's long ascendancy. Henceforth, against the background of a Liberal government's reformist measures, he was to feel increasingly
bewildered. The years immediately prior to the First War,
although they have often been depicted as an Indian summer
of calm before the slaughter, were thought by many of those
in a position of inherited privilege to represent a new era of
change and uncertainty. By November 1908 Percy Wyndham
was declaring: 'The truth probably is that the reign of the
Upper and middle class is over . . . If it has any future it can
only be realized by fighting . . . for its remaining convictions
and not by concessions.'[25] George Wyndham felt similarly
isolated, saying in 1907: 'Everything I read in newspapers
and nearly everything in modern books disgusts me more and
more with the present age.'[26] In 1908 Wilfrid Blunt, no longer
robust enough to offer a challenge, told Madeline how glad he
was to be living in rural seclusion, out of the way of his
country's progress. 'I lie all day,' he wrote on June 13th from
Newbuildings, 'on a sofa under the oak tree and thank God

I was born in Sussex and that this particular part of the county is still untouched by civilization – indeed I am sure it is less in touch with the outer world in many ways than it was fifty years ago . . . What rural population we have left is very conservative in its ways. There is no ill feeling between class and class, and no wish for rural changes. I hope, this garden of Eden may last at least for my life time.'[27]

Chapter 19
The Final Battle

George Wyndham found himself uncomfortable in Opposition. In this state he veered away from the cloudy Balfourian compromise over protection towards outright Tariff Reform, coming to believe that this alone had the strength to resist socialism, which he regarded as the true challenge. The battle henceforth, he thought, was to be between these two, and everything else should be moved out of the ring. Wyndham felt that Tariff Reform, with its appeal to imperial sentiment, had at least as strong a message for the working classes as socialism. 'I have,' he wrote to Sibell on December 20th 1907, 'a new plan altogether for a speech. After brushing the government away, I get to my old problem – the Empire and the People at home. And attack it in a new way . . . I won't begin with Empire. I will end with Empire. I begin with a child in a slum, coming back from school, on a dark December afternoon, without having had a meal, to an insanitary house. Then I say you must do something for the Race. But what? Only two plans: Socialistic and Tariff Reform. Look at (1) and I prove it will make things worse. Look at (2) and I prove it will make them better.'[1] By January 1908 Wilfrid Blunt was noting that Wyndham had become a whole-hearted Tariff Reformer.

Wyndham also, under what he felt to be threatening conditions, evolved a new and more narrow attitude towards change. He regarded with alarm the urban middle class, many of whom were radicals, and harked back to a vision of an older England in whose rural idyll the territorial gentry benignly lived alongside, and were respected by, a contented peasantry. It was in some vaguely utopian notion of a regeneration of rural England that he put his hopes for the future, telling Wilfrid Blunt that he had become 'one of a small and chastened band of medieval reactionaries'. In the 1906 House of Commons Wyndham met Hilaire Belloc, the newly elected Liberal member for Salford. Belloc, although ostensibly a radical, was in agreement with some of Wyndham's convictions. A friendship grew, urged on by a common love of literature and conversation (neither was a good listener). Belloc's stance, as revealed in his letters, was rather more mixed than that of his new friend. A defender of the traditional aspirations and values of the middle class, from which he had sprung, he believed that these had been betrayed by a new and gross materialism which had resulted in an unthinking rush for riches. He detested the plutocracy that had grown up on the back of the industrial revolution, and for capitalism and capitalists reserved his choicest abuse. His Roman Catholicism led him to see the historical origin of this materialism in the Reformation and the dissolution of the monasteries; and the Jews, for whom he nurtured a paranoiac distrust, seemed to symbolize its most extreme form.

'The great landlords,' Belloc told Wyndham in 1910, after Lloyd George's People's Budget had been finally passed, ' – when they have not sold their bodies or their daughters' bodies to the Jews – are what is best left in our society : and even when they have prostituted themselves they show by their ill ease a remainder of qualities which no other class possesses. The middle class – which is and must be (it is demonstrable like a Mathematical problem) the nucleus, basis, keel, backbone, norm (what metaphor you will) of any complex state has disappeared from England. It is the most terrifying symptom of all.'[2] Another demonstration of the way Belloc's mind operated is given in a letter to Wilfrid Scawen Blunt, in which it is remarked of an opponent: 'He is but a dirty Levantine Jew.'[3]

Belloc saw himself and G. K. Chesterton as two, almost lone, survivors of a cultivated, God-fearing, racially pure bourgeoisie. 'Chesterton,' he wrote, 'belongs to that class. He was brought up to know the classics by tradition (unlike Pearson or Winston Churchill or Herbert Samuel . . .): he sees the state now divided into a class ludicrously luxurious – and the rest – and he knows (rightly) that the beginning of that bad business was the seizing of the land at the Reformation.' Chesterton, who had met Wyndham with the Desboroughs at Taplow, also approved of him. 'Wyndham,' he wrote in his *Autobiography*, 'was not a Conservative; he was a Tory; that is, he was capable of being a Jacobite, which is something as rebellious as a Jacobin. He did not merely wish to preserve Protestantism or Free Trade, or anything grown native to the nation; he wanted to revive things older and really more international. And my first impression of the falsity of the Party system came to me, while I was still a liberal journalist, in the realization of how much I agreed with Wyndham . . .'[4]

His friendship with Chesterton and Belloc demonstrates one aspect of Wyndham's thinking at this time. Belloc and he were in disagreement upon many things. Belloc was a republican who was suspicious of imperialism. With Chesterton he had spoken out against the Boer war; and he found himself distinctly ill at ease in politics, observing of the House of Commons to Wilfrid Blunt that it seemingly had little point except 'to advertise work. It does not govern, it does not even discuss. It is completely futile.' But what appealed to Wyndham were Belloc's prejudices rather than his opinions. These were immense. Religion, or rather Roman Catholicism, bolstered up most of them, and his French ancestry propped up others. They made a formidable list, and included dislike of Germans, Jews, the new rich, Dreyfus, freemasons and religious reformers. 'I wish,' Belloc told Wyndham in 1910, 'we were of one religion. I could say so much more.'[5] Wyndham throughout his life remained a sceptical Protestant, despite his wife's high Anglicanism. But in the decade before the First War he came to share Belloc's preoccupation with 'cosmopolitan finance';

and when Belloc wrote of the 'vile international slime which has made England its working centre (and which will abandon England at the first defeat or decline)' Wyndham agreed, himself often railing against 'Levantine levies', 'fraudulent financiers', 'bounding brothers' and 'piebald hybrids'.

Belloc regarded the House of Lords, with its bought peerages and aura of riches, as 'a committee for the protection of the Anglo-Judaic plutocracy'.[6] However, with George Wyndham, he came to have a respect for its landed element, writing to Wilfrid Blunt in 1906 that, being tired of the House of Commons, 'I go in and hear the Lords. These debate in a commonsense way and very lucidly, but they are a mixed lot. I was amused to find they had no Speaker: they have therefore no master but are free. I wish I was one. It is like having a good club for nothing for life and interesting work just whenever one chooses.'[7] This was the institution that was to become the focal point of Wyndham's attempt to stand foursquare against a changing world.

After the Conservative defeat in 1906, the House of Lords came into its own as an emasculating chamber. With its in-built Tory majority, it proceeded to destroy successive Liberal bills, including those concerning education, land reform and the licensing laws with ruthless determination. The crux came with the Lloyd George Budget of 1909, in which a tax on land values was introduced for the first time. This addition was thought to be necessary because of the need for more revenue to pay for the navy and the newly conceived old age pensions. Naval expenditure had been increased by the decision to build eight Dreadnoughts as a riposte to a rapidly rearming Germany. Popular opinion had come to demand these, urged on by George Wyndham who, as an Opposition spokesman on Defence, had employed the phrase 'We want eight and we won't wait!' during a speech at Wigan in 1909. But Wyndham found it difficult to become greatly involved himself, having settled down, in Opposition, to a quiet life in Cheshire with fox hunting, his wife and son, who was now in the Coldstream

Guards, to keep him happy. On June 22nd 1909 Blunt noted in his diary, after a visit from Wyndham : 'He is rather out of it now in Parliament as he takes no very strong interest in the Budget dispute, believing the Radical bark to be worse than the bite.'[8]

Blunt thought that the Conservative party bark was also worse than its bite. 'I do not expect,' he wrote, 'the Lords will reject the Budget, as some of the extremists would have them do.' He was wrong. In the House of Lords Lord Lansdowne initially wanted to let the Budget through; but by September his party had demonstrated by their anger, which Lloyd George and Churchill had so effectively roused with demagoguery, that they would tolerate nothing less than total rejection. Wyndham was on the side of the rejectors, convincing himself that the Lords were at least as representative of the country's wishes as the Commons. On November 24th Wilfrid Blunt reported : 'Lunched with George and Sibell. They had all been attending the debate in the Lords . . . The House crowded with peeresses and, George said, the most representative assembly he had ever seen, representing as it did every grade of society from royal princesses down to Rosie Boote, Marchioness of Headfort. George quite approves of the fighting attitude of the peers and believes in his party winning at the General Elections.'[9]

On November 30th the Lords rejected the Budget by 350 votes to 70, the first time that they had sent back a finance bill for 250 years. On December 1st Asquith, who had succeeded Campbell-Bannerman as Prime Minister in 1907, moved in the Commons 'That the action of the House of Lords . . . is a breach of the Constitution and a usurpation of the rights of the Commons'. This motion was carried by 349 votes to 134. A January election was now inevitable. Without the Budget the Opposition would have entered such a contest with a fair chance of victory, for the Liberal government had been battered by four years of power and a deteriorating economic situation, but with the issue of the Lords veto, which became infinitely more controversial than the Budget itself, the Liberals had a weapon with which to go into attack.

Wyndham in his own campaign clearly desired a return to the old simplifications. In Dover, for example, he felt at ease with the poor. 'Sibell,' he wrote to his father, 'will tell you what the children of Dover were like. They swarmed like bees on our carriage. They were the children of the poorest. But they might, any one of them, have been my child or Bendor's [the Duke of Westminster]. The race has not degenerated. It has been cramped and sold to the foreigner. These half-fed, badly clothed, wretchedly poor children, had clear eyes, good features, clean limbs. They were all "gentlemen".'[10] Here, in the south, he was free of the socialists and rich radical manufacturers of the industrial Midlands and the north who formed so impregnable a bastion against Tariff Reform. 'If all England,' Wyndham declared ruefully to Wilfrid Blunt on January 26th, 'were like Sussex, Kent, Wiltshire and Hampshire what an earthly Paradise for a happy people!'[11]

The election resulted in a narrow Liberal victory. They won 275 seats, Labour 40, the Irish 82 and the Conservatives 273. Thus the Irish and the socialists held the balance of power. Previously the Irish had voted against the Lloyd George Budget, because it had raised excise duties on spirits. Now the new government secured their support for it by agreeing to curb the power of the House of Lords – a measure on which the Irish, knowing the intransigence of the peers over Home Rule, were in accord. The Budget was passed in April, as were a series of resolutions dealing with the reform of the House of Lords. Wyndham's attitude towards this was already hard. Soon after the election, on February 5th, he lunched with Blunt, who had voted Conservative in January. The diarist recorded of his cousin: 'He assures me the Conservative peers have not the least idea of throwing up the sponge about their hereditary right of veto, nor does he at all fear that the King will swamp their House with new creations. He thinks there will be a kind of deadlock in politics, which will prevent legislation of any kind for the next five years. The strength of the Tory position

is that they and the King together command the whole
national force of the country, besides half its voting strength.
They have the money, and the Army and the Navy and the
territorials, all down to the Boy Scouts. Why, then, should they
consent to a change in the Constitution without fighting?'[12]

Asquith suspected that they would not. Therefore it came as
a grave disappointment when Edward VII informed him that
he would not create enough peers to swamp the Tory majority
until the Lords had defied the government's Parliament Bill
after a second General Election. Then, on May 6th, the King
died. With the accession of George V it was resolved to make a
new attempt to come to some kind of compromise. On June
17th a constitutional conference, consisting of eight men drawn
from both parties, was convened. For the government there was
Asquith, Lloyd George, Lord Crewe and Augustine Birrell;
for the Unionists Arthur Balfour, Lord Lansdowne, Austen
Chamberlain and Lord Cawdor. All were initially full of hope
that progress would be made.

In August 1910 George Wyndham went on a walking tour of
Burgundy with Hilaire Belloc. 'Belloc and I,' Wyndham told
Sibell on August 26th, 'made a great march yesterday of 22
miles over three crests of the Cote d'Or, each nearly two
thousand feet high.' The journey had been completed with
typical Bellocian gusto. 'We had only four miles more,' Wyndham wrote, '(it was more really). And in the dark, with glow
worms by the road side and the Milky Way overhead, we sang
and shouted all the songs we knew, going down-hill through a
terrific gorge in the darkness. Then we saw a light and got to
Gevrey-Chambertin at a quarter to nine . . . The inn was
ancient. But the people were kind and complimentary on our
march.'[13] They then returned to Paris and Wyndham went on
to England, leaving Belloc to further explorations.

Here, like so many others, he awaited anxiously the results
of the constitutional conference. On November 10th, the

participants broke up, having failed to reach agreement. A second election was now inevitable. The Parliament Bill was introduced in the Lords, who 'postponed consideration' of it; and in December a dispirited George Wyndham once again found himself engaged in his customary tour of the hustings. The General Election of December 1910 was remarkable for the apathy of the electorate. The total poll fell by over a million, and the result (Liberals 272, Labour 42, Irish 84, Unionists 272) was remarkably close to that of January. Wyndham was shocked that his efforts had come to nothing. 'The Government,' he told Sibell on December 17th, 'will go on with their Revolution. I shall have to work hard, and write my views for those in whom I trust. The people of England do not realize what is happening.'[14]

Against the background of the constitutional dispute and the Lloyd George Budget inter-party courtesies were suffering a slow process of erosion. At the turn of the century, through the medium of such select groups as the Souls, rival politicians with similar intellectual and social tastes, such as Arthur Balfour and Asquith, had mingled in an easy and friendly fashion. Still, in 1909, Lord Winterton, Tory MP for Horsham, was able to give a dinner at which Wyndham, Alfred Lyttelton and Asquith were fellow guests, and write afterwards that 'in no other country in Europe would a Prime Minister have been on terms of such friendship with opponents as to permit him dining with them in public'.[15] Not until the Ulster troubles of 1912 and 1913 was bitterness to make such a gathering almost impossible. But already, on December 20th 1910, Wyndham was writing to Wilfrid Blunt, in answer to an invitation to join a shooting syndicate at Newbuildings, that he would accept 'but it must be on the understanding that Winston [Churchill] is not a member of it. I have no personal feelings against Winston. Indeed I am rather fond of him and admire his courage. But it is impossible for me to denounce my opponents for shattering the Constitution and the Union, and then, to join with any one of them for the pursuit of pleasure.'[16]

The summer of 1911 was a time of social and political tension. During its stifling months, as the temperature rose into the nineties, a series of strikes, products of the example set by the French syndicalist movements and growing British Trade Union power, culminated in the sending of troops to Liverpool where two men were killed in a clash with dockers. At Westminster, the Lords failed to reform themselves and on July 11th the Parliament Bill to curb their powers came before them for its third reading.

Here Lord Lansdowne was alarmed by the reception accorded to it by the Conservative hard-liners. In June a movement advocating no surrender had been started, having amongst its supporters Lords Halsbury, Willoughby de Broke, Salisbury, Selborne, Lord Hugh Cecil and George Wyndham. Back in February Wyndham had confided in Blunt his growing impatience with the Tory leadership. Even the admired Balfour came under his lash. 'In the House of Commons,' Wyndham told Blunt, 'there is an absolute dearth of ability. The leadership in Balfour's absence is disputed by Walter Long and Austen Chamberlain, a choice of mediocrities. Both look to Arthur's succession, and Arthur is tired of politics and affects to be unwell, though he has nothing at all the matter with him, and has taken a holiday exactly at this crisis.'[17]

Wyndham advocated a more vigorous, less prudent approach. 'His plan would be,' Blunt recorded, 'when Asquith faces them with the Veto Bill to dare him to do his worst, to say "You threaten us with a revolution, we threaten you with a counter-revolution; create the five hundred peers if you can, we refuse to have the Constitution destroyed." If Arthur would call a meeting in St James's Hall and declare war in this way he would carry the country with him, only Arthur won't. Arthur is not sufficiently interested in the issue. He is disgusted with the way things have gone, he does not want to fight. He takes too scientific a view of politics.'[18]

In the Lords in July, some speeches, notably those of Lord Willoughby de Broke, who had previously expended his excess energies on fox hunting, and Lord Halsbury, an ex-Lord Chancellor of great age and obduracy, breathed defiance. The result was that the bill was returned yet again to the Commons, decorated with amendments which Lansdowne must have known the government would not be able to swallow. In any case he and Balfour had now been informed that George V had agreed to create the necessary number of peers to get the bill through, if all attempts at compromise failed. On July 21st, therefore, Lansdowne held a meeting of Unionist peers at Lansdowne House to announce the government's intentions and the King's position. Here, after Lansdowne's failure to supply a lead and advocate acquiescence, Curzon stepped in and forcefully spoke in favour of surrender. He also succeeded in persuading the still-silent Balfour to write a letter to the moderate Lord Newton in which the Leader of the Opposition advised firmly against the die-hard revolt.

The resistance was not to be so easily quelled. On Monday July 24th there was a hysterical scene in the House of Commons in which Asquith was prevented from speaking by Tory jeers. Then, on July 25th, Wilfrid Blunt, calling at 44 Belgrave Square just before dinner, was a witness to Wyndham's final break with Balfour. 'Here,' Wyndham told him, 'you see the conspirators,' and waved his hand towards his companions – F. E. Smith and the Duke of Westminster. 'If,' Wyndham declared to his cousin, 'we had given in without a fight there would have been an end of the Tory party.' Blunt went on to note: 'George thinks they have saved that at least. They are ready for actual armed resistance, or rather, they would like that. They have chosen old Halsbury for their nominal leader because of his great age . . . otherwise there would have been jealousies. All the best men of their Party are with them, including Austen Chamberlain, whom they did not expect. The only one who has disappointed them has been George Curzon. "He is a fool," said George, "for he might have been next Prime Minister." ' Wyndham was in a bellicose mood. Blunt's entry for July 25th ends: 'George thinks war with

Germany quite possible, and he wants it.'[19]

The same day invitations were issued, in the names of Wyndham, Curzon, Austen Chamberlain and F. E. Smith, for a banquet to be given for Lord Halsbury by his supporters on Wednesday July 26th at the Arlington Street house of Lord Salisbury. At this 600 people sat down to dinner, and the rhetoric was formidable. Halsbury, Lord Selborne, Milner, Salisbury, Austen Chamberlain, Carson, F. E. Smith and Wyndham all spoke; and a message of support was read out from the crippled Joseph Chamberlain. But on July 27th Wilfrid Blunt noted : 'George's revolt is not likely to succeed. They held their public dinner to Halsbury last night, and were only able to muster some forty peers at it, while Balfour and Lansdowne have produced a list of 250, and these have threatened to vote for the Bill rather than have peers created to swamp them. The fact is the revolt is all too late.'[20]

The final debate in the House of Lords was due to begin on August 9th. Wyndham's letters show his frenzied efforts on behalf of the die-hards. On August 4th he wrote to Ward : 'Our meetings tonight at Chelsea and Holborn . . . have been passionate triumphs . . . Nothing will shake or divide, or puzzle us . . . If we are beaten by Unionist abstentions and desertions to the Revolution, all is lost except – and for this we fight – the one chance of restoring the constitution which resides in our refusal to abandon the constitution . . . We have the country with us and – what is far more – a sure faith that will survive defeat and save this nation.'[21]

On August 10th Wyndham wrote to Sibell : 'Well it will be over tonight. It is a VERY close finish. I was a little more confident yesterday than I am today, because there are more Rats – i.e. Unionists who will vote with the Government. If all do, who intend to, there will be twenty-one R A T S. If there are twenty-one R A T S, and ten Bishops; there will be a dead heat . . . That being so there is only one move left. Norfolk will speak and vote with us. He ought to carry a few with him; but on the other hand, so passionately are Curzon and Midleton working for the Government that they may detach more abstainers and turn them into R A T S. It, therefore, stands thus : if Norfolk carries three with him and frightens three into the Government lobby we shall win by 1. If he frightens five we shall be beat by 1. I have done all that a man can do and am very tired.'[22]

During the debate Morley, at Rosebery's behest, announced that the King would not hesitate to create new peers to ensure a government majority if the vote went against them. Wyndham believed that, from the very beginning, it had been this that had led to Curzon's advocacy of surrender. The ex-Viceroy could not bear, Wyndham thought, to see the peerage contaminated by such a glut of unsuitable parvenus, and snobbery, rather than prudence, was the motive behind his moderation. This moderation was the victor. At the end of the debate one hundred and thirty-one voted 'content' to one hundred and fourteen 'not contents'. The rest had abstained; but it was the thirty-seven Unionists and the thirteen Bishops who had enabled Morley's eighty-one Liberals to carry the day.

'I did all I could,' wrote Wyndham to Sibell, 'I prayed for the miracle, I mean that. I tell you, Darling, that I did pray standing on the steps of the Throne . . . The miracle did happen. Our people were true as steel; that all our Speakers spoke like Knights . . . and that Curzon and Rosebery made the Radicals whom they saved S I C K, by their cowardice and snobbishness. Many things that I loved are shattered and some friendships gone. Though they do not know it the House of Lords voted tonight for the abolition of the House of Lords, Home Rule, and the disestablishment of the Church.'[23]

After their defeat the die-hards had gone first to the Carlton Club, where some supporters of the government were hooted out of the building, and then on to the 1900 Club to seek solace in their own solidarity. To Sibell, Wyndham could not help displaying his anger and melancholy. 'Of course we can never meet George Curzon or St John Brodrick again,' he declared, 'nor can we ever consent to act with Lansdowne or Balfour if they summon Curzon to their counsels . . . I will *never* act with George Curzon. I will *never* bow the knee to the Harmsworth Press. I will *never* meet Curzon at a council convened by Balfour . . . Now we are finished with the cosmopolitan press – and the American duchesses and the Saturday to Mondays at Taplow – and all the degrading shams. When the King wants loyal men, he will find us ready to die for him. He may want us. For the House of Lords today – tho' they did not know it – voted for Revolution.'

For Balfour it was the end. Some of his strongest supporters had found themselves driven from him, like Wyndham, first by his equivocation over protection and second by his failure to supply a lead during the constitutional crisis. Leo Maxse, editor of the *National Review*, coined the phrase 'Balfour Must Go', shortened to B.M.G.; and Austen Chamberlain, one of the possible successors, was informed by Selborne and Wyndham that his leader might soon resign. On November 8th, after twenty years as the Conservative party leader in the House of Commons, he did so. George Wyndham's letter to Charles Boyd demonstrated that his admiration for his former chief could never be entirely extinguished although, politically, much had grown up between them. 'I felt,' Wyndham declared, 'the sadness of things when Arthur Balfour resigned. But he chose the moment with all the wonderful clearness of his mind, and the manner with all the kindness of his heart . . . And he wrote me an affectionate letter which I prize, and told me not to be too pessimistic. For all that, and all that . . . you can understand.'[24]

Chapter 20

The Last Years

On March 13th 1911, on the eve of his son's last political battle, Percy Wyndham had died. His father's death was a great sadness to George. Percy Wyndham had adored his son, perhaps to excess, often declaring in the midst of noisy family gatherings, 'Hush. George is going to speak.' The feeling had been returned. Blunt too was deeply moved. 'His death,' he noted in his diary for March 14th, 'leaves me without anyone now with a right to lecture or reprove me, for he was my elder by over five years, and had the position with me through life of an elder brother. George was with him when he died.'[1]

George Wyndham was now the master of Clouds. Here, in his last years, he settled into the kind of life which he regarded as his ideal – that of a cultivated English country squire. In the house he constructed a new library, using his own estate workmen, and embarked upon plans for the remodelling of the little village of Milton. He found himself turning away from politics, which had latterly proved to be such a disappointment, towards what was in effect his own kingdom of East Knoyle. Here, at least, it was possible to believe in a contented and ordered ruralism. In 1912 he was telling his friends that he would remain in the House of Commons for another two years, and then quit it forever.

The struggle over the Parliament Bill had exhausted Wyndham. On August 12th 1911, staying with the Windsors at St Fagans Castle, he wrote to Sibell in the tones of a tired and disheartened campaigner, still scarcely convinced of his own defeat. 'I do need a rest,' he declared, 'I cannot quite realize that it is of no use to write to anyone or speak, or urge and persuade any more. I begin to think of arguments and of Peers that might be brought in. And then it comes back to me with a dull thud of pain that it is all over and that we are defeated by men who knew not what they did.' In the house were some friends of the Windsors' children 'jumping over the lawn-tennis net and the chairs as I used to do'; but, although he delighted in their good humour, they also, by evoking the sense of a lost carefree world, added to his melancholy. 'I can rest here,' he wrote, 'and bathe in the sea to cleanse myself of all the dust of conflict. There is that simmer of youth about which is refreshing as one gets older . . .'[2]

Towards the end of 1911 Wyndham suffered a severe attack of influenza. 'This kind of thing,' he told Sibell, 'does not make me like politics any better.'[3] In February 1912 he was once again in fighting mood, speaking of a last assault to 'kill Dillon politically'; but this desire for activity alternated with fatigue. In February the Bellocs came to Clouds and Hilaire tired Wyndham with his perpetual effervescence. 'I enjoyed much in Belloc's visit,' he wrote to Sibell, 'but he does tire me. He rejoices in disputation for the sake of disputing, whereas I care for discussion only in so far as it extends the area of possible understanding. And he shouts.'[4] The thought of returning to Westminster displeased him. Here he had a new leader. From behind the conflicting candidatures of Austen Chamberlain and Walter Long had emerged Andrew Bonar Law, a Canadian son of the manse who believed, with Presbyterian dedication, in a loyal Ulster and Tariff Reform.

'Dined well,' Wyndham wrote to Sibell on St Valentine's day 1912, 'with Bonar Law – twenty-two of us. Dinner and house simple and suburban.'[5] In August he told her that he had begun to work again at an epic poem he had started some twenty years ago. A humiliation came when Lord Midleton, formerly St John Brodrick, tried to persuade him to speak, as his assistant, on defence matters in the Commons. This prompted a letter to F. E. Smith, a former ally at the time of the Parliament Bill. 'I would like,' Wyndham wrote on December 6th, 'your advice – as between friends – on one conundrum. St John Brodrick has been bombarding me with letters, and telegrams for three months, the upshot of which is that he has been commissioned by Lansdowne and Bonar Law to settle our army policy and to employ me as his Under-Secretary in the lower House. He objects to Amery or anyone else assisting. He writes that this charming arrangement originates with "George Curzon and some of us". I don't know who "us" refers to – presumably to renegade peers. Now I want to know whether George Curzon and St John Brodrick are the leaders of the Unionist Party. I have a pleasant home in the country and if we are to be led by the Peers who ran away, I shall "cultivate my garden".'[6]

Thus the die-hard bitterness lived on. Wyndham had previously been speaking on military matters from the Opposition front bench. Of late, however, his interventions in debate 'had become spasmodic and ineffective'.[7] It was as if the fire had gone out of him. Colleagues noted an increasing vagueness of manner, which some ascribed to drink. Those who had been his juniors, such as Austen Chamberlain, had overtaken him. In October 1912, at a weekend in the new house that Wilfrid Blunt had built for himself in Worth Forest, he was faced with another of these – Winston Churchill. Churchill, who, as an aspiring Tory politician, had written to George Wyndham for advice in 1900, was now First Lord of the Admiralty in the Liberal government. Wyndham, anxious to avoid the other's company at the time of the Budget dispute, had eventually agreed that his cousin should bring the two of them together again.

In the intervals between shooting woodcock and deer the party discussed politics. Now there could be no doubt as to who was in the superior position. Blunt, as was his custom, created a suitably exotic ambience. 'It was a fine night,' he wrote of one evening, 'and we dined in the bungalow, dressed in gorgeous oriental garments, Clementine in a suit of embroidered silk, purchased last year at Smyrna, Winston in one of my Bagdad robes, George in a blue dressing gown, and I in my Bedouin clothes ... It recalled the most glorious night's entertainments of the Crabbet Club, a true feast of reason and flow of bowl. The secrets of the Cabinet were gloriously divulged, and those of the Opposition front benches no less, from Home Rule to a reconstruction of the House of Lords by common accord after George Curzon and Asquith had been got rid of, while George Wyndham declared with great oaths that he would rather go to hell than see the British constitution made ridiculous by single chamber Government, at which point I left them for my bed. Winston was very brilliant in all this, as though he kept on at the Madeira he also kept his head, and played with George's wild rushes like a skilled fencer with a greatly superior fence.' At the end of the visit the diarist noted that 'George ... clever though he is, is a mere child in argument compared with Winston'.[8]

But 1913 began well for the Wyndhams. On February 13th George wrote to Wilfrid Blunt to announce his son Percy's engagement to Diana Lister, the daughter of Lord Ribblesdale. 'I wrote,' he declared, 'at once to you because you and one other are near to me in all that really touches my life.' Wyndham was delighted at the beauty and gentleness of his prospective daughter-in-law. But the burden of an increasingly distasteful political career was still with him. With Blunt he hoped soon to seek a momentary respite. 'I am determined,' he wrote, 'to be your guest with luck when the birds are in chorus, and in any case when the wild roses bloom. You are fortunate. To select and print poetry seems to me – after influenza in a dark drizzle damned to the hell of politics – an inconceivable extravagance of joy.'[9] In April the young couple were married. For their wedding present Wilfrid Blunt presented them with a fine edition of Ronsard, a folio of 1609 – but the gift was, in reality, meant for George.

On Monday June 2nd, the last week of the Whitsun recess,

George Wyndham went to Paris, at the Duke of Westminster's invitation, with Lady Plymouth (formerly Windsor) and her daughter Lady Phyllis Windsor-Clive. 'As a rule,' Wyndham had once written to his cousin, 'people do not know how to love; as an exception they love now here, now there; as a rarity almighty lovers find each other after both are married.' Certainly Lady Plymouth made his last years and disappointments more bearable than they would otherwise have been, sharing his friends and tastes with sympathy, and still contriving to remain on the best of terms with his wife. To the end this was true.

Belloc was also passing through Paris. Together they made an expedition to St Germain and the Buzenval woods, arranging to meet again at Clouds on June 13th. On Friday June 6th he was with Lady Plymouth and her daughter at Fontainebleau. On their return he complained of a slight pain in his chest. The next day it seemed to have disappeared. That morning he wrote to Sibell telling her of his intention to return on Sunday; but, after a night's sleep, he woke with a renewal of the pain in his chest. A doctor was called, slight congestion in one lung was diagnosed and he was advised to postpone his journey for two or three days. The pain continued, although his temperature was hardly above normal. A nurse was called, and a morphine injection administered. At seven in the evening Lady Plymouth left him to settle down to rest. Then between nine and ten o'clock she was telephoned by the nurse. She came immediately but was too late. He had died some ten minutes earlier of the passage of a clot of blood through the heart.

On Friday June 13th George Wyndham was buried beside his father in the churchyard at East Knoyle. In the House of Commons there were heartfelt tributes. 'These,' Arthur Balfour said, 'are the great tragedies of life. That I whose public work in the natural course of things is drawing to a close should have to say these few words of one whose politics from the

beginning have been as it were in close co-operation with myself, who was almost young enough to be my son, seems to me
to add deeply to the tragedy of what is a tragic situation.'[10]

To Madeline Wyndham, Balfour wrote with great feeling.
'How long ago is it,' he declared, 'since you spoke to me of
George's decision to enter political life, and to enter it as my
secretary? So much has happened since then in the big world of
public affairs – and in the smaller but more important world
of private friendships. But George remained unchanged throughout – loyal, affectionate, brilliant, chivalrous. Neither the
triumphs nor the difficulties inseparable from a statesman's
career, nor the lapse of years, nor altered circumstance could
touch in essentials his wonderful personality or check the
development of his winning gifts. The world laments the loss
of one whose greatest performances seemed yet to come. But
for his friends this loss, great though it is, seems small compared
with that which they have sustained through the tragic
severance of that affectionate intercourse which seemed almost
a part of our lives.'[11]

Wyndham's death had prevented him from entering a period
of even deeper bewilderment and unhappiness. The first two
verses of an Easter poem he wrote in March 1913 reveal his
sense of nostalgia and hopelessness, despite the beauty
of spring which was, he felt, almost alone still worthy of
salutation.

> 'I have forgotten how to sing,
> If ever I sang, so I only say
> That I am glad. For here is Spring
> And I am alive, thank God, today.
>
> I have forgotten other men's songs
> That made me jubilant long ago,
> Before I knew of rights and wrongs,
> And the death of delight in Beauty's show.'

What had happened to him? How had this figure, so full of early glitter and promise, descended in middle age to the grey introspective communings of melancholia and despair? The answer can partly be found in his temperament. Acute sensitivity and an unbalanced reaction to life's circumstances – inclined one moment to euphoria, the next to depression – were the hallmarks of this temperament. With them came, at first, unbounded optimism born of early confidence and success. When shattered this gave way to its very opposite – black pessimism, and the tendency to imagine a multitude of mysterious conspirators, anxious only to bring ruin to one's country and class.

Wyndham's political fault was, in essence, that he took too broad a view. Like most romantics he was moved more by the overall conception of a task, by its significance against the vast background of history, than by the technicalities of its accomplishment. Those who served with him in Ireland could be enthused by his visionary exhortations, yet confounded by his inattention to the details that might make this vision a reality. Failure proved too hard to bear. In the face of it, he ran off the edge of the world into a nowhere land where he might still exercise his courage and even find cause occasionally to feel full of hope, but from which the rest of his compatriots were drawing ever faster away. Balfour's suggestion to George Wyndham's mother that the best of his career was yet to come was a kind of palliative. Immediately before his death he was sick of politics. Had he lived longer, the war, with its extinction of a whole generation would surely have hardened this feeling. In June 1913 Ireland appeared to be moving towards civil war, and Europe towards destruction. Wyndham seemed almost powerless at this terrible and crucial time. Now he had at least been spared the sight of its worst excesses.

'It was a blow,' Wilfrid Scawen Blunt wrote of George Wyndham's death, 'which struck me to the inmost fibres of my heart, bewildering in its unexpectedness, and touching me on every side of my existence.' The tearing apart by death of their friendship caused the older man immense sorrow. 'He was,' Blunt went on, 'my nearest male relation, and very much my nearest friend. I had looked upon him as the inheritor after me of our family traditions, and in some measure of my possessions as trustee and knowing all. No thought had ever crossed my mind that I could have the misfortune to survive him. Although on politics we were a whole world apart, on all things else we were in perfect unison of thought and taste and literary sympathy.'[12]

'With George Wyndham's death,' Blunt declared, 'my most intimate connection with the parliamentary world ceased.' Since his last return from Egypt this connection had grown increasingly tenuous. The Liberal government of 1906 had done little to strengthen it. Sir Edward Grey, its Foreign Secretary, Blunt accused of a series of disastrous blunders. With social reform he had never had much sympathy, believing that individual effort alone, as opposed to a system of improvement imposed from above, could cure poverty. In 1885 he had sat next to Mrs Courtney, a social worker in the East End of London, at a dinner party, and, as a result of her description of her ideas and work, had written: 'To me all these matters are absolutely hopeless; system has interfered with the natural law of society, and unnatural misery is the result.'[13]

At Newbuildings, devotedly attended by Dorothy Carleton and Miss Lawrence, he could escape the turmoil of these years. But with isolation came a growing feeling of sadness and disappointment. The peace of mind which he had attained in the 1890s and early 1900s began to be replaced by an agonizing sensation of failure. He saw himself as a lonely misunderstood figure, vainly preaching the cause of conservative nationalism. As always, he was much visited. In 1911 Francis Thompson the poet, already desperately ill, came to spend a few weeks in one of the cottages at Newbuildings. He moved around as if in a dream, giving himself over, at the end of his visit, to large doses of laudanum and dying a month later in London. In

January 1914 came another literary deputation, consisting of seven more poets amongst whom were Ezra Pound, W. B. Yeats and Richard Aldington. Blunt received them in his dining room with a roasted peacock in the centre of the table, and the poets each ate two helpings of the exotic bird. Pound, the inspiration behind the expedition, read out their message of greeting.

> 'Because you have gone your individual gait,
> Written fine verses, made mock of the world,
> Swung the grand style, not made a trade of art
> Upheld Mazzini and detested institutions
>
> We who are little given to respect
> Respect you, and having no better way to show it,
> Bring you this stone to be some record of it.'

Mazzini had been mistakenly substituted for Arabi, but 'the stone' was a fine tribute. It consisted of a small marble box, engraved with a bas-relief by Gaudier-Brzeska, containing a poem in manuscript by each of the poets. Blunt understood neither the box nor the work inside it, caring little for the recent developments in art or literature. Yet he felt honoured, and when Pound came back to Newbuildings in March with Aldington, appeared at dinner in Arabian robes with two gold-mounted pistols in his belt. On this occasion he proposed a toast, 'Damnation to the British Government'. Afterwards they talked poetry and Blunt noted: 'I am trying to persuade them into some kind of sanity.'[14]

It was the publication of his diaries that made Wilfrid Blunt's rebellious past available to any who might choose to read and take example. In 1907 *The Secret History of Egypt* appeared, in 1909 *India Under Ripon* and in 1910 *Gordon at Khartoum*. In 1912 came *The Land War in Ireland* and, after the war in 1919 and 1920, the two volumes of *My Diaries*. These are journals of inimitable gusto, brilliant in observation, incisive in comment and delineation of character. Their style is full of the vigours of their writer and coruscates with his idiosyncratic prejudices. Together, they make a unique record of their time if only for the countless figures of importance in Victorian and Edwardian England who emerge from their pages enhanced by an illuminating anecdote or flash of judgement. Defenders of the Empire might deride them; but it was impossible to deny their art. In October 1914 the diaries were joined by the Collected Poems, brought out by Macmillan's. A final inclusion had been an ode to the memory of George Wyndham, entitled 'To a happy warrior'. The opening line was 'Glory be to God who made a man like this'; and later Blunt wrote, in a suitably melancholy vein :

> 'Not flowers alone
> Nor fruits were his,
> But the world's sadness
> He gathered also, its loves lost and gone,
> The tragic things that are
> As the maple leaves
> Of the past dying years.
> Crowning its funeral car,
> The glory of its passing set on fire
> In the late hedges.'

The war found him still in Sussex. He had hoped for England's neutrality and turned his face against any manifestation of militarism, refusing to sign patriotic pleas or manifestos. The slaughter appalled him; but it was too late now to indulge in the luxury of protest. In June 1919, after the holocaust was over, one of its principal poets, Siegfried Sassoon, came down to Newbuildings. Blunt received him one evening in June, lying on a narrow bed in an almost Spartan bedroom. Sassoon found the old man (he was now nearing 79) 'more fragile and less formidable than I had expected'.[15] With immense courtesy he greeted his young visitor, speaking in a soft and gentle voice, smiling to hear that the poet too was an enthusiastic horse-man.

The next evening they went out to the paddocks, Blunt wearing a white Bedouin cloak and making the journey in a small carriage pulled by an obedient pony. 'His appearance,' Sassoon remembered, 'was superb; and if anything more remarkable was to be seen in Sussex I should be glad to know where it was.' Belloc came over to join them, and there, in front of the magnificent Arab stallions grazing at peace in the calm ending of a summer's day, Blunt asked his neighbour to sing before they returned to the house. In a high tenor, Belloc launched into 'Ha'nacker Mill', and the juxtaposition of nature, old age and the simple moving words gave Sassoon an un-fogettable sensation of pathos and tranquility.

> 'Sally is gone that was so kindly.
> Sally is gone from Ha'nacker Hill.
> And the briar grows ever since then so blindly
> And ever since then the clapper is still,
> And the sweeps have fallen from Ha'nacker Mill.'

Unfortunately Blunt's last years were not entirely composed of such Elysian moments. Through his uneasy relationship with his tempestuous daughter Judith he found himself involved in a succession of acrimonious family disputes. Once devoted to her father, Judith had in the 1890s heard of an episode in his philanderings that particularly displeased her, chiefly because it involved one of her closest friends. Since that time she had turned against him with all the ardour of a convert. She came to believe that her mother had been shabbily treated, and set out to avenge her. Matters of property became one of the main points of argument. In 1919 the troubles took the form of a law suit over Lady Anne's portion of the Crabbet stud, with both father and daughter claiming control over it. Judith won the case.

The extent of their estrangement can be judged by the fact

that she heard the news of her father's death from the newspapers. The end had been slow in coming, with Blunt slipping away from life attended, in the words of Shane Leslie, 'by devoted feminine slaves, the last of a long series whom he had fascinated since Victorian days'.[16] In August 1922 he was visited by a Dominican friar, Father Vincent MacNab, who gave him the last sacraments, thus witnessing his eventual return to the faith of his childhood. 'I only hope,' Father MacNab later wrote to a friend, 'I shall have at death the same childlike faith that he had.'[17] Then, on September 10th, he died.

The burial was simple, without any religious or other ceremony. Wilfrid Scawen Blunt was wrapped in an Arabian carpet and carried by six estate workers to a grave several hundred yards from the house. Judith had come with two of her children and, together with Dorothy Carleton and Miss Lawrence, they walked behind the body. Miss Lawrence, Dorothy Carleton and Judith's daughter Anne heaped potpourri from the Newbuildings roses into the grave, and then Judith knelt beside it alone in prayer. Cockerell too was there, a pacific and steady presence. Some months later Father MacNab came to bless the site; and on September 14th Cockerell informed Judith of the terms of the will. The Worth estate had been left to Lady Mary Strickland, a daughter of Mary Elcho, and Newbuildings to Dorothy Carleton, both as life tenancies. Judith was furious. All the old bitterness, mitigated for an instant by the sadness of death, returned. Henceforth she declared a perpetual war against the memory of her father. This war only ceased on the occasion of her own death at Crabbet in 1957, at the age of eighty-four.

Epilogue

Now the world of Wilfrid Scawen Blunt and George Wyndham seems a long way distant. Since their deaths a whole age has passed, and England has changed almost beyond recognition. Blunt's old land at Crabbet is half submerged, and entirely dominated, by Crawley new town; and Clouds, the house the Wyndhams built in Wiltshire to last their family for generations, is in the hands of an institution. Yet, for all this, they are no less interesting. Both were supreme examples of the romantic temperament; and mirrored in their lives are all the attributes and disadvantages of this temperament. Enthusiasm they both possessed, and curiosity. Each was moved more by the emotions than the intellect. Each put a high value on the traditions of the past.

Of course there were differences. Wilfrid Scawen Blunt was manifestly the less conventional of the two. His background had not been so secure. An uncertain childhood, without either a permanent home or the comforts of a united and easy family life, can lead to an objective view of what others are apt to take for granted. George Wyndham, with his history of happy experiences in their midst, would be more inclined to accept the English governing class's premises and standards than would Blunt. Certainly this was true with regard to the Empire and Ireland. The one followed the line of his party, falling only when it seemed that he might be about to desert it. The other, free of the constraints of political responsibility, took a wider view, formed through personal and independent observation. Today, in the clearer light of hindsight, Blunt, with his anti-imperialism and early championship of Irish Home Rule, seems nearer to the conventional wisdom.

Enthusiasm, curiosity, a sense of history – these are some of the cards that the romantic holds in his hand. They are not, unfortunately, the only ones. There can also be a preoccupation with the external, a concern for form rather than substance. Wyndham, for instance, full of grand proposals for the future of Ireland and passing one of that country's greatest ever measures of reform, failed to read properly the everyday reports sent to him by his Under-Secretary; Blunt, crusading for Irish and Egyptian Nationalism, quickly tired of the drabness of a London election campaign and showed impatience when reminded of the poverty and distress that existed, under his very nose, in industrial England. The romantic breadth of vision – of a great beneficent empire or self-determination for oppressed nationalities – was always there. What was occasionally lacking was the capacity to delve under the glitter of a great conception to the less obvious intricacies beneath.

W. H. Auden once remarked that those writers who cry out against injustice or commit themselves to the support of some political cause, no matter how shrill their cry may be, can change nothing. They will often succeed in advancing their reputation, particularly with those who are in agreement with them, but the injustice will still stand. Towards the end of his life Blunt came to feel this. It led to depression at the thought of his own failure. The shaping of the world since his death has vindicated him, as it has come to make Wyndham's imperialism a mere antique curiosity. Yet his conservative nationalism, with its maintenance of the old landed order at home and freedom for the colonies overseas, seems as eccentric and defunct as Wyndham's struggle to defeat the Parliament Bill. Their flamboyant romanticism, with its extravagance of sentiment and language, appears out of tune with present-day reality. They share a common oblivion.

Yet in their own age they were surely of the best. Each was born into a supremely powerful and self-confident class, free of doubt or pressure; and each set out not to rest in the ease which this power and confidence could provide but to work for what they believed in. Their monuments are still with us. Egyptian Nationalism, encouraged by Blunt, eventually triumphed over Cromer's vision of an Egypt under enduring European protection and control. In Ireland the land question is settled; but Ulster intransigence, hardened by the MacDonnell-Wyndham imbroglio into a distrust of all English politicians, grows no less hard. There is, after all, a certain immutability in history. The lives of Wyndham and Blunt prove this, as they also give evidence, through their failures and successes, of two brave, adventurous and enquiring spirits. Such qualities are not merely an example for an individual age; they have a message for all time.

Notes

G.P. = Grosvenor Papers.
L.A.L.C. = Lady Anne Lytton collection of Blunt papers.
P.H.A. = Petworth House archives.

Mackail = Life and Letters of George Wyndham by J. W. Mackail and Guy Wyndham. (Hutchinson 1925).

CHAPTER I

1. Times. March 14 1911.
2. Mackail, p. 746.
3. May 19 1896. L.A.L.C.
4. October 12 1896. L.A.L.C.
5. Miss Eden's Letters, p. 250.
6. Mackail, p. 287.
7. ibid, p. 16.
8. Olivier. Four Victorian Ladies of Wiltshire, p. 99.
9. September 12 1912. L.A.L.C.
10. Mackail, p. 143.
11. August 8 1898. L.A.L.C.
12. P.H.A.
13. P.H.A.
14. P.H.A.
15. Francis Wyndham Collection.
16. Mackail, p. 128.
17. Jones. Victorian Boyhood, p. 240.
18. Mackail, p. 130.
19. ibid, p. 131.
20. ibid, p. 131.
21. ibid, p. 133.
22. ibid, p. 137.
23. ibid, p. 138.
24. P.H.A.
25. Edel. Henry James. Conquest of London, p. 328.
26. Nevill. Reminiscences, pp. 102-5.
27. Edel, op cit, p. 279.
28. Mackail, p. 140.
29. Francis Wyndham Collection.
30. Mackail, p. 140.
31. Gordon at Khartoum, p. 362.
32. Macarthy. Portraits, p. 29.

CHAPTER 2

1. Lady Wentworth. The Authentic Arabian, p. 69.

2. ibid, p. 70.
3. Letter in possession of the Earl of Lytton.
4. Finch. Wilfrid Scawen Blunt, p. 20.
5. Proteus and Amadeus, p. 24.
6. ibid, p. 24.
7. ibid, p. 25.
8. Balfour (ed.). Personal and Literary Letters of the Earl of Lytton. I, p. 189.
9. Proteus and Amadeus, p. 29.
10. Balfour. Lytton Letters. I, p. 189.
11. ibid, p. 189.
12. ibid, p. 190.
13. ibid, p. 190.
14. ibid, p. 189.
15. My Diaries. I, p. 134.
16. Brodie. The Devil Drives, p. 17.
17. Harris. Contemporary Portraits, pp. 165-6.

CHAPTER 3

1. P.H.A.
2. Lady Wentworth. op cit, p. 66.
3. Lytton. English Country Gentleman, p. 209.
4. Finch. op cit, p. 53.
5. Secret History, p. 5.
6. ibid, p. 5.
7. ibid, p. 7.
8. ibid, p. 67.
9. India Under Ripon, p. 74.
10. July 9 1876. L.A.L.C.

11. Secret History, p. 10.
12. ibid, p. 23.
13. ibid, p. 27.
14. ibid, p. 58.
15. ibid, p. 62.
16. ibid, p. 63.
17. May 10. L.A.L.C.

CHAPTER 4

1. Mackail, p. 144.
2. ibid, p. 145.
3. Gordon at Khartoum, p. 79.
4. ibid, p. 91.
5. India Under Ripon, p. 312.
6. ibid, p. 313.
7. ibid, p. 33.
8. ibid, p. 38.
9. ibid, p. 217.
10. ibid, p. 262.
11. ibid, p. 276.
12. ibid, p. 315.
13. Gordon at Khartoum, p. 413.
14. ibid, p. 459.
15. ibid, p. 59.
16. ibid, p. 362.
17. ibid, p. 453.
18. Hardinge. Old Diplomacy, p. 22.
19. Mackail, p. 149.
20. Gordon at Khartoum, p. 419.
21. ibid, p. 438.
22. ibid, p. 442.
23. Mackail, p. 177.

NOTES

CHAPTER 5

1. G.P.
2. G.P.
3. Rose. Superior Person, p. 172.
4. Mackail, p. 35.
5. Told to the author by Lady Dorothy Lygon.
6. Margot Asquith. Autobiography, p. 65.
7. G.P.
8. Mackail, p. 179.
9. ibid, p. 180.
10. ibid, p. 180.
11. ibid, p. 35.
12. G.P.
13. G.P.
14. G.P.
15. Mackail, p. 188.
16. ibid, p. 141.
17. G.P.
18. G.P.
19. G.P.
20. G.P.
21. G.P.
22. G.P.
23. Mackail, p. 192.
24. G.P.
25. G.P.
26. G.P.
27. G.P.
28. Mackail, p. 385.
29. G.P.
30. Mackail, p. 202.

CHAPTER 6

1. Edel. Henry James. The Middle Years, p. 107.
2. ibid.
3. Gordon at Khartoum, p. 423.
4. ibid, p. 414.
5. ibid, p. 415.
6. ibid, p. 428.
7. ibid, p. 472.
8. ibid, p. 471.
9. ibid, p. 501.

CHAPTER 7

1. Land War in Ireland, p. 9.
2. ibid, p. 41.
3. ibid, p. 54.
4. ibid, p. 63.
5. O'Connor. Memoirs of an Old Parliamentarian. II, p. 124.
6. Report of the Bessborough Commission, p. 598.
7. O'Connor. op cit. II, p. 123.
8. Land War, p. 66.
9. ibid, p. 73.
10. ibid, p. 76.
11. Gordon at Khartoum, p. 438.
12. Country Life XVI (1904), pp. 255-60.
13. Lethaby. Webb and his work, p. 121.
14. Country Life. op cit.

CHAPTER 8

1. O'Connor. op cit. II, p. 126.
2. Cecil. Salisbury. III, p. 347.
3. Young. Balfour, p. 101.
4. Morley. Recollections. I, p. 228.
5. Young. op cit, p. 105.
6. Wells. Experiment in Autobiography, p. 775.
7. Gatty. Recognita, p. 88.
8. Rose. op cit, p. 179.
9. Told to the author by Mrs Guy Wyndham.
10. Curtis. Coercion and Conciliation, p. 182.
11. ibid, p. 215.
12. ibid, p. 215.
13. G.P.
14. Land War, p. 301.
15. ibid, p. 296.
16. ibid, p. 298.
17. ibid, p. 300.
18. ibid, p. 301.
19. Edel. Henry James. The Middle Years, p. 105.
20. Land War, p. 303.
21. ibid, p. 307.
22. ibid, p. 328.
23. L.A.L.C.
24. Land War, p. 333.
25. ibid, p. 337.
26. ibid, p. 339.
27. ibid, p. 340.
28. ibid, p. 345.
29. ibid, p. 348.
30. ibid, p. 349.

CHAPTER 9

1. Land War, p. 358.
2. ibid, p. 367.
3. ibid, p. 368.
4. Balfour (ed.). Lytton Letters. II, p. 326.
5. Curtis. op cit, p. 206.
6. L.A.L.C.
7. Mackail, p. 217.
8. Land War, p. 381.
9. ibid, p. 376.
10. January 10 1888. Cobden papers.
11. Land War, p. 384.
12. G.P.
13. Freeman's Journal. January 16 1888.
14. Land War, p. 385.
15. Mackail, p. 287.
16. Land War, p. 404.
17. ibid, p. 406.
18. ibid, p. 406.
19. ibid, p. 407.
20. ibid, p. 407.
21. C.S.O.R.P. 1888. 4406. State Papers. Dublin Castle.
22. Times. March 23 1888.
23. Times. March 26 1888.
24. Land War, p. 413.
25. L.A.L.C.
26. L.A.L.C.

CHAPTER 10

1. Dugdale. Balfour. I, p. 185.
2. G.P.

3. G.P.
4. G.P.
5. G.P.
6. Mackail, p. 43.
7. G.P.
8. Mackail, p. 250.
9. G.P.
10. G.P.
11. G.P.
12. G.P.
13. Mackail, p. 252.
14. G.P.
15. My Diaries. I, p. 27.
16. Some Hawarden Letters, p. 252.

CHAPTER 11

1. Girouard. Victorian Country House, p. 55.
2. My Diaries. I, p. 183.
3. Mackail, p. 248.
4. History of the Crabbet Estate, Preface.
5. Gordon at Khartoum, p. 214.
6. Lytton. English Country Gentleman, p. 242.
7. My Diaries. I, p. 112.
8. Howard. Theatre of Life. I, p. 72.
9. My Diaries. I, p. 1.
10. G.P.
11. My Diaries. I, p. 51.
12. ibid, p. 52.
13. ibid, p. 52.
14. Finch. op cit, p. 278.
15. My Diaries. I, p. 138.
16. ibid. I, p. 83.
17. Howard. op cit. I, p. 72.

18. L.A.L.C.
19. Rose. op cit, p. 157.
20. Storrs. Orientations, p. 33.
21. My Diaries. I, p. 84.
22. L.A.L.C.
23. July 2 1893. G.P.
24. Lytton. English Country Gentleman, p. 245.
25. Howard. op cit. I, p. 75.
26. My Diaries. I, p. 65.
27. Balfour. Chapters of Autobiography, p. 232.
28. Asquith. Memoirs, p. 139.
29. Midleton. Records and Reactions, p. 51.
30. My Diaries. I, p. 102.
31. Midleton. op cit, p. 52.
32. G.P.
33. Wells. op cit, p. 514.
34. My Diaries. I, p. 49.
35. L.A.L.C.
36. My Diaries. I, p. 73.
37. ibid, p. 73.
38. Nineteenth Century. June 1892.

CHAPTER 12

1. Land War, p. 266.
2. ibid, p. 303.
3. L.A.L.C.
4. Asquith. op cit, p. 190.
5. G.P.
6. G.P.
7. Harrison. Autobiographic Memoirs, II, p. 174.
8. L.A.L.C.
9 National Review. Vol. xxvi, October 1895.

10. Poetry of Wilfrid Blunt, Preface.
11. My Diaries. I, p. 133.
12. ibid. II, p. 65.
13. Yeats. Memoirs, pp. 38-9.
14. G.P.
15. Mackail, p. 282.
16. Gatty. op cit, p. 2.
17. May 27 1895. L.A.L.C.
18. Essays in Romantic Literature, p. 79.
19. Connell. Henley, p. 319.
20. Eliot. The Sacred Wood (paperback edition), p. 28.
21. Boyd. George Wyndham, p. 12.

CHAPTER 13

1. My Diaries. I, p. 94.
2. Faber. The Vision and the Need, p. 75.
3. My Diaries. I, p. 37.
4. Boyle. Boyle of Cairo, p. 135.
5. My Diaries. I, p. 79.
6. ibid. I, p. 130.
7. Anstruther papers.
8. December 20 1897. G.P.
9. My Diaries. I, p. 340.
10. ibid. I, p. 340.
11. Lady Wenworth. op cit, p. 73.
12. My Diaries. I, p. 179.
13. ibid. I, p. 89.
14. ibid. I, p. 281.
15. ibid. I, p. 211.
16. ibid. I, p. 286.
17. ibid. I, p. 349.
18. ibid. I, p. 369.

19. ibid. I, p. 403.
20. ibid. I, p. 405.
21. ibid. I, p. 410.
22. Mackail, p. 301.
23. L.A.L.C.
24. Mackail, p. 441.
25. G.P.
26. My Diaries. I, p. 346.
27. G.P.
28. G.P.
29. My Diaries. I, p. 372.

CHAPTER 14

1. Boyd. op cit, p. 11.
2. Willoughby de Broke. The Passing Years, p. 165.
3. Mary Maxse. A Memoir, p. 29.
4. Gatty. op cit, p. 134.
5. G.P.
6. G.P.
7. Mackail, p. 67.
8. Lee. A Good Innings, p. 128.
9. Mackail, p. 402.
10. Mary Maxse. op cit, p. 29.
11. Mallet. Life with Queen Victoria, p. 141.
12. My Diaries. I, p. 401.
13. Pakenham. Jameson's Raid, p. 334.
14. My Diaries. I, p. 402.
15. ibid, p. 411.
16. Mackail, p. 364.
17. ibid, p. 360.
18. ibid, p. 361.
19. ibid, p. 362.

20. ibid, p. 372.
21. ibid, p. 375.
22. ibid, p. 381.
23. My Diaries. I, p. 419.
24. Cecil. Salisbury. III, p. 391.
25. My Diaries. I, p. 420.
26. Mackail, p. 382.
27. ibid, p. 383.
28. ibid, p. 384.
29. ibid, p. 390.
30. My Diaries. I, p. 427.
31. Ponsonby. Recollections, p. 78.
32. Mackail, p. 386.
33. ibid, p. 390.
34. Hansard. 4th Series. Vol. lxxviii, c. 319.
35. My Diaries. I, p. 430.
36. Mackail, p. 404.
37. ibid, p. 72.
38. My Diaries. I, p. 463.

CHAPTER 15

1. My Diaries. I, p. 414.
2. ibid. I, p. 296.
3. ibid. I, p. 463.
4. ibid. I, p. 423.
5. ibid. I, p. 465.
6. G.P.
7. Mackail, p. 384.
8. Garvin & Amery. Chamberlain. VI, p. 271.
9. Mackail, p. 407.
10. ibid, p. 408.
11. Digby. Horace Plunkett, p. 55.
12. My Diaries. II, p. 18.
13. ibid. II, p. 26.

14. March 13 1901. G.P.
15. Yorkshire Post. October 25 1901.
16. Mackail, p. 408.
17. G.P.
18. Gatty. op cit, p. 136.
19. Robinson. Memoirs, p. 138.
20. ibid, p. 140.
21. Mackail, p. 78.
22. ibid, p. 425.
23. G.P.
24. G.P.
25. Garvin & Amery. op cit. V, p. 75.
26. O'Brien. An Olive Branch, p. 161.
27. Mackail, p. 754.
28. ibid, p. 755.

CHAPTER 16

1. Mackail, p. 350.
2. G.P.
3. My Diaries. II, p. 2.
4. ibid. II, p. 2.
5. Gwynn (ed.). Letters & Friendships of Sir C. Spring-Rice. I, p. 346.
6. My Diaries. II, p. 24.
7. ibid. II, p. 46.
8. Some Hawarden Letters, p. 311.
9. Dunraven. Past Times & Pastimes. II, p. 1.
10. ibid. II, p. 14.
11. ibid, p. 16.
12. Mackail, p. 82.
13. My Diaries. II, p. 46.
14. ibid. II, p. 47.

15. ibid. II, p. 47.
16. ibid. II, p. 25.
17. Fitzroy. Memoirs, p. 136.
18. My Diaries. II, p. 48.
19. Mackail, p. 84.
20. My Diaries. II, p. 20.
21. ibid. II, p. 20.
22. ibid. II, p. 52.
23. ibid. II, p. 55.
24. ibid. II, p. 58.
25. ibid. II, p. 59.
26. ibid. II, p. 62.
27. ibid. II, p. 61.
28. ibid. II, p. 62.
29. ibid. II, p. 62.
30. Mackail, p. 463.
31. Gwynn, D. Redmond, p. 102.

CHAPTER 17

1. My Diaries. II, p. 76.
2. ibid. II, p. 69.
3. L.A.L.C.
4. L.A.L.C.
5. March 25 1905. L.A.L.C.
6. March 31 1905. L.A.L.C.
7. April 3 1905. L.A.L.C.
8. March 31 1905. L.A.L.C.
9. Some Hawarden Letters.
10. Garvin & Amery. op cit. VI, p. 467.
11. ibid. VI, p. 468.
12. My Diaries. II, p. 73.
13. ibid. II, p. 102.
14. G.P.
15. Dunraven. op cit. II, p. 24.
16. My Diaries. II, p. 107.
17. G.P.

18. G.P.
19. Adelson. Mark Sykes, p. 97.
20. Mackail, p. 91.
21. Dunraven. Outlook for Ireland, p. 272.
22. Mackail, p. 91.
23. Dunraven. Past Times. II, p. 26.
24. My Diaries. II, p. 110.
25. G.P.
26. G.P.
27. Hansard. 4th Series. cxli, c. 461.
28. Fitzroy. op cit, p. 237.
29. Garvin & Amery. op cit. VI, p. 672.
30. ibid. VI, p. 672.
31. Fitzroy. op cit, p. 241.
32. Hansard. 4th Series. cxlii, c. 431.

CHAPTER 18

1. L.A.L.C.
2. Mackail, p. 104.
3. Churchill. Great Contemporaries, p. 243.
4. My Diaries. II, p. 122.
5. Garvin & Amery. op cit. VI, p. 671.
6. L.A.L.C.
7. L.A.L.C.
8. G.P.
9. November 16 1905. G.P.
10. G.P.
11. G.P.
12. My Diaries. II, p. 129.
13. G.P.
14. January 21 1906. **G.P.**

15. My Diaries. II, p. 132.
16. Lytton. Blunt, p. 293.
17. ibid, p. 295.
18. ibid, p. 295.
19. ibid, p. 293.
20. L.A.L.C.
21. My Diaries. II, p. 153.
22. ibid. II, p. 154.
23. ibid. II, p. 173.
24. ibid. II, p. 132.
25. G.P.
26. September 17 1907. G.P.
27. L.A.L.C.

CHAPTER 19

1. G.P.
2. G.P.
3. December 10. L.A.L.C.
4. Chesterton. Autobiography, p. 264.
5. Speaight. Letters from Hilaire Belloc, p. 28.
6. Jenkins. Mr Balfour's Poodle, p. 82.
7. November 9 1906. L.A.L.C.
8. My Diaries. II, p. 262.
9. ibid. II, p. 294.
10. Mackail, p. 649.
11. L.A.L.C.
12. My Diaries. II, p. 299.
13. G.P.
14. G.P.
15. Winterton. Pre-War, p. 159.

16. L.A.L.C.
17. My Diaries. II, p. 353.
18. ibid. II, p. 353.
19. ibid. II, p. 372.
20. ibid. II, p. 373.
21. Mackail, p. 698.
22. G.P.
23. August 10. G.P.
24. Mackail, p. 710.

CHAPTER 20

1. My Diaries. II, p. 357.
2. G.P.
3. October 25 1911. G.P.
4. G.P.
5. G.P.
6. G.P.
7. Lee. op cit, pp. 128-9.
8. My Diaries. II, p. 414.
9. L.A.L.C.
10. Hansard. 5th Series. liii, c. 1294.
11. June 10. Francis Wyndham Collection.
12. My Diaries. II, p. 431.
13. Gordon at Khartoum, p. 405.
14. Finch. op cit, p. 338. Also see Norman. Ezra Pound, p. 143.
15. Sassoon. Siegfried's Journey, p. 153.
16. Leslie. Long Shadows, p. 254.
17. Blunt. Cockerell, p. 182.

Bibliography

The edition given is that which was consulted for this book.

Adelson, Roger. *Mark Sykes* (Jonathan Cape, 1975).
Afaf Lufti Al-Sayyid. *Egypt and Cromer* (John Murray, 1968).
Alexander, Michael. *The True Blue* (Rupert Hart-Davis, 1957).
Asquith, Lady Cynthia. *Haply I may remember* (James Barrie, 1950).
Asquith, Margot. *Autobiography* (Thornton & Butterworth, 1920).
Balfour, A. J. *Chapters of Autobiography* (Cassell, 1930).
Balfour, Lady Betty (ed.). *Personal and Literary Letters of the Earl of Lytton*. 2 vols. (Longmans, 1906).
Beckett, J. C. *The Making of Modern Ireland* (Faber, 1966).
Biggs-Davison, John. *George Wyndham* (Hodder & Stoughton, 1951).
Blake, Robert. *Disraeli* (Eyre & Spottiswoode, 1966).
Blunt, Lady Anne. *Bedouin Tribes of the Euphrates*. 2 vols. (John Murray, 1879).
A Pilgrimage to Nejd. 2 vols. (John Murray, 1881).
Blunt, Wilfrid. *Cockerell* (Hamish Hamilton, 1964).
Blunt, Wilfrid Scawen. *Proteus & Amadeus* (Kegan Paul, 1878).
The Future of Islam (Kegan Paul, 1882).
The Shame of the Nineteenth Century (Privately printed, 1900).
Francis Thompson (Reprinted from *The Academy*, 1907).
The Secret History of the English Occupation of Egypt (T. Fisher Unwin, 1907).
India Under Ripon (T. Fisher Unwin, 1909).
Lettre adressée au Congrès National Egyptien à Paris (Privately printed, 1910).
Gordon at Khartoum (Stephen Swift, 1912).
The Land War in Ireland (Stephen Swift, 1912).
Poetical Works. 2 vols. (Macmillan, 1914).

History of the Crabbet Estate (Privately printed, 1917).

My Diaries. I. (Martin Secker, 1919).

My Diaries. II. (Martin Secker, 1920).

Blythe, Henry. *Skittles* (Rupert Hart-Davis, 1970).

Bonham-Carter, Violet. *Winston Churchill as I knew him* (Eyre & Spottiswoode, Collins, 1965).

Boyd, Charles. *George Wyndham* (Arthur L. Humphreys, 1913).

Boyle, C. *Boyle of Cairo* (Privately printed, 1965).

Brodie, Fawn. *The Devil Drives*: *A Life of Sir Richard Burton* (Eyre & Spottiswoode, 1967).

Buckland, Patrick. *Irish Unionism*. 2 vols. (Gill & Macmillan, 1972-3).

Cecil, Lady Gwendolin. *Life of Robert Marquis of Salisbury*. 4 vols. (Hodder & Stoughton, 1921 & 1932).

Chesterton, G. K. *Autobiography* (Hutchinson, 1937).

Churchill, Randolph. *Winston Churchill*: *Youth* (Heinemann, 1966).

Winston Churchill: The Young Statesman (Heinemann, 1967).

Churchill, Winston. *Great Contemporaries* (Thornton Butterworth, 1937).

My Early Life (Odhams, 1930).

Cockerell, S. C. *Friends of a Lifetime* (Jonathan Cape, 1940).

Connell, J. W. E. *Henley* (Constable, 1949).

Cromer, Earl of. *Modern Egypt*. 2 vols. (Macmillan, 1908).

Ancient & Modern Imperialism (Address to the Classical Association, 1910).

Curtis, E. *History of Ireland* (Methuen paperback, 1961).

Curtis, L. *Coercion & Conciliation* (Princeton, 1963).

Dangerfield, George. *The Strange Death of Liberal England* (Paladin edition, 1970).

Davitt, Michael. *The Fall of Feudalism* (Harper & Bros, 1904).

Dickenson, Violet (ed.). *Miss Eden's Letters* (Macmillan, 1919).

Dictionary of National Biography.

Digby, M. *Horace Plunkett* (Basil Blackwell, 1949).

Douglas, Lord Alfred. *Autobiography* (Martin Secker, 1929).

Dugdale, Blanche. *Balfour*. 2 vols (Hutchinson, 1936).

Dunraven, Earl of. *The Outlook for Ireland* (Hodges & Figgis, 1907).

Past Times & Pastimes. 2 vols. (Hutchinson, 1922).

Edel, Leon. Henry James. *The Conquest of London* (Rupert Hart-Davis, 1962).

BIBLIOGRAPHY

Henry James. *The Middle Years* (Rupert Hart-Davis, 1963).
Egremont, Lord. *Wyndham & Children First* (Macmillan, 1968).
Eliot, T. S. *The Sacred Wood* (Methuen paperback, 1960).
Ensor, Sir Robert. *English History 1870-1914* (Oxford, 1936).
Faber, Richard. *The Vision and the Need* (Faber, 1966).
Finch, Edith. *Wilfrid Scawen Blunt* (Jonathan Cape, 1938).
Fitzroy, Sir Almeric. *Memoirs*. 2 vols. (Hutchinson, 1925).
Forster, E. M. *Abinger Harvest* (Penguin edition, 1967).
Garvin, J. and Amery, J. *Life of Joseph Chamberlain*. 6 vols. (Macmillan, 1932-69).
Gatty, Charles. *Recognita* (John Murray, 1917).
Girouard, Mark. *The Victorian Country House* (Oxford, 1971).
Graham, R. B. Cunninghame. *Redeemed & Other Sketches* (Heinemann, 1927).
Gross, John. *The Decline & Fall of the English Man of Letters* (Weidenfeld & Nicolson, 1969).
Gwynn, Dennis. *Life of John Redmond* (Harrap, 1932).
Gwynn, Stephen (ed.). *The Letters & Friendships of Sir Cecil Spring-Rice*. 2 vols. (Constable, 1929).
Hardinge of Penhurst, Lord. *Old Diplomacy* (John Murray, 1947).
Harris, Frank. *Contemporary Portraits* (Methuen, 1915).
Harrison, Frederick. *Autobiographic Memoirs*. 2 vols. (Macmillan, 1911).
Holland, Bernard. *Life of Spencer Compton, 8th Duke of Devonshire*. 2 vols. (Longmans, 1911).
Hone, Joseph. *W. B. Yeats* (Penguin edition, 1971).
Howard of Penrith, Lord. *Theatre of Life*. 2 vols. (Hodder & Stoughton, 1935).
James, Robert Rhodes. *Lord Randolph Churchill* (Weidenfeld & Nicolson, 1959).
Rosebery (Weidenfeld & Nicolson, 1963).
Jenkins, Roy. *Mr Balfour's Poodle* (Heinemann, 1954).
Asquith (Collins, 1964).
Jones, L. E. *A Victorian Boyhood* (Macmillan, 1955).
Kee, Robert. *The Green Flag* (Weidenfeld & Nicolson, 1972).
Kipling, Rudyard. *Something of Myself* (Macmillan, 1937).
Lee, Viscount. *A Good Innings* (John Murray, 1974).
Leslie, Shane. *Men were Different* (Michael Joseph, 1937).
Long Shadows (John Murray, 1966).
Lethaby, P. *Philip Webb & his work* (Oxford, 1935).
Long, Viscount. *Memories* (Hutchinson, 1923).

Longford, Elizabeth. *Victoria R.I.* (Weidenfeld & Nicolson, 1964).

Lyons, F. S. L. *The Irish Parliamentary Party* (Faber, 1951).
John Dillon (Routledge & Kegan Paul, 1968).
Ireland Since the Famine (Fontana edition, 1973).

Lytton, Earl of. *Wilfrid Scawen Blunt. A memoir* (Macdonald, 1961).

Lytton, Neville. *The English Country Gentleman* (Hurst & Blackett, 1925).

Macarthy, Desmond. *Portraits* (Putnam, 1931).

Mackail, J. W. *Life of William Morris* (Oxford, 1950).

Mackail, J. W. and Wyndham, Guy. *Life and Letters of George Wyndham*. 2 vols. (Hutchinson, 1925).

Magnus, Philip. *Gladstone* (John Murray, 1954).
Kitchener (John Murray, 1958).
King Edward VII (John Murray, 1964).

Mallet, Victor (ed.). *Life with Queen Victoria* (John Murray, 1968).

Mansergh, Nicholas. *The Irish Question* (Allen & Unwin, 1965).

Mansfield, Peter. *The British in Egypt* (Weidenfeld & Nicolson, 1971).

March-Philips and Christian (eds.). *Some Hawarden Letters* (Nisbet, 1917).

Marjoribanks, E. and Colvin, I. *Life of Lord Carson*. 3 vols. (Gollancz, 1932-6).

Maxse, Mary. *A Memoir* (Privately printed, 1946).

Midleton, Earl of. *Records & Reactions* (John Murray, 1939).

Morley, Viscount. *Recollections*. 2 vols. (Macmillan, 1917).

Morris, William. *Signs of Change* (Reeves & Turner, 1888).

Nevill, Lady Dorothy. *Reminiscences* (Edward Arnold, 1906).

Newton, Lord. *Lord Lansdowne* (Macmillan, 1929).

Nicolson, Harold. *King George V* (Constable, 1952).

Norman, Charles. *Ezra Pound* (Macdonald, 1969).

O'Brien, Conor Cruise. *States of Ireland* (Hutchinson, 1972).

O'Brien, William. *An Olive Branch in Ireland* (Macmillan, 1910).
Evening Memories (Maunsel, 1920).

O'Connor, T. P. *Memoirs of an Old Parliamentarian*. 2 vols. (Benn, 1929).

Olivier, Edith. *Four Victorian Ladies of Wiltshire* (Faber, 1945).

Oxford and Asquith, Earl of. *Fifty years in Parliament*. 2 vols. (Cassell, 1926).

Pakenham, Elizabeth. *Jameson's Raid* (Weidenfeld & Nicolson, 1960).

Pakenham, Thomas. *Year of Liberty* (Hodder & Stoughton, 1969).

Ponsonby, Arthur. *More English Diaries* (Methuen, 1927).

Ponsonby, Frederick. *Recollections of 3 Reigns* (Eyre & Spottiswoode, 1951).

Reinehr, Mary. *The Writings of Wilfrid Scawen Blunt* (Milwaukee, 1940).

Robinson, Sir Henry. *Memoirs, Wise and Otherwise* (Cassell, 1923).

Rose, Kenneth. *Superior Person* (Weidenfeld & Nicolson, 1969). *The Later Cecils* (Weidenfeld & Nicolson, 1975).

Rothstein, Theodore. *Egypt's Ruin* (Fifield, 1910).

Sassoon, Siegfried. *Siegfried's Journey* (Faber, 1945).

Solow, Barbara. *The Land Question and the Irish Economy* (Harvard, 1971).

Speaight, Robert. *Hilaire Belloc* (Hollis & Carter, 1957). (ed.) *Letters from Hilaire Belloc* (Hollis & Carter, 1958).

Storrs, Ronald. *Orientations* (Ivor Nicholson & Watson, 1937).

Thornton, A. P. *The Imperial Idea & its Enemies* (Macmillan, 1959).

Thorold, Algar. *Labouchere* (Constable, 1913).

Wells, H. G. *An Experiment in Autobiography.* 2 vols. (Gollancz & Cresset, 1934).

Wemyss, Lady. *A Family Record* (Privately printed, 1932).

Wentworth, Lady. *The Authentic Arabian Horse* (Allen & Unwin, 1945).

Willoughby de Broke, Lord. *The Passing Years* (Constable, 1924).

Winterton, Earl. *Pre-War* (Macmillan, 1932). *Fifty Tumultuous Years* (Hutchinson, 1955).

Wyndham, George. *The Development of the State* (Archibald Constable, 1904). *Essays in Romantic Literature* (Macmillan, 1919).

Wyndham, Guy (ed.). *Letters of George Wyndham.* 2 vols. (Privately printed, 1915).

Wyndham, Hugh. *A family History.* 2 vols. (Oxford, 1939 & 1950).

Wyndham, Violet. *Madame de Genlis* (Andre Deutsch, 1958).

Yeats, W. B. *Memoirs* (Macmillan, 1972).

Young, Kenneth. *Balfour* (Bell, 1963).

Zetland, Marquis of. *Cromer* (Hodder & Stoughton, 1932).

Index

Index

STIRLING
DISTRICT
LIBRARY

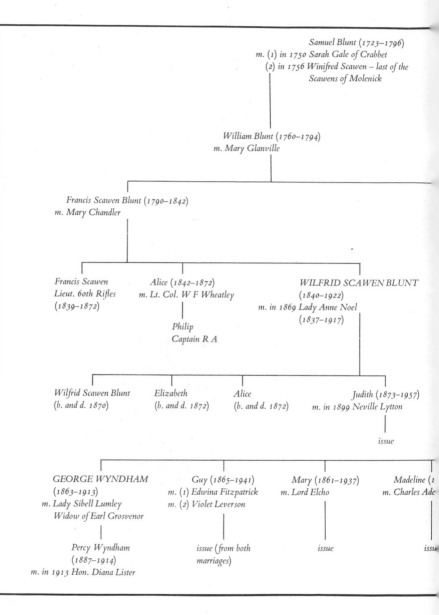

Samuel Blunt (1723–1796)
m. (1) in 1750 Sarah Gale of Crabbet
(2) in 1756 Winifred Scawen – last of the
Scawens of Molenick

William Blunt (1760–1794)
m. Mary Glanville

Francis Scawen Blunt (1790–1842)
m. Mary Chandler

Francis Scawen
Lieut. 60th Rifles
(1839–1872)

Alice (1842–1872)
m. Lt. Col. W F Wheatley

Philip
Captain R A

WILFRID SCAWEN BLUNT
(1840–1922)
m. in 1869 Lady Anne Noel
(1837–1917)

Wilfrid Scawen Blunt
(b. and d. 1870)

Elizabeth
(b. and d. 1872)

Alice
(b. and d. 1872)

Judith (1873–1957)
m. in 1899 Neville Lytton

issue

GEORGE WYNDHAM
(1863–1913)
m. Lady Sibell Lumley
Widow of Earl Grosvenor

Guy (1865–1941)
m. (1) Edwina Fitzpatrick
m. (2) Violet Leverson

Mary (1861–1937)
m. Lord Elcho

Madeline (1
m. Charles Ade

Percy Wyndham
(1887–1914)
m. in 1913 Hon. Diana Lister

issue (from both
marriages)

issue

issue